Praise For *Fly Fishing For Dummies*

Peter Kaminsky is one of those rare writers who knows how to develop a genuine rapport with his readers. As you read *Fly Fishing For Dummies,* you find yourself becoming friends with the author; and by the end of the book, you're not only Kaminsky's buddy, but you're also, suddenly, quite knowledgeable in the sport of fly fishing. It's all here, in easy-to-read, understandable terms: from choosing gear, to learning how to cast, to reading water, to catching fish. This is a keeper.

—Jay Cassell, Editor, *Sports Afield* magazine

Would-be fly fisherman, here's your chance. With relentless wit and a sharp eye for what's useful and what's merely fashionable, Peter Kaminsky has peeled away all the mysticism, social tone, and other impediments to learning about this sport. What's left, and what fills this splendid book, is all you need to know, and why it's so much fun.

—Paul Schullery, author of *American Fly Fishing: A History* and *Shupton's Fancy: A Tale of the Fly-Fishing Obsession*

Is fly fishing difficult to learn? Not with a resource such as *Fly Fishing For Dummies*. Well-written and superbly organized, this book is a great primer on fly fishing's essential elements.

—Joe Healy, Editor, *Saltwater Fly Fishing* magazine

Praise For Fishing For Dummies

I've known Peter for years and am a big fan of his writing style. *Fishing For Dummies* taught me some new tricks — and made me laugh along the way. Buy this book — you'll enjoy it.

—Tom Rosenbauer, Vice President, Merchandising, The Orvis Company, Inc. and author of *The Orvis Fly Fishing Guide*

With his trademark blend of supreme scholarship and keen wit, Peter Kaminsky has commited an act of true piscatorial worth.

—Gary Soucie, Editor, *American Angler* and author of *Traveling with Fly Rod and Reel* and *Hook, Line and Sinker: The Complete Angler's Guide To Terminal Tackle*

If you are a beginning angler, this is the first book you should read. Pete Kaminsky has a keen reporter's eye and the sensitivity of your favorite teacher (the funny one who understood how you felt as a stranger). Here he draws on his vast experience, covering all kinds of fish and fishing, but in small bites, easily digested. . . . This is the most personal text book you are ever likely to find. Even the know-it-all angler will find something new. So, if you are not a fishing nut now, don't worry, Pete will get you there.

—Joan Stoliar, Director, Project Access

After decades of technically overarching, "how-to" angling literature that turns off as many people as it instructs, we now have a book that provides meaningful advice to those who have always wondered, but were probably afraid to ask. As with Kaminsky's other writing, this is truly first-rate. Readers will appreciate Kaminsky's mastery of the subject matter and the humor with which he presents it.

—Charles F. Gauvin, President & CEO, Trout Unlimited

TM

BESTSELLING BOOK SERIES

References for the Rest of Us!®

Do you find that traditional reference books are overloaded with technical details and advice you'll never use? Do you postpone important life decisions because you just don't want to deal with them? Then our *For Dummies*® business and general reference book series is for you.

For Dummies business and general reference books are written for those frustrated and hard-working souls who know they aren't dumb, but find that the myriad of personal and business issues and the accompanying horror stories make them feel helpless. *For Dummies* books use a lighthearted approach, a down-to-earth style, and even cartoons and humorous icons to dispel fears and build confidence. Lighthearted but not lightweight, these books are perfect survival guides to solve your everyday personal and business problems.

> *"More than a publishing phenomenon, 'Dummies' is a sign of the times."*
>
> — *The New York Times*

> *"...you won't go wrong buying them."*
>
> — *Walter Mossberg, Wall Street Journal, on For Dummies books*

> *"A world of detailed and authoritative information is packed into them..."*
>
> — *U.S. News and World Report*

Already, millions of satisfied readers agree. They have made For Dummies the #1 introductory level computer book series and a best-selling business book series. They have written asking for more. So, if you're looking for the best and easiest way to learn about business and other general reference topics, look to For Dummies to give you a helping hand.

Wiley Publishing, Inc.

5/09

FLY FISHING
FOR
DUMMIES®

FLY FISHING FOR DUMMIES®

by Peter Kaminsky

Wiley Publishing, Inc.

Fly Fishing For Dummies®

Published by
Wiley Publishing, Inc.
909 Third Avenue
New York, NY 10022
www.wiley.com

Copyright © 1998 by Wiley Publishing, Inc., Indianapolis, Indiana

For general information on our other products and services or to obtain technical support, please contact our Customer Care Department within the U.S. at 800-762-2974, outside the U.S. at 317-572-3993, or fax 317-572-4002.

Wiley also publishes its books in a variety of electronic formats. Some content that appears in print may not be available in electronic books.

Library of Congress Cataloging-in-Publication Data:

Library of Congress Control Number: 98-84305

ISBN: 978-0-7645-5073-7

20 19 18

About the Author

Peter Kaminsky caught his first fish, a 30-pound grouper, on a party boat in the Florida Keys. It was the first time he went fishing, and that grouper won $45 for the big fish of the day. Kaminsky was hooked. He was Managing Editor of *National Lampoon* at the time. Soon after, he began to write for *Outdoor Life, Field & Stream,* and *Sports Afield.* In 1985, he began his regular contributions to a *The New York Times* "Outdoors" column. Kaminsky also writes "The Underground Gourmet" in *New York* magazine and is a frequent contributor on food and dining in *Food & Wine* magazine. As a television producer, Kaminsky has created many prime-time specials with Jerry Seinfeld, Mary Tyler Moore, Bob Newhart, and a fellow angler who is sorely missed, John Candy. Kaminsky is a graduate of Princeton University and lives in Brooklyn with his wife and two children, all of whom fish.

Dedication

For Bobby Shamis, with whom I spent a great afternoon bait fishing in Dania, Florida.

Acknowledgments

To begin at the beginning, thanks to Geoff Norman for putting a fly rod in my hand and pointing me to the Beaverkill one April morning a long time ago. Tony Atwill for good times, good advice, and good photos. Josh Feigenbaum for the willingness to drop everything and go fishing whenever the chance arose. Tom Akstens for taking Lily in a canoe, putting Lucy on a brown trout, and making sure that this book is less error filled than it was when it left my Macintosh. Melinda, for never saying no when I feel the need to fish. And the biggest thank you to Scott Bowen, who took time off from being a future prize-winning novelist to assist in creating this book. Now all he needs to do work on his double haul.

Publisher's Acknowledgments

We're proud of this book; please register your comments through our Online Registration Form located at www.dummies.com.

Some of the people who helped bring this book to market include the following:

Acquisitions, Development, and Editorial

Project Editor: Tim Gallan

Acquisitions Editor: Stacy S. Collins

Copy Editors: Michael Bolinger, William A. Barton, Tamara Castleman

Technical Editor: Tom Akstens

Editorial Manager: Leah Cameron

Editorial Assistant: Donna Love

Production

Project Coordinator: E. Shawn Aylsworth

Layout and Graphics: Lou Boudreau, Kelly Hardesty, Angela F. Hunckler, Jane E. Martin, Anna Rohrer, Brent Savage, M. Anne Sipahimalani, Deirdre Smith, Kate Snell

Illustrators: Precision Graphics; Ron Hildebrand, Hildebrand Design

Proofreaders: Christine Berman, Kelli Botta, Michelle Croninger, Rachel Garvey, Rebecca Senninger, Robert Springer, Sandra Wilson, Janet M. Withers

Indexer: Sherry Massey

General and Administrative

Hungry Minds Consumer Reference Group

> **Business:** Kathleen Nebenhaus, Vice President and Publisher; Kevin Thornton, Acquisitions Manager

> **Cooking/Gardening:** Jennifer Feldman, Associate Vice President and Publisher; Anne Ficklen, Executive Editor; Kristi Hart, Managing Editor

> **Education/Reference:** Diane Graves Steele, Vice President and Publisher

> **Pets:** Kathleen Nebenhaus, Vice President and Publisher; Tracy Boggier, Managing Editor

> **Travel:** Michael Spring, Vice President and Publisher; Brice Gosnell, Publishing Director; Suzanne Janetta, Editorial Director

Hungry Minds Consumer Editorial Services: Kathleen Nebenhaus, Vice President and Publisher; Kristin A. Cocks, Editorial Director; Cindy Kitchel, Editorial Director

Hungry Minds Consumer Production: Debbie Stailey, Production Director

Contents at a Glance

Cartoons at a Glance

By Rich Tennant

page 332

page 313

page 227

page 5

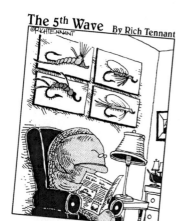

page 55

Cartoon Information:
Fax: 978-546-7747
E-Mail: richtennant@the5thwave.com
World Wide Web: www.the5thwave.com

Table of Contents

Introduction

*F*orget about what you've heard about fly fishing in the past. If you believe what you read, fly fishing requires the touch of a surgeon, the body mechanics of Tiger Woods, and the spirit of a Zen master. I know this isn't true because I am an okay fly fisherman and I fit none of those qualifications. But fly fishing has this aura about it that may have more to do with writers than with fishing. A lot of fly fishermen write about fishing, so naturally, they try to make it seem that it is the most demanding and soul-improving method of catching a fish. However, for me, I find that angling with a fly rod is far and away the most pleasant way to fish. In fact, I will go even further than that and say that it is my favorite thing to do — period.

Bait fishing can be as demanding. Spin fishing with lures requires every bit as much knowledge of fish behavior as well as a wide acquaintance with all kinds of lures. So you really can't defend the position of most fly fishing snobs that their sport is more demanding and challenging. The real difference between fly fishing and every other form of angling with a rod is that with most conventional rods, the weight of your bait or sinker or lure carries the line, whereas in fly fishing *the weight of the line* carries the fly. This crucial difference requires that the fly rodder learn to cast in a special way, moving the line through the air like a very long bull whip. This maneuver calls for a certain amount of timing and a whole lot of practice. Most people cannot pick up a fly rod and begin to cast right away, but they can, after a few flicks, begin to use a baitcasting or spinning rod in short order. But having taught many, many people to fly fish over the years, I promise you that I can have you casting and catching fish on your first day. You may not cast very far and you may not catch very many fish, but you will be fly fishing. After that, the rest is just practice.

Bad Students Wanted

Do you remember the kid in class who never did any more than he or she was told to do? The kid who tried to get by on a minimum of work and a maximum of relaxation? Well, that is my philosophy of fly fishing. If you were interested, there are thousands of flies to learn how to tie and hundreds of insects and bait fish to get familiar with. You could spend your whole life learning about these critters and very little time fishing. In this book, I promise you that I will simplify the number of flies you need to carry around, the number of casts you need to master, and the number of insects and other bait that you need to identify. You can, as I do, make it through your fly fishing life in fresh and saltwater, for all kind of species, with 20 flies, a half dozen casts, and three knots.

My goal in this book is to winnow through the gazillions of pages that have been written about fly fishing and boil it down to the stuff you need to know to begin fishing enjoyably. After that, you can spend the rest of your life learning everything else, or you can just keep fishing. I strongly believe that after you get the basics down, the best education you can get comes from spending time on the water.

Reasons Why You Should Fly Fish

- It takes you to beautiful places.
- The gear doesn't weigh a lot.
- The fish don't care if you tell bad jokes.
- You can do it all by yourself.
- You can do it with friends.
- Ted Williams is a fly fisherman and he was the last guy with a .400 batting average.
- Harrison Ford fly fishes and he got to kiss Princess Leia in *Star Wars*.
- You can have the thrill of the catch and let the fish go free and unharmed.
- Because people know that fly rodders release their fish, you can have a lousy day, get skunked, and then lie about how many fish you caught and released.
- On the other hand, you can also keep your catch, and most fly roddable fish are delicious to eat. In this case, it is harder to arrive home empty-handed and lie about how well you did.
- Learning to tie flies gives you something productive to do with clothes-dryer lint.

Who Needs This Book?

There are three kinds of people who can use this book:

- People who have never fly fished.
- People who have done some fly fishing.
- People who have fished a lot.

For those of you who have never held a fly rod, you will find enough to get you started. You don't have to learn everything all at once. If you're already a fly rodder, you'll find plenty of tips and techniques that you can turn to right away without going through the basics all over again. And you master anglers will also find this book a handy reference for all kinds of questions. So depending on where you fit on the scale of never fly fished, fly fished some, or fly fished a lot, you can skip those parts of this book that aren't important to you right now.

How to Use This Book

This book is a reference; you don't have to read it from cover to cover. I suggest that you find a topic that interests you in the table of contents or index and go from there. I've peppered the chapters with cross-references to related topics in other chapters (and even other books). If you want to read this book from front to back, feel free, but like I said, skipping around is good, too.

How This Book Is Organized

No mystery here: Each chapter in this book presents self-contained coverage of a specific subject. Related chapters are grouped into parts. Here's a summary of each part:

Part I: The Basics

The first chapter of this part is for those of you who have never fished. The rest of the chapters cover your equipment: rods, reels, lines, leaders, and so on. If you're a beginner, you should read every word. More experienced anglers should skim these chapters for tips and tricks, but you can also skip right over all of Part I if you want to get into some of the deeper stuff right away.

Part II: The Fish and the Flies

There are a whole lot of fish in the sea, but most of them are of absolutely no interest to the fly rodder. Learn about trout, bass, other freshwater fish, plus the saltwater fish that are really making lots of news in the world of fly fishing. Find out how to tie flies if that interests you, or at least discover the all-time winners among the thousands of flies out there. Also, this part lists my favorite places to fish for trout, bass, and saltwater fish.

Part III: Fly Fishing Essentials

How to cast. How to wade safely. How to read the water. How to tie a few basic knots. How to dress. How to get a fish on your line. How to land that fish and, if you want to, how to release it. These are lessons that have taken me a lifetime to learn from the world's great anglers, and now I pass them on to you in one fun-to-read section of this book.

Part IV: The Part of Tens

Every *For Dummies* book ends with a group of chapters that are, in essence, top-ten lists, and this book is no exception. In this part, I present some interesting Internet sites, my favorite fishing books (besides this one), and the magazines that will keep you up-to-date on where and how to fly fish.

Icons Used in This Book

This icon flags information that will save you from making the same mistakes that took the rest of us years to unlearn.

Having the right fly, rod, hat, shoes, and so on can make all the difference between success and a miserable day. This icon flags the stuff you *really* need.

From a hook in your finger to a dip in the stream, text next to this icon will show you how to stay dry, comfortable, and safe.

With more and more people pressuring fewer and fewer fish, we all need to learn some basic rules of the road.

Part I
The Basics

The 5th Wave   By Rich Tennant

"Jerry! Over here — the bass are running!"

In this part . . .

Before I can discuss the act of fly fishing, I need to show you the equipment. After covering the general concepts of angling in Chapter 1 (a great starting point for absolute beginners, by the way), I devote the remaining chapters in this part to such topics as rods, reels, lines, leaders, and other important equipment.

Chapter 1

What Every Fly Rodder Needs to Know

In This Chapter

▶ Finding out what fish *really* want

▶ Discovering what information you need (and where you can *find* it)

▶ Getting a license (and why you *need* one)

*I*f you're reading this book, you probably have some interest in catching fish. Perhaps you have never tried to catch one, or you may have caught many and would like to improve your skills. Either way, whether you're a novice or an experienced angler, the equation remains the same — catching a fish requires three things:

✔ A fish

✔ A fisherman or woman

✔ Some fishing gear

What Is a Fish?

A *fish* is a cold-blooded animal that lives underwater, has fins, and breathes through gills. Some fish, such as eels, may not look as if they have fins, but they do. Other fish, such as manta rays, may look more like futuristic designs for jet fighters, but they, too, live in the water, navigate with fins, and breathe through gills.

As far as the angler (that's you) is concerned, fish eat other fish, insects, and the occasional unlucky mammal, reptile, or other animal that finds itself in the water. Although some fish subsist on a diet of plants, *fishing* is the art of convincing a fish that the thing at the end of your line is an edible animal.

Whether you use a bait, a lure, or a fly, a fish usually strikes because it thinks that your offering is an easy meal. At other times, a fish, like any protective parent, may strike because it may think that your imitation animal endangers its young (and very few species can stand to see their babies eaten).

What does a fish look like?

A fish biologist may need to know hundreds of parts of the anatomy of a fish. As an angler, you're only interested in a few of these parts — the parts that are illustrated in Figure 1-1.

The torpedo shapes of most game fish allow them to move easily through tides and currents. The fins propel and guide their movements; and sometimes, as in the case of spiny rays, fins serve as protection. Gills enable fish to breathe by extracting oxygen from the water. The lateral line is a special sensory organ that enables fish to detect vibrations in the water (like the kind of vibrations that are made when you clank an oar on the bottom of a rowboat or when you tramp along the rocks in the bottom of a stream).

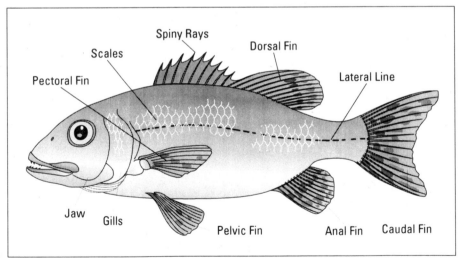

Figure 1-1:
Your average fish.

What does a fish want out of life?

On an average day, a fish has only two requirements:

- ✔ Finding something to eat
- ✔ Avoiding being eaten

In other words, food and shelter are at the top of the priority list of every fish. At certain times of the year, making babies also acquires some importance. But by and large, in looking at any fishing situation, you should ask yourself these two questions:

✔ What will the fish be looking for in the way of food?

✔ How will the fish avoid danger from predators while it is looking for food?

Figuring out the food

Answering the first question can tell you a great deal about what kind of fly to use to trick a fish into biting down on your not-very-good-tasting hook. Often, when you a see a fish feeding, a close look at the water can tell you what food is available. After you have figured out what food is available, your job is to tie something on your line that looks like that particular type of fish food. If a fish is taking something big, such as herring or shrimp, guessing the right food isn't very hard. However, as any frustrated angler can tell you, four or five kinds of food — little insects, bait fish, crawfish, worms, and the like — are often in the water at any given time. In these cases, some concentrated observation should help you to figure out what the fish are eating. Most of the time, fish seem to follow this unwritten rule: If a choice between large food and small food can be made, then pick something to eat that is so small that it is invisible to any angler that may be hanging around.

Finding a safe hideout

All other things being equal, a fish would spend all of its time in a safe place, where predators can't see it or reach it. But to get food, fish, like people, need to get out of the house and go shopping; and that time that a fish is away from home is when the angler has an opportunity to catch the unwary fish. Although a fish in pursuit of a juicy meal may be a little less cautious than a fish lying under a rock, safety is always a prime concern; and no fish worth his (or her) fins *ever* chases food without having some kind of escape route close at hand. After you know what and where these escape routes are, you are well on the way to knowing where and — more importantly — where *not* to fish.

A fish can use one of three ways to escape being caught:

✔ **Hide in the dark.** Look for fish in or near shadows. Also, expect fish to be feeding when the light is low (at dawn and dusk — and sometimes even at night).

✔ **Hide under something.** If food is around, expect to find fish under nearby rocks, fallen trees, and undercut banks.

✔ **Get down.** If you are a bear, a bird of prey, or an angler, chances are you are not going to go very deep into the water to chase a fish. Therefore, even on a bright sunny day with no tree limbs or rocks to crawl under, a fish may stay in plain view in deep water.

Fishing versus Angling

A *fisherman* or *fisherwoman* is a person who fishes. People catch fish by using all kinds of gear (from spear guns to nets to bare hands). An *angler* is someone who angles (an Old English word for *fishing*) with a rod and reel. This book is about angling. Figure 1-2 shows a *fly rodder* on the right, someone who angles with a fly rod.

Your main tool as an angler is, of course, a fishing rod. Rods come in all sizes, and they are made from many different materials. Some rods are made from graphite or other space-age composites. Some rods are made of fiberglass. Other rods are made of bamboo. Which rod is best for you?

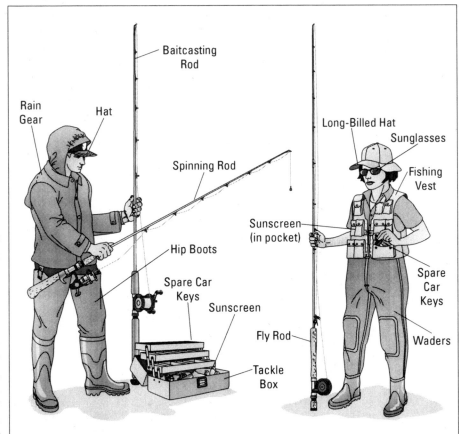

Figure 1-2: The almost-complete angler. Two anglers, well equipped for spinning, baitcasting, or fly fishing.

Was St. Peter a fly rodder? I sure hope so!

Although no one is sure exactly when people started to use fishing rods, we do know that Stone Age people used pieces of flint, bone, or wood to make fishing implements called *gorges*. Basically, a gorge was a double-pointed, bait-wrapped, narrow piece of flint, bone, or wood that was tied around its middle to a line. The fish would eat the bait, and (when the angler pulled on the line) the gorge would stick in the fish's throat, enabling the fish to be landed. It's probably safe to assume that these cave folk made these tools for fishing (otherwise it would have been a pretty big waste of time when they could have been out there chasing mammoths or giant sloths). The first real proof we have of people actually fishing with rods comes from drawings of the ancient Assyrians and Egyptians. Whether the "Phishing" Pharaohs used bait or lures or possibly flies is an open question.

Those anglers of old used a wooden rod with a line attached to the end. It was very much like today's cane poles that many young anglers first use to fish for panfish at every lake and dock. We know that people were using reels by the 12th century because pictures of rods and reels appear in China shortly before Marco Polo visited there. And the art of fly fishing was already well advanced in England when, in the 15th century, the most famous fisherwoman of all time, Dame Juliana Berners (an English nun), wrote her *Treatise On Fishing With An Angle* during this time.

By the time that Izaak Walton wrote *The Compleat Angler* in the 17th century, fishing knowledge about the fish that lived in the rivers of Europe was very advanced, but Walton never saw a rainbow trout, a largemouth bass, a bonefish, or a bluefish. The 20th century has introduced such wonderful rod materials as fiberglass and graphite, which enable the modern caster to achieve distances that only a champion could have hoped for in Walton's day. This century also saw the birth of the outboard motor, which works even better than the strongest rod in getting you within fishing range.

Your choice of rod depends on the type of fishing you do. Figure 1-3 shows the three basic types of rods. Like everything else these days, you can spend a little, or you can break your piggy bank on the purchase of your rod. Take my word for it: If you're a novice, you don't need to break your piggy bank. Buying the most expensive rod would be like buying the great racehorse Secretariat so that he could pull your milk wagon: You'd wind up with more horse than you need, and you probably wouldn't know how to get the most out of Secretariat anyway. Save the expert gear for the experts and start off with a good, serviceable starter kit. Reputable manufacturers (such as Orvis, Reddington, Cortland, and Sage) have very good beginners' kits that contain rod, reel, and line. At 1998 prices you can get started fly fishing in the $100-$150 range. After you use a beginners' outfit to get the feel of fishing, you are ready to move up from the entry-level kits to the more sophisticated and pricier stuff.

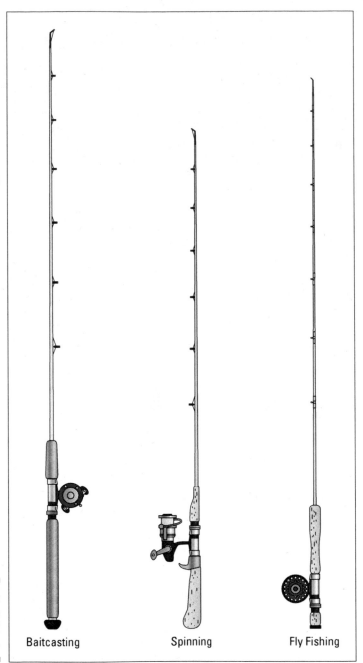

Figure 1-3:
Some
standard
rods.

Baitcasting   Spinning   Fly Fishing

GEAR

Avoiding the heartbreak of rodbreak

Although both cars and fishing rods are products of modern technology and use similar materials, I've noticed that cars have a nasty tendency to break and/or lose fishing rods. The minute your rod gets near a car, the rod is in danger of being mugged. If you put a rod on top of the car while you take off your boots, I promise you that one day you will drive off with the rod on the roof and that the rod will fly off and be lost forever (if not crushed by the truck behind you). If you lean a rod against your car's tailgate or rear bumper, it will someday find a way of wedging itself into the hinge of the trunk or tailgate. When you close the trunk or tailgate, you will be reminded of the rod's location by the crunching sound that it makes as it breaks in two. If you try the old standby of putting the rod on the vehicle's floor beside the front passenger seat and placing the rod so that its tip is pointing toward the back seat, I can almost guarantee you that you will break off the rod tip someday. Basic rule of thumb: If a rod *can* be broken by putting it in or near your car, the rod *will* be broken.

The cure for your rod-catching "Car Disease": *Break down* (disassemble) your rod and put it in a case; or if you are placing your rod in the back of a pickup truck, lay the rod down flat on something soft.

How Do I Learn? Who Do I Ask?

If you never fished at all before you began to read this book, you may have started fishing a little bit later than most. If so, don't worry. (I didn't really start to fish until I was in my 20s.) Still, the best time to begin to fish is when you are a little kid and a parent, grandparent, uncle, or big brother or big sister gets you started with a simple rod and a worm or some balled-up bread on a hook.

But if you weren't lucky enough to begin fishing as a youngster, you can become an angler (or a better angler) in any number of ways.

Parents

Fishing with Mom and Dad is a good place to start, but Mom and Dad need to be patient. Type-A parents who hover over their children, correcting and criticizing, are not very good fishing instructors. Parents who stop teaching and start fishing the minute that they see a fish to catch are better off not teaching. Jack Hemingway, oldest son of the late American author Ernest Hemingway, is a fishing fanatic. Jack's dad, Ernest, was a famous fisherman as well as a great writer, so you would be inclined to think that Papa

Hemingway was one heck of a fishing teacher. Well, Jack once said that in all the years that he went marlin fishing with his dad, he (Jack) was actually allowed to hold the rod exactly once! Before you decide to teach your child to fish, make a resolution to let your youngster do the fishing while you do the watching.

Friends

Friends are great teachers. Or maybe it is more accurate to say that you can learn a great deal from friends. I have always learned (and continue to pick up tricks) from fishing buddies. The thing to remember about friends, like the thing about parents, is that fishing is not a competition between anglers. Fishing is a contest between an angler and a fish. Many people have difficulty accepting pointers and advice from friends. If you want to be a good angler, learn to accept help and advice. This *doesn't* mean that you have to listen to every opinionated gasbag who comments on your style. After you pass the beginning stage, you can always go off by yourself. It's perfectly fine to say, "I'm going to try that next pool for a while. I'll meet you later by the big rock," and in so doing, get out of earshot of any self-appointed font of wisdom.

But not your boyfriend

Guys have about as much patience teaching fishing to women as they do teaching driving. You may luck out and have a terrific, unselfish guy to learn from, but just as often, asking your boyfriend to teach you to fish is as good as asking for an argument. If any of your women friends know how to fish, ask them for help. I think of myself as a pretty liberated guy and a patient teacher. I have taught my eldest daughter a lot about fishing, but I was amazed one summer afternoon on the Lamar River in Yellowstone Park to watch how rapidly and easily she picked things up from a woman angler who joined us for the afternoon. There wasn't a whole lot of competitiveness, and I have to admit that my daughter learned more in that afternoon than I could have shown her in five afternoons.

Guides

Wherever you find good fishing, you can usually find professional guides to take you fishing. Many anglers try to impress their guides with stories of the places they've been and the fish they've caught. They bristle when their guides try to improve their fishing techniques. This is downright silly. A good guide is on the water from 200 to 300 days per year. Any guide can teach amateur anglers something. Apart from listening for a guide's advice, anglers can also learn by keeping their eyes open. As the great Hall of Fame catcher, Yogi Berra, once said, "You can observe a lot just by watchin'."

Guide service can cost anywhere from $50 to $600 per guide per day. Some guides are patient, but others are like Marine drill sergeants who feel that they have to subdue every angler into an obedient zombie. To find a good guide, personal endorsements are best. Articles mentioning good guides often appear in outdoor magazines. Many guides advertise. Professional outfitters can also give you references to guides. Tackle shop owners often have relationships with guides, so if you like and/or trust a tackle shop owner, that owner can also be a good source for recommendations.

Because people usually hire guides for special trips, I strongly advise you to take the time and effort to check out your prospective guide before you end up in a boat with someone who makes your skin crawl. Before you book a guide, talk to him or her on the phone if you can. Ask about the guide's policy if you have to cancel your booking. Ask the guide how he or she deals with bad weather. (Some guides cancel because of wind, rain, or cold. Other guides go fishing no matter what the weather and expect you to pay in full.) Finally, remember this: Only a rare guide *guarantees* fish. Don't expect the guide to feel sorry and give you a refund if you don't catch anything. If the fishing is crummy, you may get a discount or a refund, but that practice is the exception rather than the rule.

Schools

These days, you can take lessons for all the things that people just used to pick up somehow as part of everyday living: cooking lessons, parenting lessons, personal trainer sessions, and (most importantly for this book) fishing lessons. Fly fishing, being a pretty pricey sport, is taught at all kinds of schools. You need to look for two kinds of fishing knowledge in a fishing school:

- **Fishing technique:** How to cast. How to hook, fight, land, and sometimes release a fish. When I began fishing, I went to a casting clinic for two days, and attending that clinic was the most valuable thing I ever did on the way to becoming an angler.

- **Fishing lore:** How does one read the water? What are the fish taking? What different flies should you try and when? These questions are the kind that a beginner's course can start to answer. That being said, I find that people are more often frustrated by lack of technique than they are by lack of lore. After all, you can usually get a friend or relative to take you fishing. But if you can't use your rod and if you don't know how to tie your hook to your line, your fishing session isn't going to be very productive.

TIP

Prime learning directive: Use your eyes!

I can give you no more valuable piece of advice than this: *Watch the water!* Can you see fish feeding? How are they feeding? Are they slashing through a school of bait? Are they lazily cruising, looking for the odd bit of food? Are birds feeding on bugs or bait in the water? Where does the current go? Does the water contain currents within currents, and are fish feeding in the seams between currents? What places look as if they would provide the best protection for a fish who wants to be near food and safe at the same time?

No matter how good an angler you become, you can always be more productive on the water if you stop to look first. We all want to rush from the car and immediately heave our lines into the water, but you can do a million percent better if you study the water *before* you start fishing.

Magazines and books

"The Big Three" North American outdoor magazines (*Field & Stream, Sports Afield,* and *Outdoor Life*) have all been around for more than a century for a good reason. They are good, and readers know it. They are full of useful information for both anglers and hunters. They deliver many how-to and where-to stories. I still pick up tips from all of them. There is a growing number of magazines devoted specifically to fly fishing. *Fly Fisherman* is one of the oldest and best. See Chapter 20 for a list of ten great magazines and how to subscribe to them.

Four Things That I Wish Somebody Had Told Me about When I Started

So you know what a fish is, what it likes to eat, and where it lives. You have your brand new rod and reel, and you are ready to go. Let me clue you in to a few things to avoid in *all* fishing situations!

1. Bad vibrations

When it comes to fishing (with apologies to any Grateful Deadheads who may be reading this), there are no such things as "good vibes." In fishing, all vibrations are bad. I am talking about clanking oars on the bottom of your aluminum boat, running your motor near feeding fish, or wading through a quiet pool like a 250-pound fullback busting through a gang of linebackers. Check out the special sensory organ called the *lateral line* shown back in Figure 1-1. This organ basically enables fish to "see" vibrations.

Why would a fish want to see vibrations? Predators make vibrations. To a fish, vibrations mean that danger is nearby (like, for example, an angler).

2. Trying to do more than you really can

Trying to cast absolutely as far as you physically can is one sure way to guarantee a lousy cast that will land in the wrong place and spook fish, or hang up on a tree limb. Trying to wade in rougher water than you can comfortably handle guarantees a dunking or at least a few pretty hairy moments exiting from the stream. Taking your boat into heavier water than it was designed to handle is one way to wind up as shark food. Fly fishing is not a sport of extremes. Stay within your capabilities.

3. Shadows of evil

Hawks throw shadows on the water. So do bears, eagles, ospreys, otters, alligators, raccoons, fishermen, and anything else that eats fish. Through thousands of generations of breeding, those fish that weren't afraid of shadows were eaten. In this way, natural selection has bred extreme caution into any fish that you will be interested in catching. So take note of the sun (or on bright nights, the moon) and be careful to keep your shadow away from the fish.

4. Your Budweiser hat

Don't get me wrong. I have nothing against loud, garish clothes. After all, if you can't escape the Good Taste Police when you are out fishing, you need to find a new pastime. However, Day-Glo fishingwear on a stream or lake is not the ideal camouflage. If you're out for a day trolling on the ocean, well, go ahead and wear whatever you want.

The Dog Ate My Homework (Or Why You Need a License)

I do not pay many taxes happily. However, I don't have a problem with paying for my fishing license. Clean streams, public access, stocking, disease eradication, senior citizen programs, and juniors programs all are paid for, in large part, by fees paid by anglers. In this age of downsizing and trimming of government programs, you can be sure that some legislators would go after funds now spent on fishing if sportsmen and women were not on the pay-as-you-go system of yearly fishing licenses.

Rules change from place to place, but in general, only small children and senior citizens are exempt from license fees. Some states do not require them for saltwater fishing but many — a growing number — do. Almost every state requires that you have your license in your possession when fishing.

If your are an out-of-stater on a fishing trip, chances are that you must pay a higher fee for the privilege of fishing than in-state residents do. I have no idea why this practice isn't considered unfair gouging, but it is the law, so don't fight it. After all, who needs hassles on a fishing trip? The point, or at least one of the points, of going fishing is to leave those kinds of problems back in the everyday world.

Advice from an old-timer

Remember that fishing is one of the few things in life that you can keep improving as you grow older. As the patron saint of angling, Izaak Walton, wrote three centuries ago,

"Angling may be said to be like the Mathematics, that it can ne'er be fully learnt; at least not so fully, but that there will still be more new experiments left for the trial of other men that succeed us."

Chapter 2
Choosing a Rod

Fly rodding may be steeped in tradition, but fly rods themselves aren't. When Izaak Walton fished the chalk streams of southern England, there were no fancy split-cane bamboo rods. A rod was a branch cut from a willow or ash. Bamboo, which most of us think of as the tradition-steeped rod of the olden days, came along in the late 1800s and dominated the sport for about 100 years. Bamboo is fun to cast and there is something strangely pleasurable about fishing for a live animal with a rod material that was once alive — as if its living spirit lingers and directs your hand.

When fiberglass came along, many more people could afford to get into fly fishing. Nowadays, the successor to fiberglass — graphite — is the finest casting material ever known. The essential act of fly fishing is the cast, and the essential pleasure of fly fishing (aside from catching fish) is laying out a great cast. Graphite has enabled more fly rodders to become better casters.

When I teach people to cast, I won't promise that they will be casting like pros right away. But, in most cases, I can have them in a stream, catching fish on their first day, and there is nothing like a little success to turn a ho-hum student into an eager learner.

Anatomy of a Fly Rod

The fly rod (shown in Figure 2-1) gets the fly to the fish. It uses the line to do this. The principle of the rod is like a bull whip or a wet towel that you roll up and snap at your friends during gym class. (***Note:*** If you are 50 years old and reading this and you still snap towels at your friends, you might not be the sedate fly fisher-person that I gave you credit for.) All seasoned anglers agree that a good fly rod is as light as it can possibly be while still doing its job.

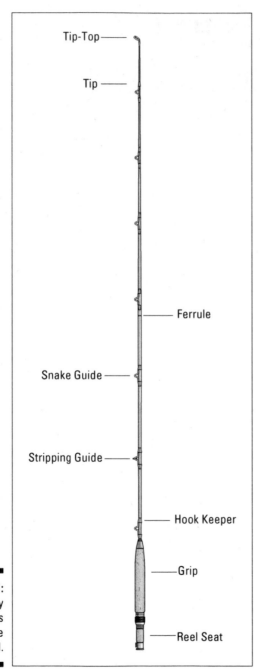

Tip-Top

Tip

Ferrule

Snake Guide

Stripping Guide

Hook Keeper

Grip

Reel Seat

Figure 2-1:
The key
parts
of the
fly rod.

- **The reel seat:** This part holds the reel to the rod and is discussed further in Chapter 3.

- **The grip:** Usually made of cork, it allows you to hold the rod in the proper way for the kind of casting you need to do.

- **The hook keeper:** A place to hook your fly when the rod is strung up and ready to fish.

- **The butt:** The bottom half, or third, of the shaft of the rod. As with the tip, on some rods the butt really bends, while on others it doesn't.

- **The stripping guide:** This is the first guide that your line passes through as it comes off the reel. On most rods, the stripping guide is lined with ceramic to cut down on friction, which can shorten your casting distance.

- **The ferrule:** A male-female connection (like, for example, an electric plug) that joins one part of the rod to the other, allowing for a smooth and secure bend.

- **The snake guides:** Thin wire guides that help the line run straight and true without the least amount of friction. They basically form a metal squiggle, which is roughly a snake-like shape. If you have a spinning or a baitcasting rod, you will notice that these rods have circular guides (like the stripping guide) the whole way up the rod, but the line that you use with conventional tackle is much thinner and not as prone to friction as the wider fly line is. (Therefore, the fly rod guide must be thin to compensate.)

- **The tip:** The last foot or so of rod. It can bend a little or a great deal and is critical in determining the action and sensitivity of the rod.

- **The tip top:** A round guide that directs the line out into the world and hopefully toward the fish.

Most fly rod handles are cork, a very light material that balances well with fly rods. Cork also provides a surface that offers friction for good contact but is comfortable to the human hand. You will find that as a material, cork gives you a touch on the rod that you don't experience with the foam rubber or plastic grips of spinning and baitcasting rods.

You can see some of the standard grips in Figure 2-2. Other grips are available, but they are just variations on these themes.

- **The Standard:** A nice contoured feel that gives you gripping surface where you need it and curved spaces where your hand fits snugly.

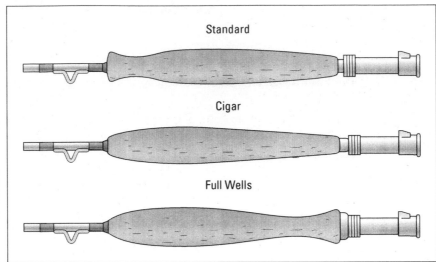

Standard

Cigar

Full Wells

Figure 2-2:
The most
popular fly
rod grips.

 ✔ **The Cigar:** The Cigar grip is a pleasant hand-filling shape (just like a
   real cigar) which allows you to raise your forefinger for a tighter loop in
   short, delicate casting situations.

 ✔ **The Full Wells:** The tapered front will allow you to raise your thumb
   comfortably, making for a more powerful cast with extra punch. This
   grip also allows for greater force in fighting the fish.

You have to cast your way

Casting a fly is like throwing a baseball: Everyone has a different style. I have
a kind of three-quarter, sidearm cast that is miles away from the classic
English style of straight up-and-down arm motion where they teach you to
keep your elbow snug to the ribs. It's all a matter of finding a casting style
and a rod that works for you. Some rods that more traditional casters love
give me a problem. Some rods work for me at short distances, but when I
really want to lay some line out there, I feel an unresponsive or "dead spot"
(just like you'll find in a golf club or tennis racquet) that has more to do
with how I cast than the rod I'm using. So when someone asks, "What rod is
right for me?" I can recommend, but in the end you are going to have to feel
your way into this and get the rod that feels best for you.

If no one had said it before, then I am sure that some fly rodder, somewhere,
would have come up with the saying, "Different strokes for different folks."

Don't forget the women and children

The fly rod grip was devised by fishermen, not fisherwomen. Right now, there is a debate going in fly rodding about whether or not women should have their own rods — that is, rods made specifically for them. One of the main points to consider is that a woman's hand is often smaller than a man's hand. Can the average woman fit her hand on a rod made for either sex? For the most part, she can and always has in the past. But now with many women becoming serious fly rodders, they are looking into having their rods customized to their hands, rather than having to customize their grip to the rod. The same holds true for children who also may be more comfortable with a smaller diameter grip. Handles were altered for tennis racquets, so it makes sense that we do the same for fly rods.

The Four Jobs of a Rod

Everybody knows that a rod is for catching fish. To do this, it must be stiff but supple, strong but delicate. If fishing were just a matter of cranking fish in, you could use a broom handle. But angling for a fish is a four-part job:

✔ **Getting the fly to where the fish is.** That is — delivering the goods. The goal here is achieving distance and the right amount of delicacy to present the fly properly. With some fish, this task makes all the difference, and with some, like a pack of bluefish, they could care less about presentation as long as the fly looks like food.

✔ **Setting the hook.** Because not every take is a visual one, a rod has to be sensitive enough to let you feel the fish as it takes your fly and strong enough to set the hook.

✔ **Fighting the fish.** The rod is a big lever that transmits a great deal of force, and because of its ability to bend, it transmits variable force as required, acting as a shock absorber when the fish suddenly turns or bolts off again.

✔ **Lifting the fish.** With very few exceptions, there comes a time in every contest with a fish, when you will have to lift its head out of the water. This last factor isn't a big deal with a bluegill, but when you get to a 125-pound tarpon, it is definitely a consideration.

The way in which a rod accomplishes these four tasks varies. Sometimes the delivery has to be as light as a snowflake. Sometimes you just heave and hope. To accommodate the different tasks involved and to accommodate the differences in anglers, all kinds of rods are available. In time, if you fish enough, you will discover how to feel the differences in rods. You may like some rods but not care for others. Your personal fondness for a particular rod doesn't mean that one rod is necessarily better than another (although there are both winners and stinkers out there). It just means that one rod is better for you and the kind of fishing you want to do at any given time.

When big is better (and when it isn't)

Personal differences aside, choosing a rod usually comes down to what kind of fish you want to catch and the kind of water that fish lives in. Smaller fish live in smaller waters and usually eat smaller food. Smaller flies require lighter line, and so does calmer water. You want to make as little a splash as possible. The calmer the water, the spookier the fish. In this situation, which is all about delicacy, you need a lighter rod to throw lighter, less water-disturbing line. With bigger water and bigger flies, the main task is delivering the fly to the general neighborhood of the fish. A heavier rod can carry heavier line and therefore can deliver more force, in the same way that a bow and arrow that takes more oomph to bend can shoot farther and penetrate deeper. For big water, big fish and big flies go with a heavier rod. Also remember, a great angler can subdue even very big fish with a light rod, but if you are going to release the fish, a heavier rod will subdue it more quickly, which means that the fish will revive more quickly. You can literally kill a fish from exhaustion if you fight him on an unsuitably light rod. See the chart later in this chapter ("Matching the rod to the fish") for my recommendation in matching the kind of fish you are fishing for and the weight of the rod.

Line weight and rod weight: The bottom line

Rods are rated by the weight of the line they throw. Lines are graded by an ancient system, probably English, that has no relation to anything else. For example, if you remember that with hooks, the smaller number means a larger hook, then it should come as no surprise that the original line measurers took the exact opposite point of view and made the lowest numbers equal the lightest weight. Things like this system probably go a long way toward explaining how fly fishing got such a reputation for being complicated. The lowdown is this: Line weights range from 1 to 14; the higher the number, the heavier the line. You can manage a nice, delicate presentation of a very small dry fly only with a very light rod. But when you need to shoot an 80-foot cast to a swirling striped bass, you are getting up into the 10 weight class.

The long and short of it

Next, you must consider the length of the rod. Shorter rods, from 6 to 7^1/$_2$ feet, offer much control and are good for accuracy and delicacy, particularly on small streams. There was a time in the last 20 years when it was thought that shorter rods were somehow more sporting. I never subscribed to that notion. For trout, I have always been partial to 8 feet as a length, although the newer graphites achieve optimal performance with a 9-foot length. Either length lets you get a good bend in the rod during the fight but keeps the cast high and allows you to hold line off the water in drag-producing situations. As I get into saltwater, I like rods a little over 9 feet. Ten-footers are kind of necessary for tarpon and other big game, but remember: The longer the rod the more tiring it will be to cast. Even though the rod itself may be light, bear in mind that a long rod is like a lever that applies pressure to your wrist and arms. A 1-foot difference in length can add up to a lot of extra force required over the course of 200 or 300 casts in an afternoon's fishing session.

While you are gearing up, bear in mind that people usually *overestimate* the distance that they need to cast. Most trout fishing happens no farther than 30 feet out, and even with bone fishing or striper fishing in the surf, you are not going to be able to control a cast of more than 60 or 70 feet of line. So while it may be nice to have a rod that can cast 90 feet, the bigger questions are: Can you cast that far? And should you?

Where the action is

Action refers to the flexibility of a rod: how much of it bends. There are three basic types of action (shown in Figure 2-3):

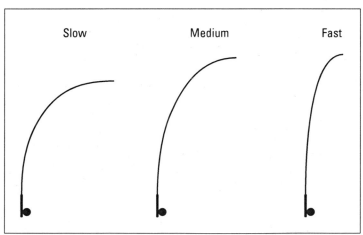

Figure 2-3: The three basic rod actions: slow, medium, and fast.

Slow   Medium   Fast

- ✔ **Slow action:** The rod bends through its entire length from handle to tip.
- ✔ **Medium action:** The top half of the rod flexes.
- ✔ **Fast action:** Only the tip, or top third of the rod, flexes when casting.

Each kind of action has a different impact on your casting and the way you fight a fish.

A slow action requires less strength to bend the rod and offers a softer feel on the cast. All other things being equal, a fish can fight longer and harder against a slow action rod, so this sort of rod is not well matched to bigger-game fish, such as salmon or tarpon. From 1 weight through 4 weight, you will find panfish are a lot of fun with a slow rod, and trout up to 14 inches long are well matched against this kind of rod.

Not surprisingly, medium action is recommended for beginners because it can handle a variety of casting distances and styles, and it is most easy to deal with when first learning to cast. You are probably looking at 6 and 7 weights in the 8- to 9-foot range. These are good for most trout and medium-sized bass.

A fast action rod offers good casters the ability to create lots of line speed and therefore to cover more water more accurately. A fast rod demands good timing and motion from the angler, and can create very tight casting loops which are necessary for distance casting. A fast action rod also has a bit more backbone with which to fight a fish. I like a fast 4 weight for most of my trout fishing and a fast 9 weight for most of my inshore saltwater fishing. This is not, however, a rule of thumb. For many long-time trouters, or new flycasters, saltwater flycasting demands a longer pause between your backcast and forecast: This pause is time to let the line roll out and really bend the rod, loading it up with peak potential energy. The slower rod would be the choice for these anglers.

A Rod for All Seasons

Question: Why is a rod like a potato chip?

Answer: You always want one more.

Here are some guidelines that can help you pick that first rod which, I guarantee, will very soon become a few rods.

Trout

In general, fishing in small streams with overhanging branches often leads to a tangle of rod and line. Watching anglers fish in this setting is almost like watching people in an old slapstick movie. The angler looks in front for obstacles, and then, with equal care, looks back. Then he or she looks around again (just so Mother Nature doesn't have a chance to sneak in any trees or shrubs while their backs are turned). Then the angler very carefully casts and — boing! — the line is hung up in a tree behind Mr. or Ms. Fly Rodder. Apart from your being very conscious of where your line is going to go when you cast, a short rod with a fast tip enables you to cast with very little line out of the guides (which is what you have to do when you fish small streams).

There is an old saw about dry-fly fly rods having fast action and wet-fly fly rods having slow action (see Chapter 6 for a fuller explanation of dry and wet flies). I don't agree. A fast tip makes for a tighter casting loop, which is good, especially with small flies. But you need to be careful when setting the hook with a fast rod, especially when using light tippet (the final, lightest part of your leader). If the rod doesn't have much give, your leader will break. To avoid this situation, you need to learn to strike with firm, but not explosive, pressure. As far as wet flies go, when you are fishing a nymph upstream, which is an increasingly popular and effective method of fishing them, you need the same sensitivity that a fast tip has for the dry-fly angler. Then, in most cases, I want a rod that will allow me to keep my cast high and, once it has landed, will let me lift line off the water so that the heavy line doesn't drag the fly across the current. What my recommendation gets down to is this: I like a longer, faster rod for most trout situations. An 8-foot 6-inch 4 weight is first choice, and then I go with an 8-foot 6 weight when I need some more punch.

Bass and pike, and light saltwater

Flycasting has a great deal to do with *line speed* (how fast the line moves through a cast), which many anglers, unfortunately, confuse with *arm speed* (whipping your arm). When you are fishing with big, air-resistant flies (and when you add them to the amount of line you need to carry in the air for distance casting in saltwater), you don't want to do a great deal of hurry-up casting with a bunch of false casts (waving line in the air to build up line speed). Fast trout rods tend to reinforce this tendency of speeding up, and the one thing I tell trout fishermen when they begin saltwater fly fishing is to slow down. A slower, somewhat softer rod encourages an angler to let the fly line have that extra second or two in the air to *load up* (flex) the rod fully. The result in your cast is less false casting and longer distances. Ideally, for bass, I like a fast tip with slower action throughout the body of the rod. A 9-foot, 9-weight rod is a versatile saltwater choice; make that an 8 weight if you want to catch some freshwater bass and pike while you're at it. If you have good upper-body strength, you might like a $9^1/_2$-footer that helps keep your backcast aloft nicely when you wade in deeper water.

Heavy saltwater: Tarpon, sharks, and other monsters

Now we're talking about big rods capable of long casts and possessing the backbone to fight, subdue, and lift big fish. You need a long, 10 to 14 weight rod for these mega fish. The bigger the fish, the heavier the rod you'll need. (See Chapter 12 for more about fishing for big saltwater gamefish.)

Matching the rod to the fish

Though there are no hard and fast rules, Table 2-1 is a good general guide to figuring what kind of rod you might need depending on what kind of fish you are going after.

Table 2-1	Fly Line Weights and Common Game Fish	
Type of Fish	*Line Weight*	*Situation*
Trout, bluegill, and crappie	1–4	Small streams and creeks, and quiet ponds
Larger trout, bass, and smaller saltwater game fish	5–7	Rivers, lakes, larger ponds, and gentler saltwater
Pike, big bass, steelhead, salmon, bonefish, stripers, and bluefish	8–9	Big rivers, lakes, and saltwater flats
Striped bass, bluefish, and tarpon	10–12	Surf, open water, and flats
Big tarpon, shark, and billfish	12–14	Deeper, open water, and flats

Two-part rods

Years ago, two-part rods were the standard. But now with the strength and performance of graphite, three- and four-piece travel rods are available that hardly lose any strength to their multi-part design and still cast smoothly. And, let me tell you, when you are traveling great distances with lots of connections and puddle-jumper airlines, if you give the airlines enough chances to lose your rod, they will. You can snort and fume and they can offer to replace the rod, but if you have traveled 5,000 miles to some Pacific island or up into the Alaska wilderness, what good is that going to do you when you're 500 miles from the nearest tackle shop? Be smart — keep your rod with you.

Does tire-kicking do any good?

One of the time-honored ways of testing out a rod in the tackle store is to bend the rod while holding the tip against the ceiling of the store (provided the store has a low ceiling). I don't think that this experiment tells you much. Another favorite pre-purchase ritual is to hold the rod in one hand and wiggle it back and forth to see how much it bends. This experiment does give a little better idea of what to expect from a rod, but it tells you little more than does kicking the tires on a car.

You wouldn't buy a car without a test drive. The same thing goes for a rod. Try it out. See how it feels and how you handle it. Of course,

if this is your first rod and you don't know how to cast yet, you won't have any basis for comparison, so you will be forced to go with the recommendations of others. Get your recommender to try the rod, if possible. Of course, if the recommender is employed at the tackle shop, you are somewhat at his or her mercy. In this case, stick with a name brand. Don't buy a bottom-of-the-line rod if you can afford not to. And (unless you have money to burn) don't buy a top-of-the-line rod because you may not be able to tell the difference between it and a bottom-of-the-line rod at this stage of the game.

Rod Care

A good graphite fly rod may last longer than you if it is well-maintained and does not meet an early death in the clutches of the evil automatic car window. This section covers the crucial care that a rod requires.

Be finicky about ferrules

Keep an eye on the *ferrules* (the place where two rod pieces join) and keep them clean. If the fit of the male and female ferrules seems a tiny bit loose or worn, coat the male with candle wax. This increases the diameter ever so slightly, which is usually just enough for a good fit.

Use a rod case

Use a case to carry your rod. No exceptions. Do it. If you don't, you will break your rod someday. I know because I have broken a number of rods, and you know what? Not one of those tragedies ever happened when the rod was stowed in its case. They happened when I was safely transporting them in my car. In the old days, I had a semi-excuse. After all, if you are traveling

The panty hose test

The great rule of panty hose is: "If it can snag on something, it will." Lefty Kreh, perhaps the greatest flycaster and one of the leading pioneers of fly fishing, no doubt heard this many times around the house. Always looking for a way to get the edge in fishing, Lefty took a piece of panty hose and ran it inside the guides. If the panty hose caught or stuck, he knew the guide needed replacing (which you can have done at many stores). In the interests of your marriage, I advise the male fly rodder to check with his spouse *before* ruining a good pair of panty hose.

from place to place in the course of a fishing session — 10 minutes here, 15 minutes there — you would never get any fishing done if you had to clip your fly, reel up your line, take off your reel, put your rod in its bag, and put the bag in the case every time you moved. Then some genius came up with the idea of The Breakdown Case: a simple case that allowed you to leave the rod strung up while still giving maximum protection. These cases aren't cheap — at least $50 — but they are much cheaper than a new rod.

Getting stuck

You get to the river and you see a beautiful trout rising in midstream. You go to put your rod together and the rod doesn't want to go together. It needs a little lubrication, but you don't want to gunk the rod up. Doug Swisher, author of *Selective Trout,* taught me how to fly cast. That took some doing. He also taught me to rub the male part of the ferrule along the side of my nose, right on the bony part. The skin oils should give just that little bit of lubrication that you need. Later, when you get home, wash off your nose oils and other accumulated gunk with a soapy rag.

Getting unstuck

Although one-piece rods are neat, 99 percent of the readers of this book either have (or will have) rods that break down into two or more pieces. Going on the time-honored principle, "If something bad can happen, it will," you can count on a pair of ferrules getting stuck together someday. When this happens, remember the following do's and don'ts.

Don't use pliers. A rod is usually a hollow tube, and pliers are *guaranteed* to break your rod. It may not break right then and there — although it usually does — but take my word for it: You will injure the fibers in the rod, and it will break one day.

The same goes for twisting the stuck ferrule apart like a screw-top soda bottle. First, this technique probably won't work; and second, you could easily snap one of the guides. *Do* use a gentle twisting motion when you disassemble a rod; but if that technique doesn't work, try one of the following methods.

The squat-bend-and-push maneuver

As shown in Figure 2-4, put the rod behind your knees and, with your arms next to and just outside your knees, grip the rod firmly on either side of the ferrule. Then push your knees outward until the ferrule comes unstuck. Don't get violent about it or you may fall down (and probably break the rod in the process). Just a firm, small push should do the trick.

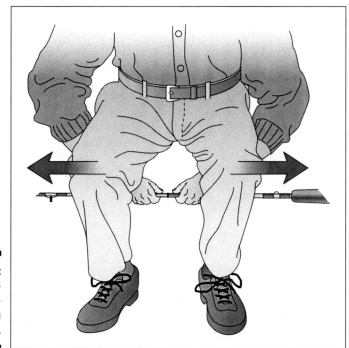

Figure 2-4:
The squat-
bend-and-
push
maneuver.

Ice is nice

If you have any ice handy, put some in a plastic bag and place it around the ferrule. Leave it for a minute or two. Then remove the ice bag, grab the female (outer) part of the ferrule, and let your hand warm it for half a minute. The part in your hand should expand while the inside of the ferrule remains contracted from the cold. This temperature contrast often frees up the ferrule so that it can be separated easily.

The last word

Two final bits of care and maintenance. Always rinse after fishing in saltwater. Otherwise, your reel can become corroded to the reel seat and your guides can get pitted. And lastly, don't gunk up your grip. Suntan lotion, fly grease, pizza oil, and Blimpie dressing can all get in the pores of your handle and ultimately rot it out or render it terminally slimy. You should clean your handle as often as you brush your teeth — ideally after every use.

Chapter 3

Reels

A *reel* is one of those things that you think about only if it doesn't work. Part of the reason for this situation is that, in general, reels are very well designed and, for the most part, very well made. With a minimum of care, a reel can last a long, long time.

A reel serves a couple of purposes:

✔ It stores line. How else could you possibly fish with 100 or 200 yards of line if it weren't stored on a reel?

✔ It introduces a new level of skill and enjoyment to the sport by giving the fish the option of taking line off the reel. You can fish with lighter line than anglers could use back in the days before the advent of reels, when they were limited to just 20 feet of line (or thereabouts) attached to the end of the rod. A reel allows for the give and take of line that tests the skill of the angler.

MFP (Maximum Fishing Pleasure) and the Balanced Outfit

As with most everything else in life, the key to enjoyment is the right balance — in this case, a well-balanced outfit of rod, reel and line. Bigger fish (or fish that tend to run for a long distance) require a great deal of line and a bigger, beefier reel. In general, the guideline is that the smaller the fish, the lighter the outfit you need. Then, of course, skill comes into the equation. As you become a more accomplished angler, you'll be able to use lighter equipment to conquer bigger fish.

Your resource for advice here is your tackle dealer. Contrary to many buying experiences these days, I find that clerks at most tackle shops know their subject (which is more than I can say for the people in most computer departments). Anglers are always asking many questions, and clerks are used to answering them. If in doubt, ask. My only strong piece of advice is don't get the cheapest equipment you can find if you can possibly afford to pay a little more — you're going to use that gear for a long time, and only the good stuff lasts. Mid-range fishing equipment is usually pretty serviceable, but as my Grandma used to say, "Cheap is cheap." And cheap breaks.

Fly Reels

The fly reel, shown in Figure 3-1, has the simplest mechanism of all the kinds of reels made, including spinning and baitcasting reels. A spinning reel can have dozens of moving parts. A fly reel has just a handful.

Notice how the fly reel mounts below the rod. With most reels, you can configure your reel for winding with either the left hand or right hand. Because I cast with my right arm, I like to hold the rod in my right hand and reel with my left. This way, I don't complicate my life by needing to change hands to fight a fish and can use the strength of my more powerful arm to assist the rod

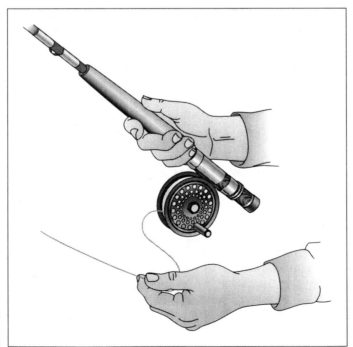

Figure 3-1:
A fly reel.

during the fight. On the other side of the equation, some anglers such as Lefty Kreh like to reel with their strong arm when fighting big fish. Lefty maintains that you do more physical work with the reel when fighting a large fish than you do with the rod. Still, I've found that I do better in all situations cranking with my left hand. If you're unsure how to configure your own fly reel, ask the people in the tackle shop to set it up for you at the time you buy it.

What does a fly reel do?

Sometimes when I go fishing out in the Rockaways (a long barrier island that protects the Brooklyn and Queens shores from the full force of the Atlantic and its storms), I avoid the Expressway and drive up the narrow spit of the Rockaways. To my left is a long promenade running along Jamaica Bay, a rich fishing ground. All along that promenade, I see anglers. Never do I see any fly rodders there. Mostly I see bait guys, with their plastic five-gallon buckets of the kind that you find lying around construction sites. I'm in New York City, however, so I'm not surprised to see that the fishermen use a lot of shopping carts to transport their gear to the water's edge. Every now and again, I see a fisherman without any pole. Instead, he has a hand line, swinging it around to get up speed and then letting it go. If a fish hits, he retrieves the line by wrapping it around a soda or, more likely, a beer can. Basically, that soda can is a reel, or at least a spool, which is the main line-storing part of a reel.

The first function of a reel is to store the line. Before reels, the angler fished with a fixed length of line, about one and a half pole lengths. The reel enables the fly get out there farther in the water than just two pole lengths, and it enables the fish to run great distances, tiring as he goes. *Gear ratio* (how many cranks it takes to move the reel through one revolution) which is so important in constructing a spinning or baitcasting reel, is a secondary consideration with a fly reel — or does not come into play at all. The capability to control drag is a significant factor in a fly reel — more so if you're fighting bigger fish.

Is there a choice of reels?

The basic fly reel is a *single-action reel,* which means that one turn of the crank handle equals one revolution of the spool. Some reels are also *anti-reverse,* which means that, after the fish takes line, the spool doesn't turn. Sounds good, but somehow, these reels tend to fall victim to gear-wrenching grit. You can also buy *multiplier reels* that employ the same kind of gear-driven principle that you find in baitcasting: One turn of the crank produces a number of revolutions of the spool. I've never found a need for this kind of reel. A regular old single-action reel is the overwhelming choice of every professional fly-rod guide that I know.

Drag: A Weapon against the Fish, Not the Angler

In most freshwater fishing situations, setting drag is not a critical issue for fly rodders. Most reels have a simple ratchet-like clicker, controlled by a dial on the solid-faced side, that keeps the reel from turning too quickly and tangling the line. Within limits, the clicker is somewhat adjustable. Some fresh reels use *disc drags* that operate much the same way that disc brakes do. Inside the reel is a disc of leather pressed against the spool. Reels with disc drag are useful for fighting big freshwater fish (namely salmon) or big saltwater fish because the reels apply drag in a more smooth, fluid way, creating a very steady, even tension on the fish, thus reducing the possibility of line breakage.

Using your tools to stop the fish (Hint: Your hand is a piece of tackle, too)

In fishing for most trout and bass, you can use a combination of the following techniques to apply drag:

- Use the drag from the reel.
- Raise the rod tip to create an angle that increases *line resistance* (which, insofar as the fish feels it, is the same thing as *drag*).
- Cup the revolving spool and use the palm of the hand as a brake pad.

You should quickly get the hang of the interplay of these forces. The one thing you *do not* want to do is grab the line with your fingers and try to apply drag that way. You'll break off any decent fish if you do. At the end of the fight, however, you may secure the line by simply using the forefinger of your rod hand to press the line against the rod, as shown in Figure 3-2. This trick enables you to grab or net the fish more easily. If the fish wants to lunge for another run after you're in this position, let it go. That way, you still have a chance of getting the fish in again. If you try to prevent the fish from taking that last run, you'll lose it in almost every case.

Dealing with drag when saltwater fishing

If you're playing and landing larger saltwater fish, you require a more reliable and adjustable drag. When I started fishing, a wonderful American reel called the *Pfleuger Medalist,* which had a very simple drag, was still made. I caught thousands (well, at least hundreds) of fish, including bonefish, with this reel. I still have the reel. It still works, and I've never

Figure 3-2:
Use your finger on the line to help when landing the fish, not during the fight.

had to replace the drag. But, alas, the day of the classic Medalist is gone for most anglers. Today's Medalist is, in my opinion, a pale imitation of the original. These days, a *good* saltwater fly reel has a more-complicated drag than that of the Medalist — a drag made especially for saltwater — and more corrosion-resistant materials than were available in the earlier days of salty fly rodding.

TIP

Fishing for sport utility vehicles

A smooth drag is *so* important in fighting a big fish. I'd guess that a significant number of lost fish have less to do with the strength of the fish and more to do with a funky drag. A good idea, when you're not fishing, is to back off on your drag. Keeping the drag tight all the time will put undue pressure on it when such pressure isn't necessary. A good way to test your drag is to tie your leader around the rear bumper of your car. Then have a friend or relative drive away at a steady speed of ten miles per hour. If the drag responds smoothly, without any sudden jerks, it's in good shape. If it's not smooth — now's the time to give it some attention. (Note: Don't try this stunt with a friend who thinks that just the funniest thing in the world would be to peel rubber and roar down the street. Reels weren't made to go 0 to 60 in five seconds. In fact, doing so in cars isn't always a good idea either.)

Why Is a Reel Like a New Business?

A reel, just as does any fledgling business, needs sufficient backing. With a business, this backing is the kind that goes into the bank account. On a fly reel, *backing* refers to how much braided-nylon *running line* the reel can hold. The amount of backing it can hold is another key factor that you need to keep in mind in choosing a saltwater fly reel. Saltwater game fish can *run,* and if you've been a trout fisherman all your life and are about to go out for blues or albacore, you need to be aware that saltwater fish are bigger, run faster, and fight harder than freshwater fish. The nice thing about having enough backing to let a fish run to its heart's content is that, for the most part, the ocean isn't a collection of line-breaking booby traps such as the fallen trees, underwater grass, and mid-stream rocks that you encounter in a trout stream. You can let those salty fish run and then crank 'em in. A good saltwater reel, therefore, must enable the line to peel off smoothly, but very rapidly, and also have enough backing to outlast a good-sized run.

Be seated

The *reel seat* is the fitting that attaches the reel to the grip of the rod. Figure 3-3 shows the most common types of reel seats. The following list describes these reel seats in more detail:

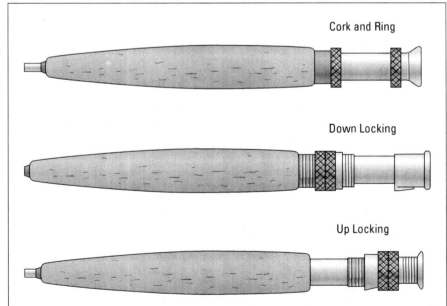

Cork and Ring

Down Locking

Up Locking

Figure 3-3:
The three
most
common
types of
reel seats.

- **Cork and ring reel seat.** This type of reel seat represents a very minimal setup. I got this type on one of my earlier rods because it's made for the lightest possible rod. Actually, I was fooling myself. The weight that's important is the weight between your hand and the tip of the rod — that's the arm of the lever. The reel also can become unseated all too easily — and if you go on the principle that, if a bad thing can happen, it will, you can pretty much count on your reel falling off just as you tie into that trout of a lifetime.

- **Down locking reel seat.** This configuration is the one that I like on my trout and freshwater bass rods. The double screw locks down the reel tightly and securely.

- **Up locking reel seat.** This configuration is the one that works best for me in saltwater. The double ring locks very tightly, and the up locking arrangement keeps the reel away from the bottom of the rod. If you jam the rod into your gut to help you fight a big fish, you want that reel out of the way.

The full-figured reel

Be wary of what reel makers say is the maximum amount of backing that a saltwater fly reel holds — not because reel makers are shady but because how you fish with a reel creates some serious variables. Length, for example, differs from fly line to fly line, so be aware that you may load a line that's longer than the one the manufacturers use to determine backing capacity. How much backing a reel holds is relative to the kind of fly line with which you load it, and if you load up with floating line — which takes up more space than sinking line — you reduce your backing capacity. Don't ever overload a reel: That's just asking for trouble. Put on the correct amount of backing and then load your fly line. Make sure that, after you've fully loaded the reel, you retain an eighth-inch to a quarter-inch space between the edge of the reel frame and the last coil of line. Somewhere between 150 and 250 yards is the correct amount of line and backing to load, depending on the fish you want to catch.

The school of hard knocks

Whenever you're walking through rough country or out onto a jetty, you should always protect your reel by using padded reel covers made specifically for fly reels. Buy them and use them even while walking from the car to the fishing area or from fishing hole to fishing hole. I've wrecked three expensive reels in my life after I took some spills on slippery rocks. And the more expensive the reel is, the easier it seems to wreck. Make sure that you cover and pad all your reels. If you're like me, you probably have many orphan sweatsocks in your drawer. You can always slip one or two of these over your reel.

Don't eat your hat

Have you ever gone to the beach and bitten down into a nice sandwich and been unpleasantly surprised to find little grains of sand on your nice roast beef and onion lunch? Sand has a similar effect on reels. One or two grains can ruin the most expensive reel. My basic rule is that you don't put your reel anyplace you wouldn't put your food. I do make one exception to that: I'd never put a liverwurst sandwich on my hat, but I would put my reel there. A hat is usually a dirt-free — or at least grit-free — article. If you need to put your reel down on the ground, put your hat down first and lay your reel on it.

Maintenance

A fly reel can be an expensive piece of equipment, so you'll want to take care of the ones you have. The following sections provide some maintenance advice.

As the dentist said, rinse often

Whether or not your reel is designed specifically for saltwater, you need to rinse it after every use in the ocean. No matter what anyone tells you or what any manufacturer promises, no fly reel currently made is 100 percent corrosion-proof in all its parts. If you rinse your reel in freshwater and dry it after every use, your reel will be fine. If you don't, you'll become a very familiar and free-spending customer at the tackle shop. Every now and then, remove the line and backing and wash them down in freshwater, too, if you've been a serious salty dog.

Don't forget to oil

Because reels are made with moving metal parts, they need to be lubricated. Sewing-machine oil works well for gears. I like to lubricate spools and spool posts with silicone lubricant, which holds up under a wide temperature range. I use silicone lubricant on everything from my ice-fishing gear to the gear that I store in the trunk of my car in a Florida parking lot.

Chapter 4

Between the Rod and the Fish: Hooks, Lines, Leaders

In This Chapter

▶ The complete short hook encyclopedia

▶ The right line

▶ What makes a good leader

A rod is important, but without a line to deliver the fly, a leader to tie onto the fly, and a hook to tie the fly on, your space-age rod is just an expensive stick. Fly fishing offers a number of choices for each kind of fish that you pursue, but the good news is that it's a heck of a lot simpler than baitcasting or spinning. You have no sinkers to speak of, no swivels, and no intricate combinations of hooks and loops and sinkers. Basically, in fly rodding, you point, you cast, and you fish — a very uncomplicated setup.

Fly Lines

A fly line is a totally different animal from all other kinds of fishing line. In spinning and baitcasting, the weight of your terminal tackle pulls the line off the reel and carries it to the fish. In fly fishing, it's just the opposite: The weight of the line carries the relatively weightless fly to the fish.

Way back when, fly line was made from braided horsehair. If you wanted a heavy line, you braided more hairs. The modern fly line is a smooth, plastic coating around a core of braided nylon or dacron. Most lines are 70 to 90 feet long and are spliced to another 100 yards or so of thinner backing line (usually braided Dacron). Whenever you buy line or a reel, have the people at the store put the backing on and splice it to your line. You can do the job yourself, but why hassle with it?

Is weight good or bad?

Weight is good up to a point. The weight of the line is what bends the rod, and the bend of the rod as it springs forward is what shoots the line toward the fish. Fly lines come with different ratings according to their weight. A *1 Weight* is a very light line that you use with an extremely delicate rod. As the numbers go up, so does the line's weight. Most trout fishermen prefer something in the 4- to 6-Weight range. Rods are rated according to the weight of the line they throw. My first fly rod was a 6 Weight, and I caught trout, bass, an 18-pound pike, many bonefish, and two barracuda on it. (The second barracuda finally broke that rod after 10 years of casting.)

Although I can't give you any hard and fast rules, Table 4-1 lists my recommendations for line (and rod) weights for some common game fish (all of which are described in Part II).

Table 4-1	Fly Line Weights and Common Game Fish
Line Weight	*Type of Fish*
1, 2, and 3 Weight	Panfish, trout
4 and 5 Weight	Trout, freshwater bass
6 and 7 Weight	Trout, bass, small blues, stripers, bonefish, pike
8 and 9 Weight	Salmon, stripers, bonefish, permit, bluefish, redfish
10, 11, and 12 Weight	Tarpon and other big game fish

The line-weight table gives you a bunch of general guidelines. They're not commandments. My favorite bass guide, Jack Allen, feels that, with graphite rods, you can usually go up or down one line weight from the recommended number and still remain well within the optimum performance range for your rod. And in heavy wind — or if he wants more of a fight on light tackle — Jack's been known to put 8-Weight line on a 5-Weight rod. My friend Tom Akstens, who teaches fly fishing up in the Adirondacks, says that he thinks that all newcomers do better if they overload their rod by one line weight.

Does color count?

In most situations, I'm not sure that line color means very much to the fish. From the point of view of the fish looking up at the fly line, all he sees is something dark, lit from behind. So floating lines can be whatever color you like. Visibility — for the angler not the fish — is, however, an important consideration, in which case something bright that stands out can aid you in visually tracking the movement of your fly. With sinking lines, however, the story's different: Now your line is in the area of the fish's best vision — the water. Lines that blend in with the background are less likely to put a fish on guard.

For fishing on the flats, I tend to favor one of the new clear monocore lines. These lines are often manufactured with a see-through finish that's virtually invisible — a feature that's very important in dealing with bonefish and permit, for example, which are so skittish that I'm sure they can hear you think.

Taper tips

Most fly lines have a *taper* — that is, they're fatter in one part than in another. These days, the most common taper is *weight forward*. This type of line is heavier in the *head,* which is the first 30 feet or so of line to come through the guides of your rod. The principle behind a weight-forward taper is that you want to get a lot of leverage on the rod to develop momentum quickly, and then, after you've developed a rapid line speed, the weight of the head will carry the rest of the line. In other words, the weight-forward line is ideal for *delivery* of the fly.

You'll see some fly lines marked with a *saltwater taper* or *bass-bug taper*. These, too, are weight-forward lines with a more exaggerated taper. Most fly rodders, myself included, use weight-forward lines exclusively. A *shooting head* is 30 or so feet of heavy weight-forward line attached to running line. In the hands of a powerful caster, enough line speed is developed with the head that it can pull a lot more of the thin, light running line with it, resulting in a fast forward cast that travels farther.

Less common these days than it once was is the *double taper*. This design is thin in the head, gradually fattens out, and then slims again. The idea is that you have a good amount of line in the air to develop line speed (momentum), yet the line that lands nearest to the trout does so more delicately than the weight-forward variety. I keep thinking that, someday, I'm going to become a sensitive-enough angler that I can appreciate a double taper, but my experience so far has been that, if I want more delicacy of presentation, I just go to a lighter rod and line.

Sink or swim

Now that fly fishing no longer exclusively means dry-fly fishing for trout in a stream, fly rodders have begun to use different kinds of lines for different fishing situations. Often, this situation means using some kind of weight to get down to fish that aren't surface feeders — for example, stream-borne trout hanging on the bottom, bass three feet down in a pond, or stripers 15 feet down in San Francisco Bay. In the old days, you used weighted flies or tied some split shot onto your leader to reach those fish, and these methods still work in many situations. But then came lead-core line (with the inner core literally made of lead), which made for the least-pleasant casting imaginable. I once spent a week using a 13 Weight with a lead core while fishing for tarpon in the bocas (river mouths) of Costa Rica. A total, tiring bummer!

Today there are more streamlined and more castable sinking lines, the most common being the following:

- **Intermediate** line sinks very slowly so that you can fish it as a floater or a sinker. This type is far and away my preferred line for saltwater fly fishing in the northeastern United States. It gets the line below the surface chop and keeps you in contact with your fly.

- **FS,** or **full sinking,** lines get down fast and deep. The best are the *teeny* lines that have come on the market in recent years. They're slim, so they cut through the wind, and they aren't so hellish to pick up and cast as the old lead-core lines were.

Threading your fly line

I remember when I got my first computer. It had all these "simple" instructions to get me up and writing in no time. These instructions told me where the on-off switch was and how to plug the thing in, all of which I pretty much could have guessed, because, after all, a computer is just an electrical appliance, like the toaster or dishwasher. What the instructions *didn't* tell me was which end of the disk went in first. I guess the manufacturer took it for granted, but if you think about it, the *disk* was the one piece of gear that was totally new.

So as far as fly rods go, the big difference between them and other fishing rods is the line. Usually, after you thread line through your spinning or bait-casting rod, you pick up the end of the line and thread it through the guides. If you try to do so with heavy fly line, the line will find a way to slip back down and make you start all over again. As shown in Figure 4-1, the easy way to string up your rod is to pull off about six feet of line, double it over, and then pull the doubled line through the guides. (Don't make me explain the physics. This approach just works better.)

Figure 4-1:
If you
double over
the heavy
fly line,
stringing
up your rod
is easy.

TIP

Out of the garage and into the stream

As time goes by, you may find that your fly line doesn't shoot for distance the same way it once did. Don't worry. Your casting isn't getting worse. The problem is that your line is dirty and gunked up. First, wash it in soap and water. You don't need to remove it from the reel to wash it. You can just strip line into a bucket of soapy water or pull the line through your hand while holding a soapy rag. Rinse in clean water. After the line is dry, spray it with some Armor All, commonly used to brighten up the vinyl on your car's dashboard. The protective slick coating is very slippery and will act as a good lubricant to increase your casting distance measurably.

Leaders

After the fly, the most critical element of the fly-fishing setup is the *leader*, which is the nylon monofilament line that attaches the fly line to the fly. Remember that a fly line is big and thick, and a fly is delicate and small. The leader must also be light; otherwise, it'll overpower the fly, giving it a lifeless action. Add to this situation the fact that a big, fat fly line landing next to a spooky fish is guaranteed to send it straight for cover. A leader that makes as little disturbance as possible increases your chances of connecting with a fish.

As shown in Figure 4-2, the thick section of the leader that joins to the fly line is called the *butt*. What happens between the butt and the fly is a gradual *taper* as the leader gets progressively thinner and lighter. The result is a smooth and even transfer of force from the rod to the line and down through the leader. The last section of the taper is called the *tippet*.

For the average dry-fly leader, the butt and taper sections each make up 40 percent of the leader, and the tippet is the remaining 20 percent.

Figure 4-2:
A typical
leader.

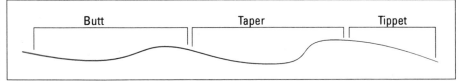

Butt   Taper   Tippet

Leaders are usually between 7 and 12 feet in length. You can buy them knotted or knotless. The taper of a knotted leader is made up of progressively lighter lengths of mono knotted together. The knotless type is just a single strand that smoothly tapers.

If you change flies a lot, you end up cutting off and replacing tippet. Using a knotted leader is a handy way to remember what thickness you're fishing. On the other hand, if you're just starting out, knotless is pretty simple, so just keep it simple.

Match your leader to your fly

A little fly requires a light tippet. If you use a heavy tippet with a little fly, you have a classic case of the tail wagging the dog or, in this case, the line wagging the fly. This setup will never catch a fish.

The rule for matching fly to leader is to divide the fly size by four to figure out the appropriate leader. A big size #8 fly gets a sturdy 2X tippet. Size #16 gets a 4X. And if the trout are finicky, you can always go a little lighter. Try 5X for that size #16, for example, if the trout act interested but don't strike.

The X file

If you ever catch a nice trout — make that *when* you catch a nice trout — someone will probably ask you, "What did you take it on?" This query is actually two separate questions: The first is "What fly?" and the second is "What tippet?" Tippets are rated according to their thickness, which is directly related to their strength. Where the spin fisherman may say, "I caught it on 12-pound test," the fly rodder's equivalent answer would be "1X."

Why *X?* What does that letter mean in fly fishing?

The simple answer, as is true of much in fly fishing, is that the English figured out the system. And you know that, if you give the English a chance to measure anything, they do so differently from the rest of the world.

In the old days, leader tippets were made of silkworm gut. They were sized by being passed through a die that shaved down the thickness of the gut. If you ran the gut through the die once, it was 1X; twice through gave you 2X and so on. The more shavings the tippet got, the thinner the leader. So the higher numbers represent thinner, lighter leaders.

Beginners usually fish somewhere in the 3X to 5X range. The heaviest tippets are 1X and 2X.

What tippet should I tie?

During the course of a normal fishing session, you may change flies a dozen times as you try to find something to interest the fish. Each time that you do so, you'll cut back on your leader by eight inches or so. At a certain point, you're going to need to lengthen your leader by adding some more tippet. The problem? How do you know how thick the tippet you tie on should be? If you're not traveling around with a micrometer, you really don't know how heavy the leader is that you're lengthening. As you fish more, you'll be able to come close by guesstimating. At least you'll be able to tell the difference between 2X and 5X. But still, to get that smooth transition in your loop and the right presentation of the fly, you need a balanced leader. So do your best at guessing and then try the following test. It *never fails.*

Grab hold of your leader with two hands. The left-hand length is the old leader, and the right-hand length is the section you just tied on. Push both segments toward one another, and the leader will form a loop. The leader on the left isn't balanced. The thick part overpowers the thin part, and you get a lopsided loop. The right-hand loop, however, is balanced — a smooth, uniform oxbow. To make the loop on the left like the loop on the right, simply clip off the new tippet and tie on a length that's one size thicker. Then repeat this test until you have a uniform oxbow.

How strong do the line and leader need to be?

After you learn how to play a fish, you may be surprised at how much fish you can subdue with a relatively light line. Notice that I said *"subdue."* You fight the fish with your rod, reel, and line. Line isn't designed to *lift* fish. You use special tools such as nets, gaffs, tailers, and special leaders for that task (see Chapter 15).

Look at it this way: Say that you weigh 140 pounds. If I stuck a hook in your lip, I'll bet you that I'd need to exert a lot less than 140 pounds of force to lead you around. In fact, we human beings are so wimpy that a pound or two of pressure applied to the right location should have you following along quite nicely. Fish are a little tougher, but still, I've caught 100-pound tarpon on 20-pound tippet. (I've also lost five-pound trout on two-pound tippet.)

If you're fishing a sink tip in shallow water, you may not want a long, delicate leader or an unweighted fly. Think about it: Your tip gets down where the fish are, and your long leader and weightless fly float to the surface. The sink tip helps get you in the fishing zone. A weighted fly keeps you there.

Everything You Need to Know about Hooks

A *hook* is a rather simple device — a pointed piece of metal that you attach to your line. The conventional tackle angler has many hooks to choose from, depending on what kind of fish and fishing is on the agenda. In fly rodding, the choice is simpler. The hook needs to be big enough to hold the materials of the fly and light enough, in the case of dry flies, not to sink under its own weight. The most popular hook shape in fly fishing is the *Model Perfect,* and you can find a number of good manufacturers of quality hooks, among them Mustad, Daichi, Orvis, Tiemco.

Figure 4-3 features the different parts of a typical hook's anatomy.

Figure 4-3: The anatomy of a hook.

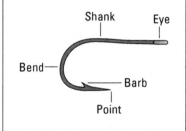

Following are the most important parts of a hook:

✔ The *point* is where tackle meets fish. As in many situations in life, the first impression is an important one. If you don't have a good, sharp point on your hook, you can have the most expensive rod in the world but you won't catch fish.

✔ The *barb* is a type of a reverse point that's designed to keep a fish on the hook after the fish bites. Bigger is not better with barbs. Big barbs can make setting a hook difficult if the hook meets up with a tough-mouthed fish, such as a bonefish. Or big barbs can make too big a tear in the mouth of a soft-mouthed fish such as the American shad. Many catch-and-release anglers fish with barbless hooks, or they bend the barb down with pliers.

✔ The *bend* is the curved part of the hook and has two elements: the *bite* and the *gap.* I think of the *bite* as the depth that the hook penetrates. I think of the *gap* as the width of the area that your hook clears after being set. A relatively wide gap may get around the snout of a billed fish or dig in beyond the width of a thick jawbone. The downside is that the wider the gap is, the easier the fish can bend the hook so that it escapes. If this event occurs, some anglers console themselves over losing the fish by saying something like "Gee whiz! Straightened it right out!" The implication is that the fish that straightened the hook must have been *one huge fish* — a fish that no angler could have held, including the expert who made the comment. The fact of the matter is that you really shouldn't lose a fish after you hook it. Yet losing a fish this way happens to everybody. Developing a sense of how much pressure your tackle can take is part of becoming an educated angler.

✔ The *shank* connects the bend to the eye. A shank can be long or short. As is the case with gap, having more length means that a hook is easier for a fish to bend. So why aren't all hooks short? The answer has to do with what goes *on* the hook. A fly such as the Griffith's Gnat is supposed to imitate a generic small insect and, therefore, is very short. Lefty's Deceiver imitates a long, lean bait fish and, therefore, is tied on a longer hook.

✔ The *eye* of the hook (the loop through which the line passes) may be turned up, turned down, or straight. The garden-variety hook — the kind that most anglers use most of the time — has a turned-down eye. Some exceptions to the rule exist, however. Traditional salmon flies tie onto turned-up hooks, and some anglers prefer turned-up eyes on very tiny flies, because small flies have little gap and bite to begin with, and a turned-up eye provides a bit more gap.

When bigger is smaller

The bigger the hook, the more weight it has; and the more weight it has, the more hackle it needs in order to float — and that extra amount of hackle is not a good thing because it just junks up the look of the fly. Whenever one fly rodder asks another what the fish are taking, the answer is often something like, "A size 16 Adams." Flies don't come in sizes. Hooks do. But hook size has become so linked to fly size that everyone thinks in these terms, so here's the deal: The *higher* the number, the *smaller* the hook. A size #6 hook is much bigger than a size #28 hook. And by the way, hook sizes are counted by twos. No odd numbers until size 1. Actually, the measuring system changes at 1 to the system called the *aughts* (written 1/0, 2/0, and the like) in which the zero is pronounced old style — *aught*. In the aughts, the higher the number, the bigger the hook. A 2/0 is big, a 6/0 is really big. Got that straight? Like getting a wisdom tooth pulled, after you get hook sizes sorted out in your mind, the good part is that you never have to do it again.

Get to the point!

As I write these words, I've just walked in from the bass pond in back of my parents' house. I used the same popping bug that caught fish on my last visit to that pond. The water had a bit of chop on it — just the kind of conditions that make bass a little less spooky and more eager to hop on a nice slurpy popper. Within 10 minutes, I'd raised (seriously attracted) and missed six fish. I wrote this disappointing experience off to tentative takes from the bass and slow reflexes on my part.

I was wrong. As I went to change flies, I noticed that all the freshwater hooks in my box were rusty. Then I remembered that, while I was wading for striped bass in the surf one recent night, my flies had become soaked and I hadn't bothered to rinse them off. The saltwater hooks showed a little salt staining, but the freshwater hooks (which included my bass bugs) had become rusty and *dull*. Dull hooks never catch fish.

Some anglers think that they have a sharp hook as long as the hook's point pricks the skin. But a hook is more than a needle. Even though the point of a hook is relatively small, the point has some area and *edge* to it. That edge, just like the edge of a knife, needs to be sharp to cut into the fish beyond the end of the barb. Driving the hook home to this depth is called *setting the hook*. How to do this, when to do this, and how hard to do this are all-important elements of angling technique. But you never get a chance to show off all your mind-blowing techniques with dull hooks.

As I said, a hook has an edge to it, just as a knife has. Sharpen a hook just as you'd sharpen a knife, using a file or sharpening steel. Special *hook hones* and files are made expressly for this purpose. If your experience is like mine, I know that you may neglect sharpening *until* you lose a good fish. Before you even tie on a fly, however, you're always best off running your file along the edge of your hook to get it good and sharp. And (no matter what any-body tells you to the contrary) you *can* sharpen stainless steel.

Spark-plug files (which you can find in any auto-parts store) make good hook sharpeners — which makes sense if you consider that spark plugs' points (like fishhooks) are small, have a narrow gap, and are made of metal. Fly rodders who find themselves out in a stream with a dull hook and no file may want to try using the striker on a matchbook cover to touch up their hooks.

Unhooking yourself

I've never met you. I don't know how old you are, how big you are, where you come from, or how well you fish. But I do know one thing about you: If you fish, someday, somewhere, you will hook yourself. You have a number of choices. Sometimes you can continue to push the hook all the way through the wound and out again. This action is somewhat painful, but it is doable. In nearly every other case, the following steps, which I checked out with my brother the doctor who is also a fly rodder, will do the trick.

This looks as though it shouldn't work, but it does. You need to have confidence or you may not do very well. Try practicing this method on a piece of raw meat until you understand what you're doing. After you get the idea, it all makes sense.

The following steps, illustrated in Figure 4-4, show you how to remove a hook that's embedded in some part of your body:

1. **Take a 2-foot length of at least 25-pound test line and tie the ends together so that you have a circle of line.**

   If you don't have 25-pound test line, double a few strands of 10-pound or 12-pound test line.

2. **Loop the line over your wrist and form a small loop between your thumb and forefinger.**

3. **Take this small loop and put it around the hook in the center of the hook's bend.**

4. **With your other thumb, press down on the eye of the hook.**

   This action should open the wound enough for you to gently back the barb out of your flesh. Getting the barb clear of the flesh is *very* important. If you don't get the barb clear, you shouldn't continue with this procedure.

5. **Finally, pull on the small loop with a sharp jerk.**

   The hook should come free with relatively little pain to you.

Of course, prevention is the best practice, and you can deflect many wandering hooks with a hat and a pair of glasses. Wear them.

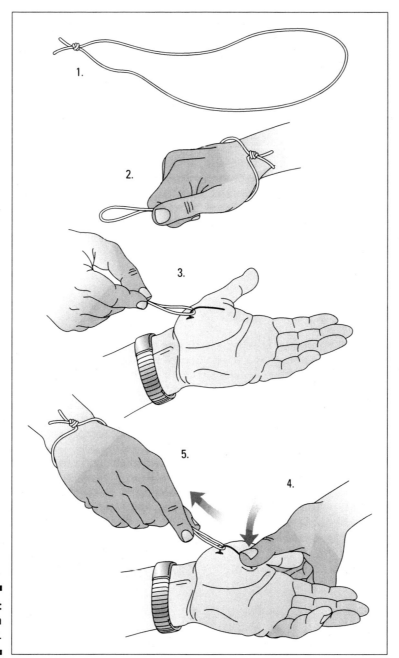

Figure 4-4:
Getting a
hook out.

Big Exception!!

Don't ever try to remove a hook anywhere near your eye. Get medical attention for this as soon as you can. I reiterate that the best way to prevent this kind of injury is to wear glasses or sunglasses.

Get rid of your barbs

One way to avoid needing to go through the whole hook-removal operation is to *debarb* (remove the barbs from) your hooks. Debarbing also helps speed up the releasing process if you're fishing catch-and-release. Simply take a pair of pliers (needle-nose pliers work best) and crimp the barb against the hook's tip. Remember that you're not using a wire cutter here, and you're not trying to take the whole point off the hook. On most hooks, a small amount of pressure on the barb does the trick.

Sinkers: A Necessary Evil

A fly weighs next to nothing. That's one of the beauties of fly fishing. But if the current's moving at a good clip and the fish are hanging on the bottom, a floating fly isn't going to do much good. In this situation, you may need to resort to some kind of weight to get your fly down to the fish. Sinking line isn't always the answer. After all, if the fly line sinks and the fly has a tendency to float, you may wind up having your line on the bottom and your fly somewhere above it and out of fish range. In these instances, you may need to bite the bullet and put a little weight on your leader. You basically have two choices. One choice is to use *twist-on* weights, which are about as long as a matchstick and that, as the name suggests, you just twist around your line. I've never done very well with these kinds of weights. The other alternative is to use a piece of split shot, just like the kind that you use in conventional fishing. I like the kind that has a little tab in back that enables you to open the shot and remove it after you no longer need it.

Part II
The Fish and the Flies

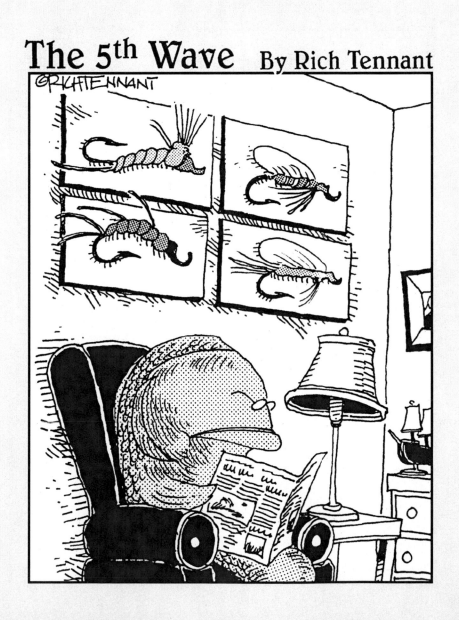

In this part . . .

This part is a little weird. True, it's about the fish you're after and the flies you use to go after them, but I haven't grouped all of the fish in one chapter and all of the flies in another. I wanted to structure this part in a way that you will find more useful, so I devote the first few chapters to trout, the flies they eat, the flies you can buy or tie to catch them, and the great rivers where you can find them. I do the same for that other great game fish: bass. I also talk about many of the other game fish in fresh and saltwater that you may be tempted to take with a fly rod.

Now that you see the logic to this part, if you're after trout, read Chapters 5 through 8. If you want bass, see Chapter 10. Many of the other freshwater game fish are covered in Chapter 9, and you can find a great intro to saltwater fly rodding in Chapters 11 and 12.

Chapter 5
Trout and the Bugs They Love

*O*nce upon a time, when the only fish you fished for with a fly was a trout, a *fly* was a bit of feather and fur on a hook. It was always meant to look like an insect, a very particular kind of insect, the mayfly. But these days, fly fishers angle for trout, bass, striped bass, redfish, bluefish, blue marlin, bluegill, dolphin (fish), ladyfish, tarpon, fluke, flounder, salmon, and on and on. The list gets longer every year as more and more people take up this challenging and satisfying sport. So a *fly* no longer means something that looks like an insect. In the same way that someone who makes CDs is still called a record producer (or the way that a person who makes videos is called a filmmaker), anglers who use a fly rod to deliver concoctions that look like shrimp, eels, bait fish, baby robins, frogs, mice, and crabs still refer to the thing on the end of their line as a fly.

So even though a *fly* once meant just that — something that looked like a winged insect found in trout streams — it may be more accurate to give a fly a wider definition so as to take into account where the sport is today and where it is going. *A fly is something you fly fish with* is as close as I can get to a real if not a very exact definition.

Having said that considerable mouthful on the question of "What is a fly?," it remains true that during the past 300 or 400 years, *fly fishing* meant *trout fishing*. Only in the last century or so have other fish attracted the attention of fly rodders. So although it is true that a fly is no longer just an imitation of a mayfly, it is also true that the vast majority of flies and all the terminology in fly fishing came out of trout fishing. And even today, most fly rodders are trouters, and most artificial flies were originally devised to entice trout to the hook.

The following is a look at the mayfly which, from birth to death, through all the phases of its life, is of paramount interest to the trout and the fisher of trout. The point to bear in mind is that wet flies, dry flies, and nymphs, terms that you come across again and again in fly fishing, all have their origin in the life cycle of the mayfly.

The Short, Happy Life of the Mayfly: Swim, Eat, Fly, Mate, Die

I have often envied the mayfly. Not that I'd want to be one: They only live about a year. However, when you compare the way a mayfly's life goes with the way your average human gets in and out of this world, I like the romantic mayfly script better.

In the beginning

A mayfly starts out as an egg on the bottom of a stream. (So far no great shakes; but stick with the story until the end, and you can see what I am talking about.) Soon, the egg hatches, and out crawls a many-legged little critter known as a *nymph,* or immature mayfly. When you see trout with their noses down, rooting about on the bottom of a stream, they are often feeding on nymphs.

About one year to the day from when it began life as an egg, the nymph is ready to hatch and become a full-fledged mayfly. When fly rodders talk about a *hatch,* they don't mean what happens when the egg becomes a nymph. (Technically speaking, going from egg to nymph is a hatch; but this type of hatch isn't of much interest to trout, and therefore, it is of even less interest to trout fishermen.)

Dry fly time: The big show

The hatch of most interest to fly rodders occurs when all the mayflies of a particular species shed their old skin, rise to the surface, sprout wings, dry themselves off, and (for the first time) fly. Millions of mayflies may hatch in a single stretch of a stream. This process, which takes a few minutes for each individual fly, normally takes a few days to play itself out on any given stream. Usually, a hatch begins in the warmer waters downstream and moves upstream, which has relatively cooler waters.

In this period of time, between when they begin to shed their skin and when they first take flight, the mayflies are at their most vulnerable. Look at it this way: If I were the trout and you were the insect, you'd have a pretty hard time defending yourself just as you were trying to pull a sweater over your head (or better yet, just as you were trying to wriggle out of a wet suit). Fly rodders sometimes call this stage the *emerger stage.*

When a hatch is on, the trout know that plenty of easy-to-catch food is around, just for the taking. When the mayfly has broken out of its old nymph case, it is often known as a *wet fly* or *emerger.* Many mayflies never make it to full-blown, flying-around Mayflydom. For one reason or another, they can't shed their cases and they just float on the surface as stillborns — stillborn but still tasty to the trout.

Most of the time, the mayfly does make it out of the case; most of those that do rest for a while on the surface of the water, drying their wings and just generally getting their bearings. You can easily tell if an insect is a mayfly at this point because its two wings are folded back and stick up in the air like the sail of a sailboat. To the hungry trout, this is the sitting-duck phase. The insect is now a full-fledged mayfly or *dun.* And the artificial fly of choice at this time is often the dry fly. The mayfly may beat its wings every now and again in order to dry them. This further attracts the attention of the hungry trout.

Because the mayfly instinctively knows that it may be gobbled up at any moment, it is in a hurry to get off the water. Because the trout knows this, too, it will feed purposefully as long as there are mayflies on the water.

As a general rule, most fly rodders find dry-fly fishing the most satisfying way to take a trout. I think that this attitude has a great deal to do with the fact that when a trout eats your dry fly, you get to see the whole thing. As with topwater lures, a visual-surface take is incomparably exciting. Many writers, and many more anglers, run off at the mouth about all the extra skill and smarts you need to be successful with the dry fly. Baloney! Fly fishing is just more fun because you get to see all the action.

Spinners: Ending happy

If our mayfly manages to survive the hatching stage and the wing-drying stage, it is ready for one last change into the *spinner phase.* Shortly after hatching, a mayfly flies around for the first time and heads for a streamside bush or tree. After it reaches that sanctuary, its tail grows longer and its wings lose their milky translucence and become clear. Then, that evening or possibly the next day, the spinners fly over the stream and mate in midair.

The male, having done his assigned job, drops to the surface of the stream and dies. The female deposits her eggs in the stream (where they cling to a rock, hatch, and start the nymph cycle all over again). Following this, the female joins her husband-for-a-day on the surface of the stream. At this time, a trout sees a huge amount of fresh mayfly meat that has no chance of escaping. At this stage of the hatch, known as a *spinner fall,* an angler can encounter some amazing fishing. In the case of some flies, the biggest mayfly (which is called the Green Drake) and the smallest mayfly (the *Tricorythodes* or *Trico),* for example, the best fishing in the whole hatch is during the spinner fall.

So much for the life of the mayfly (as shown in Figure 5-1): It begins as a little crawler on the bottom of the stream; then on the last day of its life, it sprouts wings, flies up into the bright, summer sky, and (in a grand climax) mates for the first time while in midair, following which it immediately dies and falls to the surface of a clear-flowing stream. See what I mean about the mayfly having a better life script than most folks?

Get wet!

Okay that's the theory, now let's see how it works out in the stream. One of the very first things I do is to pick up a stream rock and look on its underside. You should see a bunch of little critters scurrying around. In a healthy trout stream, these are often mayfly nymphs. They look like the world's smallest clawless crawfish. Every one of those nymphs will grow up to be a mayfly. Actually, they would like to grow up to be mayflies. Some will get eaten long before they have that chance. The important thing to remember is, after you have been fishing for a while, you will begin to be able to identify nymphs, and depending on how developed they are, you will have a good idea of what is going to be hatching.

The one with the most flies wins

"Artificial flies are all named. There are the Professor, the Hackle, the Ibis, the Yellow Sally, and several other breeds. Whenever a bilious angler has no luck and nothing to do, he sits down and concocts a new swindle in feathers and christens it with a nine-jointed Indian name, and, at once, every angler in the country rushes in and pays $2 a dozen for samples."

Henry Guy Carlton

Figure 5-1:
The mayfly
begins at
nymph
stage and
then
hatches to
become an
emerger,
a dun,
and finally
a spinner.

Get net!

If nymphs are important when they are hiding in rocks, they are super-important when they are floating in the stream because, more often than not, if there are a lot of one kind of nymph floating in the water, chances are it indicates that a hatch has happened, is happening, or will happen. This is important information to have because it will tell you what kind of flies to expect and what you should have in your box. A little aquarium dip net is an invaluable tool to carry in your vest. Dip it into the obvious feeding lanes, in the back eddies, or any other place where your two eyes or your experience tell you that there are nymphs in the water. Look at what you find and very soon you will begin to understand what to expect in the way of mayfly activity.

Some Nymph Basics

In a healthy stream, most trout eat more flies in the nymph stage than in their later phases. A good nympher will outfish a dry-fly angler as a general rule. But most fly rodders prefer the dry fly because of the excitement of watching a trout rise to the fly. I am not going to get in the middle of that argument, but I will say this: No matter how you like to fish, if you know where to look for nymphs and how to identify them, you will be more productive. You can break down the hundreds of mayfly nymphs into four basic groups. The following sections can help you do this.

Crawlers

The classic shape that most fly rodders think of when they think of nymphs is in the crawler group. Crawlers live in various stream types, both moving and still water. They prefer to take cover in vegetation, in bottom gravel, and under stones — in other words, places where it pays to be able to crawl around. They are not great swimmers. Some of the more important flies go by the common names of Hendricksons (a Hendrickson nymph is shown in Figure 5-2), Pale Morning Duns, and Tricos.

Clingers

Clingers (an example of which is shown in Figure 5-3) have shorter, more compact bodies than crawlers. They prefer swift currents because of their high oxygen requirements, and so they need to be able to hang on to something. Their heads and bodies are flat to deflect fast water. Most

Clingers have large suction-cup-like gills. Some of the more important species (the ones that trout key in on and anglers should too) move to quieter water when they are getting ready to hatch. At this time, you will see the nymphs around shoreline rocks. Important Clingers include March Browns and Quill Gordons.

Figure 5-2:
This typical crawler, a Hendrickson, is the center-fold of Nymphdom.

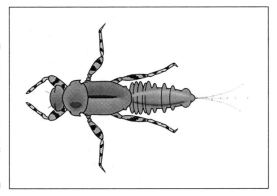

Figure 5-3:
The Clinger is a classic fathead (no offense intended).

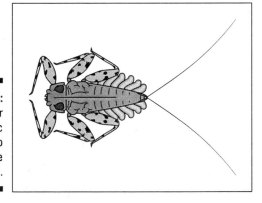

Burrowers

Burrowers are larger nymphs that inhabit the silt and mucky bottoms of pools and quiet places in rivers and cold lakes. They burrow and hide in soft bottoms. They tend to be bigger and have long, tusk-like mandibles (jaws). They also have noticeable plumed gills that they wave to extract oxygen from the water. The Giant Michigan Mayfly and the Green Drake, shown in Figure 5-4, are two of the biggies in this group.

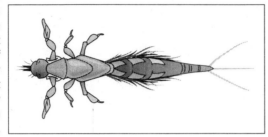

Swimmers

Larger members of the swimmer group live in swifter, rockier water where they cling to rock bottoms. Smaller types prefer medium-fast to slow waters, where they hold on to bottom structures. Swimmers all have smooth bodies, long, delicate legs, and gill plates down the top of their abdomens, as shown in Figure 5-5. Their tails are fringed with hairs and used as paddles to dart through the water. Blue-Winged Olives and Isonychia (shown in Figure 5-5) are both members of this group.

Figure 5-5:
Swimmers
move
quickly,
and the
trout will
take them
aggressively.

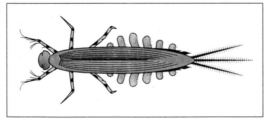

TIP

Get wet again

Go back to the stream and pick up some rocks again. If you want, go back to the same little stretch of creek that you went to at the beginning of this chapter. Chances are, when you noticed the little mayfly nymphs running around, you didn't pay much attention to the little sticks and bits of leaves stuck to the bottom of the rocks. This is good news to the caddis. It means it has done its camouflaging act well because those bits of debris are actually cases that protect caddis *larvae* while they mature. Of course trout, as anyone who has ever fished for them has discovered, are far from fools, which is why if you ever look at their stomach contents, you will see that they have gobbled up a good amount of these cases to get at their delicious innards. Still, the trout must miss a few, which explains the millions of caddis in trout streams.

Caddis Flies: Not Sexy, but They Work

If the mayfly is the supermodel of the trout food universe, then the caddis is the unglamorous, overalls-and-workboots assembly line worker. They aren't colorful like mayflies. When they return to a stream, lacking the ballet dancer grace of the spinner, they remind me more of an old Volkswagen running out of gas. But trout love them. On many streams, they are the primary insect in the trout's diet, and because they aren't always as particular about stream quality in the way that mayflies often are, rivers that once boasted great mayfly hatches now have much greatly increased caddis populations.

Caddis flies have a life cycle comprised of three stages, as shown in Figure 5-6. Step one for most caddis is inside those cases. The little worm within is called a *larva,* usually white-bodied with a black head. There are some larvae that don't build cases and take their chances just like respectable mayfly nymphs and they can be brownish, greenish, or orange. This is all you need to know about the larva because there is not much you can do with an artificial fly — which moves — that will imitate a larva in its case that sits there like a bump on a log (which is just what it looks like).

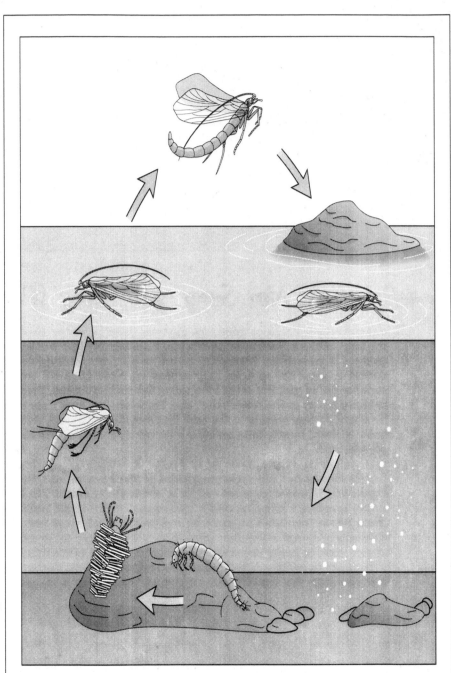

Figure 5-6:
The life
cycle of the
caddis.

Next, the worm becomes a *pupa*. It leaves its protective case and rises to the surface. Some caddis zip to the surface rapidly and pop right through the surface of the stream to emerge as mature flies. Others drift along. They are fished like nymphs at this stage. For many years, when I was primarily a wet-fly fisherman, I would tie a mayfly nymph and a caddis pupa on the same leader, figuring that it increased my chances of giving the trout something that they were interested in.

Finally, the pupa rises to the surface and breaks out of its case to become a caddis fly. None of the long-drawn-out orchestration of the mayfly here. The caddis is a wham-bam-thank-you-ma'am kind of insect. It just hops out of its hatching suit and takes off in a hurry. Perhaps this great haste explains the splashy rise that a trout makes when chasing caddis pupae on their way to the surface. The caddis are in a hurry, and the trout are too. When they reach the surface, many caddis species hop a few times as they try to jump-start their flying motor for the first time. If there are a lot of caddis on the water and they are all hopping about, this movement can stimulate trout feeding. Skittering a dry fly along the surface can often summon up a strike. The main thing to note about the caddis in distinction to the mayfly is that its wings, when at rest, are folded in a tent-like v-shape. This v-shaped fly is a *tent* or *down-wing* fly as opposed to the mayfly, which is known as an *upright-wing* fly. The caddis has two pairs of wings, four in all.

Most caddis like to save their mating for one big party when they form huge swarms over the stream. Shortly after, the females bounce their way up stream laying their eggs right in the surface film. Trout will respond aggressively to this phase of the caddis.

Stone Flies: The Biggest Bugs

Years ago, when I first started fly fishing, there was a fly shop in New York run by the world's most irascible fly shop owner, Jim Derren. Jim was a lifelong angler and fishing buddy of some greats of the sport from the Golden Days of the Catskills, back in the 1930s and 40s. Jim's shop was in the untroutiest place on the face of the planet, a windowless, third story, little room in a Manhattan office tower. When you walked in, it was always a good idea to give a second or two (after opening the door) to make sure that no waders or fly boxes came tumbling down from the huge, unorganized piles. Jim was the kind of guy who didn't trust anybody else's information. I remember asking him for a fly that a friend had told me about and Jim said, "Your friend is a horse's ass!"

I quickly figured out that if I wanted information, I had to grin and bear it. "Sorry 'bout that," I said, "What do you recommend?"

"Here, take these," he said as he flipped me a few large nymphs. "They're stone flies. The Esopus Creek is full of them."

That marked my introduction to the largest insects on the Esopus, which was my home creek. I won't insult your intelligence the way Jim did mine (and my friend's), but I will tell you that the stone fly (shown in Figure 5-7), which has four wings like the caddis, is important trout food. They are not particularly good dry-fly insects because many of them hatch at night and even more of them crawl out of the water before they hatch on convenient rocks. In midsummer, in the Catskills, you will see their cases drying in the sun. They are easily the biggest nymph cases of the year. Though the dry doesn't produce that well, a nymph is a good fish taker in many rivers. When I am in a pure exploration mode, I will sometimes tie a mayfly, a stone fly, and a caddis fly nymph on the same leader and work my way down through a riffle. The more swift water in a stream, the better, as far as stone flies are concerned because they rely on heavily oxygenated water, which is what you are more likely to find in swift-flowing free-stone streams.

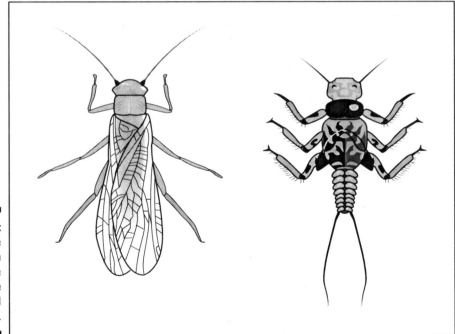

Figure 5-7:
The stone fly nymph and the mature winged stone fly.

The Two-Angler-Instant-Stream survey

If you fish with a buddy (most of us do) and you find yourself on a new stream (which also is pretty common), here is a tip that I picked up from Al Caucci, who invented the Compara-dun (along with his partner Bob Nastasi).

Your high tech gear is a piece of mesh or common household screening stapled to two lengths of broom handle. This allows you to roll up the screen like a scroll when not in use. One angler takes the screen and gets in position downstream of the angler without the screen. The upstream angler kicks up some rocks on the stream bottom (or some gravel or mud), and the downstream angler traps debris in the mesh. Then you take your gear to the streamside and look in the mesh to see what insect life is there. From this simple investigation, you will instantly know what kinds of nymphs and pupae are in the stream, and in all likelihood, there will be stillborn duns, spinners, emergers, and so on. If you have been doing your streamside investigations for a while, you will also know what hatches to expect. Even if you don't remember the name of one insect, you can still take out your fly box and compare it to what's in the mesh. Very soon, you will begin to know a lot more about bugs, at least the kind that trout like, than you ever thought you would. And there is nothing like actually catching a few fish to get you wanting to learn more!

Salmon flies: The greatest hatch

The salmon fly is the biggest insect that trout eat. When it hatches on many rivers in the Rockies and Sierras all, or at least most, of the rules of dry-fly-fishing go out the window. Big flies and sloppy casts that land with a *splat* will often bring up really big fish. In the same way that the huge size of the Green Drake or the Hex will bring out big eastern trout for their once-a-year dry-fly binge, the salmon fly on rivers like the Madison and the Yellowstone can produce absolutely torrid fishing for big trout. These bugs can be 2 inches long and fished on hooks up to size 2.

This is a late-spring-to-early-summer hatch that comes off pretty dependably at the same time every year. The classic pattern for the dry is the dark stone fly, but things change from river to river, so my advice is go into the local fly shop and ask. They probably won't call you a horse's ass, but if they do, so what? You've been called worse without catching any fish. Ignore the abuse and go fishing with confidence.

Grasshoppers: Trout Candy

Although no one catches a trout on every cast, or even every 20 casts, there are times when it is easier than others. Grasshopper time, which usually begins somewhere in August and continues through September's first frosts, is the closest thing to no-brainer trout fishing that I know. A grasshopper, shown in Figure 5-8, is a big insect — bigger than any bug in the stream — and when a breeze or an over-enthusiastic jump carries him into the stream, he is the bug version of a fish out of water: He is a big meal, basically helpless, struggling and making a commotion as he tries to scramble out of the water. To my way of thinking, this is the grasshopper's way of holding up a big "Eat Me" sign.

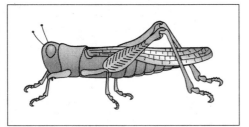

Figure 5-8:
The grasshopper, a favorite trout food.

When hoppers are on the water, this imitation is the first fly I will try. In fact even when they are not on the water but have been there for a few days previous, I will still try one because the trout are tuned in and even a dead piece of water can yield aggressive, hungry trout when you cast a hopper. And whatever you do, make sure that your hopper imitation has some yellow on its belly. Although hoppers in the field may come in a variety of colors including green, brown, yellow, and black, the hopper that the trout will take always seems to have some yellow. It must be like red to a bull or something like that, because the color seems to trigger a response.

For hoppers to be any good as trout attractors, you need to have live hoppers blowing on the water. This will not happen when the hoppers are young and can't leap any higher than the grass they live in. They need to get some loft so that the wind can catch them and carry them into the stream. So if you walk through a field and you scare up a lot of high-leaping, big, fat hoppers, you might give serious consideration to tying on an imitation for your first fly of the day.

Just because there are hoppers in the field, however, doesn't mean that there are hoppers on the water you are going to fish. I can recall many times in my early fly rodding days when I would walk across a hopper-filled field on my way to a favorite pool on the Esopus Creek in the Catskills. I would invariably scare up a mess of hoppers, but I never caught a trout using a hopper in this particular pool. This puzzled me. It was flat water with a gentle, even flow. The trout could surely see my hoppers, and according to the books, a twitch of the fly should have summoned up a surge like a bass slamming a plug. What I had neglected to keep in mind is that although the field was filled with hoppers, the bank on both sides was bordered by a thick stand of shrubs and trees that blocked the path of the hoppers as effectively as a brick wall. Lesson: If they can't get to the water, the trout can't eat them, can they?

Don't tell your husband anything!

On my first fishing trip to the west with my wife, I remember spending an afternoon on Slough Creek catching trout after trout on hoppers. Without moving more than 30 feet, I completely fished every wrinkle in a riffle that fed into a big pool. On the outside of the riffle, as the water calmed, I took a number of cutthroat trout. On the *current seam* — the clearly defined boundary between faster and slower water — I took a number of fat rainbows up to 21 inches. They were not easy to keep on, however. They hit with a rush and immediately took to the air. You needed a fair amount of technique and experience in striking and playing big fish to have any chance. I probably lost half and landed half. Melinda couldn't hold on to any.

We decided to walk downstream and try our luck elsewhere. We forded the river, following the footprints of a herd of buffalo that grazed on the far shore. They loped away from us, the baby bison scampering with their moms as they followed the lead bull.

We walked along a very calm stretch. The river must have been 15 feet deep in spots. You could see fallen trees on the bottom. It didn't look trouty to me, but it did to Melinda.

"I think there has to be a nice trout that would just love to see a hopper right about there," she said as she pointed her rod to the skeleton of a sunken fir tree.

"Yeah if we were fishing for bass," I said in a husbandly know-it-all way. Still my inner angler must have sensed something because I reflexively cast a hopper and — I can still see it in slow motion — a huge cutthroat rose purposefully and really smacked my hopper.

"Darn," Melinda said. "I was going to cast for that fish!"

I still feel pangs of guilt, all these years later, at having stolen that fish from under Mel's nose, and I still cast hoppers in unlikely places because — hey — you never know.

Chapter 6

Great Mayflies (And Why Trout Love Them)

*H*aving fished in most of the trout-loving world, I can tell you with certainty that you will *never* learn all the mayflies on a stretch of water. The good news is you don't have to. If you recognize some of the major hatches and know how to fish them, the general rules apply to the whole range of hatches. All I can say is: If *People* magazine devoted an issue to The World's Biggest Box Office Mayflies, these would probably be in it. I have included Latin names not because you will be quizzed on them, but because as you begin to fly fish for trout more, you are going to run into people who sling Latin. So knowing the names will prevent you from looking clueless and, in some cases, you might actually like learning these names.

I have also included some notes on fishing techniques that I have found to be particularly useful with these mayflies. If you have already done some fly fishing, they should make sense. If you haven't, you will find full explanations later in this book in Chapter 13.

How Big (Or Small) Is a Mayfly?

The size of most mayflies is usually expressed as the size of the hook that you use to tie an imitation of the fly. Figure 6-1 lets you see how flies measure up to each other. Accurate size becomes more critical, or easier to mess up, as flies get smaller.

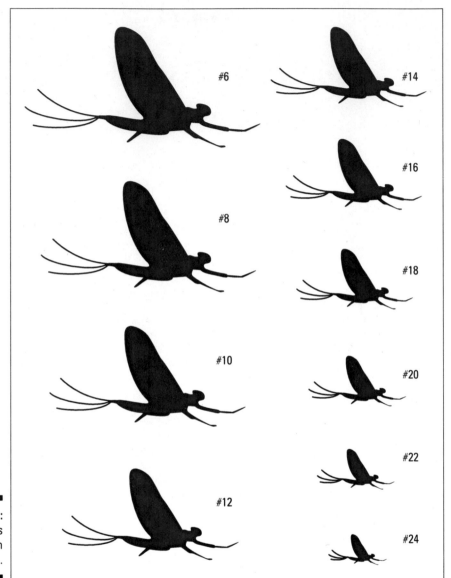

Figure 6-1:
Mayflies
come in
many sizes.

Start downstream

Mayfly hatches depend on water temperature. As the water warms, the hatches begin. Usually, this means that the hatch starts downstream and moves its way upstream to water that is cooler. You can extend the period that you can fish a favorite hatch by a week or more if you start early and follow the hatch upstream.

The Quill Gordon: As Unpredictable as the Weather

(Latin name: Epeorus pleuralis)

The Quill Gordon hatch, though it is often a washout fishing-wise, is heavily anticipated by East Coast trouters because when it happens we know — after enduring months of winter — that we have a shot at some fly fishing — no guarantee, but at least a shot. The hatch usually begins mid-April in more southerly streams. When the water temperature holds at 50°F for several days, the hatch begins and continues despite dips in temperature. Emergence peaks are in the early afternoon from 2 to 4 p.m. on cold or cloudy days and after 5 p.m. on hot days.

Quill Gordon nymphs are a dark gray-brown. They have high oxygen needs and inhabit riffles, rapids, and fast, gravelly runs where they can cling to the bottoms of rocks and boulders. They move to the downstream sides of rocks before emerging. Cast a weighted nymph pattern on the downstream side of obstructions where nymphs congregate. Or, during the hatch, fish an emerger in the film. Finally, fishing down and across (see Chapter 13) can induce a take as the fly ascends at the end of its swing through the current. The Gold Ribbed Hare's Ear will work fine for this hatch.

Duns have grayish-yellowish bodies with dark-brown markings and dark-gray wings. Early season trout congregate at the heads of pools to eat drifting duns, but because these are the first mayflies of the year, the trout need to get tuned in, and they are often tentative feeders especially in the early stages of the hatch. Nasty cold weather may be a bummer for the fishermen, but it can be a bonus to the fishing because it makes it hard for the newly hatched duns to get off the water. The dry fly can be fished in sizes #10 – #14. A Compara-dun and the classic Hackled Catskill fly with quill body both work well on this hatch.

The spinner is yellowish with dark-brown marks and gray wings. They appear three or four days after the first hatches. Spinners return to lay their eggs over riffles during the warmest part of the cool days or the coolest part of the warm days. Look carefully for rising trout quietly sucking down spinners. Because this is likely to happen over more broken water, you may have trouble making out what's happening, but look hard. There isn't a lot of food in the water at Quill Gordon time, and the trout need food. If you feel frustrated at not seeing spinners readily, don't give up. It took me 20 years to start seeing trout taking spinners. It was just one of those things I never could see very consistently. It is very subtle. My best advice: Stare until you can't anymore, and then stare some more. One of these days, you will recognize the rise to a spinner, and once you do, you won't forget it.

The Hendrickson: When the Fishing Gets Serious

(Latin name: Ephemerella subvaria)

There is probably no hatch more wildly anticipated by trouters in eastern North America than the Hendrickson. There are a number of reasons for this. First off, the Hendrickson usually pops on the first really great weather days of the year: Their emergence is pretty much a guarantee that the cold snaps of early spring are gone for good. Secondly, although it is not the first mayfly of the year, it usually is the first one the trout turn on to in a big way. The Quill Gordon, for example, is earlier, but not as predictable. Trout have to warm up to the idea of eating mayflies, and some years, it takes a few hatches before they get really bug-minded.

The Hendrickson hatch starts in April and can last through early June. It kicks in when the water reaches 50–55°F. In colder weather, the hatch will occur at the warmest time of day. In hot weather, the flies emerge in the cool of dusk. Or, to put it another way, it happens during the nicest part of the day. During the peak of the Hendrickson, the major hatching happens between 2 and 6 p.m. and lasts anywhere from a half hour to three hours.

Hendrickson nymphs are dark brown and, when they are hatching, you will often see them climbing on rocks in plain view. I like a Gold Ribbed Hare's Ear nymph for this mayfly, and I fish it in the film if I see surface activity, or quarter casting down and across, if I don't.

The dun, when seen in the air, looks pink with purple wings that give off flashes of gold as the newly hatched flies try to take wing. When trout key in on Hendricksons, they rise rhythmically, sucking in the struggling duns as they float in the current. Pick your trout, time its rise, and cast a few feet upstream a second or two before the trout rises. For sure, you will mess this cast up the first few times, but you will learn more from your mistakes than from any detailed instructions I can give you now. I like the classic Pink Hendrickson fly and the Compara-dun fly patterns in sizes #12 and #14 hooks.

The Hendrickson spinner fall can be extremely exciting, productive, and challenging. You'll see the spinners mating in the air just before dark or early in the morning. They are dark brown with gray wings. Trout will take the spinner during the spinner fall, or you can see them eating spinners any time in the eddies where dead insects collect. I find that it requires very delicate casting — which means shorter, rather than longer — to take fish during the spinner fall. I love it, but it's tough. A mahogany body with grayish CDC wings is my most effective (and visible) tie for this phase of the hatch.

One note of caution: Although it can be a great hatch, it is one of those things, like so much else in trout fishing, where you have to put in your time on the water. In 25 years of Hendrickson hoping, I can truthfully say that I have hit this hatch well only two times. I remember early in my trout days getting a call from Marsha Norman up on Vermont's renowned Battenkill. "They're happening!" was the two-word report that got me into my vintage Volvo on a five-hour dash north. I spent two days driving up and down the river, counting flies as they came off: two here, three there. I may as well have been counting whooping crane flyovers. If you are there every day in Hendrickson time, you will (in all likelihood) experience some fishing that will rival anything you have ever seen. The only catch is that you have to be there when the bugs are *and* the trout have to be in a Hendrickson mood. Like a Royal Flush in poker, the odds aren't that good on any particular hand, but you will get one sometime, and it will feel great, and you will remember it.

Hey, who was Hendrickson anyway?

Well, he wasn't the guy who tied the fly, although that's not a bad guess. He was the guy who fished with the guy who tied the fly. Roy Steenrod was a brakeman on the rail line that ran along the Beaverkill. At the end of the last century, he was one of the most respected anglers on the stream. He would often guide Dr. Hendrickson on the river, and when he originated the fly (which traditionally was tied with urine-stained fox fur!) he named it after his best client. Not a bad way to get a tip, although I don't know if that was the reason.

March Brown: Big Enough to Care About

(Latin name: Stenonema vicarium)

The March Brown is one of the most important and the first of the really big Eastern mayflies. It is popular among trout fishers because it looks like a sitting duck. I find it terribly exciting. Emergers hatch sporadically all day, so there can be hours of fishing that peaks at dusk. You can watch one of these big flies burst out of its case and ride down 100 yards of pool, fluttering, skittering, and making a spectacle of itself. Sometimes this activity will trigger a big trouty slurp, and sometimes nothing happens. But the thought that something just has to happen is part of the fun of this hatch. In eastern North America, the March Brown hatch starts in mid-May and lasts through early to mid-June, or into July in the upper-midwestern U.S.

The nymph has a dark amber to dark-brown body with three long tails. Nymphs live in swift water and riffles. They move to slower water to hatch. A weighted nymph fished along the bottom can produce if you know that the bugs are in their hatching phase. During the hatch, I like to begin with an emerger in the surface film or a plain old traditional March Brown wet fly fished *dead drift*. Dead drift means that it is cast upstream and allowed to float downstream at the same speed as the current: In other words, the way a natural fly would be seen by the trout.

The duns are large and have tan bodies with brown mottling and grayish wings. They flutter on the surface when trying to rise, a movement that can trigger strikes from big trout. You may see bugs hatching in midpool with no response from the trout that you know are there, but then those same flies that make it through a whole pool without being chomped on will get swept into the pocket water and riffles below the pool. I find that I score well in this situation because the food is more concentrated and the trout in this more active water are less wary and more eager to pounce on big food.

As with all mayflies, you can fish the spinners, but there is usually so much other activity at March Brown time that I usually ignore the spinner fall.

Green Drake: The B-52 of Mayflies

(Latin name: Ephemera guttulata — try saying that five times)

The Green Drake is the largest eastern North American mayfly, and most fly rodders consider it the climax of prime time dry-fly-fishing. The thinking goes like this: Fly fishing starts when it is still cool and nasty in April with the Quill Gordon. The flies get bigger as we go through the Hendrickson and

March Brown hatches and culminate in the humongous Green Drake. After that, according to the traditional school of thought, the weather gets too hot and the mayflies too undependable for great fly fishing and, by July 4, the streams ought to be left to the die-hards.

Well, I agree with the days-getting-nicer and mayflies-getting-bigger part of the script, but I think in the last few decades, stronger, smaller diameter leaders and more knowledge of small flies has meant that there can be good trout fishing all through the summer and well into the fall. Still, the classic hatches are great fun, and the Green Drake *can* be spectacular. That depends of course on whether the trout are cooperative. When they are, the Green Drake can seduce the biggest brown trout in the heat of the day to take a mayfly on the surface. Big trout don't often do this, preferring to feed on larger crustaceans and bait fish in the depths or in the dark hours. The hatch begins in Pennsylvania in mid-May and lasts until late June as you move north into New England. There is a similar, but distinct fly known as the Western Green Drake that I have fished in Colorado and, with great success, on the Fall River in northern California in June.

Nymphs are amber-olive or tan-olive. They burrow into soft-bottomed pools and mud banks of slower flowing rivers. In fast water, they burrow into silt and debris between rocks. They also burrow in fine gravel. The nymphs hatch sporadically, and because of this, trout do not often key on the nymphs as they do with other more concentrated hatches. Likewise, the duns seem to attract trout some days while on others it seems that the safest place a Green Drake can be is on a pool full of trout.

Duns have a yellow body with brown marks and light gray wings. Trout are very picky with Green Drakes, so be careful about selection — catch a few naturals and consider their size and color with what you have in your flybox. I like the Compara-dun in sizes #6–8. Traditional hackled dry flies seem a bit clumsy and unconvincing on this hatch.

Now for the real fun part. The Green Drake spinner, also known as the *coffin fly,* is among the most magical of flies. It is huge and white with emerald green eyes. Rather than gathering into a mating swarm after each day's hatch, the Green Drakes save their mating until thousands of them have hatched out over the course of a week or so, roosting in streamside trees and shrubs. When they finally go into the mating and dancing, there are huge clouds of them over the water. The trout can respond like bluefish in a feeding frenzy.

No flashlight, no ruler, no scale

I was on Spruce Creek in the limestone country of central Pennsylvania. The rich water and insect life produce big brown trout, bigger than any stream-borne trout I have ever come across. I had fished all afternoon during a season when the cicadas clattered in every tree in the forest. They fell into the stream like black hailstones. The trout were not that interested. I guess if you only saw a potential food source once every 17 years (the hatching cycle of this periodic cicada), you might not know what to do with it either. There were huge trout in the stream, finning among the waving stream grass. I nymphed, fished emergers, tried to pound them up with all manners of dry flies. At twilight, the lightning bugs filled the air with their little golden lanterns and the fields smelled full of the promise of summer. A couple of my friends sipped a drink on their patio. They watched me fish and, every so often, commented on a big fish. Then the coffin flies rose from the trees and took up their position over the pool. They mated, fell to the stream, made a ruckus laying their eggs, and (sure enough) the trout went bananas. I tied on a coffin fly and cast repeatedly. With so many naturals on the water, it seemed that my fly was always lost in the crowd. And in the failing light, I began to lose hope. If a fish were to strike, I feared I would miss it. But a fish did strike, and I did feel it (or sense it). I struck back.

"A big one, guys," I called to my friends as the fight began. I was into one whale of a head-shaking, bulldogging brown trout. I kept whooping and shouting to my friends who never said a word. Maybe they didn't want to jinx me or distract me, I thought. After a fight of ten minutes or so, I brought the fish in. There was very little moonlight, and I could barely see the fish. I felt it though. I called out to my friends for a flashlight, a ruler, and a scale. They didn't answer. Meanwhile I didn't want to keep the fish out of the water too long, especially after that fight. I remember thinking that it weighed about as much as my Mom's poodle, Ginger, who was roughly ten pounds. It was just a guesstimate, but definitely the biggest brown trout I had ever caught. I revived it in the shallows and let her slip into a calm backwater in the pool. I rushed up the bank to see what had happened to my buddies, but they were gone.

I guess they had picked up and left earlier, which explained the lack of a cheering gallery during the contest. So there I was, having caught my biggest brown trout with no way of recording it or at least showing it to a credible witness. "If a man catches a big fish and there is nobody to show it to," I thought, "it's kind of like the tree that falls in the forest with no one to hear it."

I knew what had happened, though, and that's what mattered the most.

Pale Morning Dun: All Summer Long

(Latin names: Ephemerella infrequens, Ephemerella inermis, and — in the eastern U.S. — Ephemerella dorothea and Ephemerella invaria)

The Pale Morning Dun is one of the more poetically named mayflies. Actually it is a whole group of closely related flies. It is also one of the most beautiful with a butter yellow body and lavender wings. It is not only a highly important Western mayfly, but also the savior of many a day on some eastern U.S. rivers, such as the Delaware. It is one of the few summer hatches that comes off in the heat of the day on cooler streams, which works nicely if you have to be home for the barbecue at nightfall. Its hatch times vary with altitude, latitude, and weather but can occur anytime from late spring through summer.

The nymph is dark to light brown. It makes several runs at the surface before it wriggles out of its shuck. In the same way that a person undressing can trigger interest in its mate, trout key in on ephemerella just below the surface as they take off their hatching suits. Trout are often very picky about the size and color of these nymphs, requiring the use of a very good imitation. The great Catskill angler, Art Flick, often ignored the dry fly and fished a wet fly all through the hatch. These days, more anglers prefer a specific emerger pattern. Either way, emerger or wet, fish it straight upstream (like a dry fly) or down and across, giving it a little action as the fly swings in the current.

The beauty of dry land

Anglers will walk three miles along the bank of a crowded river instead of crossing a half a mile of dry land to get to a less pressured creek. Maybe just being near running water has a soothing effect on the angler, just like a kid needs a favorite teddy bear in order to be able to sleep in a strange house. This came home to me one afternoon on the Lamar River in Yellowstone Park. The Lamar is an often overlooked river. Most anglers prefer nearby Slough Creek, which is a beautiful but often overcrowded stream. I had long dreamed of taking my eldest daughter to fish the stream where her mom and I had honeymooned. But the Slough of 15 years ago was a more peaceful place than today's Slough where the parking lots look like those of a prosperous dealer in used sport utility vehicles. I thought about trudging upstream, but a few return fly rodders told me that even more people were upstream. I decided to head for the Lamar. We walked across a half mile of hot, sagebrush-dotted valley and came to a section of beautiful river with riffles and slower bends. A herd of buffalo grazed on the far bank. For the next three hours, we practiced our casts on rising trout who were feeding on PMDs. We fished the hackled patterns that I had picked up in a fly shop in Cook City. They should have worked, but trout were finicky on this hatch. Finally, I waded out chest high and cast a Compara-dun in a little patch of quiet water just behind a boulder. Socko! I was into a pretty cutthroat. In the next 20 minutes, before a thunderstorm drove us to shelter under an overhanging bluff, we raised a dozen fish. As dusk fell, we returned to the car. The parking lot was filled with tourists looking through their binoculars trying to get a glimpse of the wolves that had recently been released into the Lamar Valley. I wondered, in the dying light, if they took Lucy's bouncing ponytail as the tail of a loping wolf.

Try to capture a few flies (remember your trusty dip net) and then match size from your fly box. The only dry fly that I have had consistent success with is the Compara-dun in sizes #16–20. This is true even in swifter pocket water where, with other hatches, you don't always want a no-hackle fly like the Compara-dun.

The spinner has a medium to dark-brown body and falls at dusk, which lasts nearly an hour, usually over swifter water. I position myself downstream in calmer water where the trout (and I) are looking for easier pickings.

Trico: Major Snack Food

(Latin name: Tricorythodes stygiatus)

The tiny Trico presents one of the most challenging hatches to fish, and when you see just how tiny they are — about the size of a Tic-Tac breath mint — your first reaction will be something between depression and despair.

Take heart. The Trico hatch isn't so tough once you learn to cast delicately. I suppose you can fish the nymph or the dun, but I never do. Like most anglers, I wait for the spinner fall. Trico hatches and spinner falls can occur daily in the morning from late June through October, and into November in milder zones.

If you get to a stream and see a lot of Tricos hatching, go get a cup of coffee, lie down by the stream bank and take a nap, or maybe clean out all the candy bar wrappers and cheeseburger bags that accumulate on the floor-boards of any well-used fishing car. When you get back to the stream, you will (in all likelihood) see a cloud of Trico spinners. This is a mating swarm. The Tricos are having a blast. Very soon, they will begin to fall back to the surface of the stream in one big clump. Though each fly is teeny, the sheer amount of dead mayfly meat is enormous. The trout know this and turn on to the spinners bigtime.

Although Tricos are found in many freestone streams, spring creeks (especially those with lots of limestone-enriched waters) give off bumper crops. Whatever the stream, the basic fact is that you will be fishing in quieter water. You really need the kind of situation where the fish gather in pods and then get into a rising rhythm in gently flowing water.

Fishing a spinner (anywhere from #20–24), I find that presenting the fly from upstream allows me to drift it in front of the trout without exposing any of the leader. Even a very light leader with such a small fly can be a turn-off. I discuss how to make this presentation in Chapter 13; but just bear in mind that if quiet waters dictate a gentle approach, then approaching from upstream just doubles the need for caution. For similar reasons, if you are a real slap-the-line-on-the-surface kind of caster, you will be in trouble. You need a delicate touch and a tight loop. So cast within your limits. False cast away from target fish, and fish each cast completely, taking the fly off the water a good distance from your target fish. If you are a fly tier, you can turn up the hook eyes to get more gap because Trico imitations are so small. Don't think about fishing with tippets larger than 6X (see Chapter 4).

I know this sounds hard, but take it slow and easy and I swear you can do it. To make things just a little easier, some commercially available flies tie a little orange tuft on top of the black body of these flies to help you track the path of the flies downstream, which means you aren't going to lose your fly in the crowd and miss a strike.

My favorite technique is to take a position a little upstream and off to one side of the trout's feeding lane and float the fly down to the lead fish. After you take him, go to the next dish downstream. On Silver Creek, in Idaho, I have parked myself in a float tube this way and taken half a dozen fat fish out of a feeding pod (group of fish) before floating downstream to the next pod.

Callibaetis: Banker's Hours

(Latin name: The same — Callibaetis)

Okay, you don't feel like making it out for the Trico spinner fall. They're too small or maybe you fished until ten the night before, grabbed a burger in one hand and drove two hours with the other, and you didn't feel like starting all over again early in the morning. If so, the Callibaetis was designed for you. Western spring creek anglers can lay in bed if they like and still be on the stream in the early afternoon. It's a nice size fly #14–16, which shows up really well on the surface of spring creeks. The nymphs do quite well in the algae grass of these rivers, and when they hatch, the trout will stay on them all afternoon. I rarely see this fly discussed when people put together lists of the so-called super hatches, but it is a fly that consistently produces on many of the West's blue ribbon waters. It doesn't require the daintiness of the teeny flies like Tricos or little Blue Winged Olives.

The duns have a gray-brown freckled appearance, and because of that, I often fish one of the most traditional American dry flies, the Adams, when I fish this hatch. The Adams wasn't tied to imitate the Callibaetis, but the trout don't know that — the mix of colors in the Adams looks like a Callibaetis, which is the important thing. (Don't you just love putting something over on someone?)

Look for spinners in the morning. Also, if nothing else is happening on the water, I suppose you can fish nymphs, but if you are on classic dry-fly water, and most Western spring creeks are, then I think you will have more fun fishing dry flies.

Giant Michigan Caddis: The Champ

(Latin name: Hexagenia limbata)

This 747 of a bug is called a Caddis, but it's actually a mayfly. And what a mayfly! It is so big that it is sometimes tied on #4 hooks. Every part of the country has its unique hatches that anglers try to catch at least once in life. The stone fly hatch on the Yellowstone is one. Green Drake time on the Delaware is another. Over in England, they dream about the time in late spring known as "Duffers Fortnight," when the big Mayfly hatches on the beautiful chalk streams of the south (there is only one bug in England that they save the name *Mayfly* for, a bug about the size of a Green Drake). And in the midwestern U.S., they wait for "The Hex," a fly that can reach sizes of $1^1/_2$ inches.

The Hex hatch begins mid-June and lasts through July, going into August on some rivers. Some hatches occur on cold water lakes with silty bottoms in the northeastern U.S. and Canada. (Lake Placid in the Adirondacks offers fine dry-fly-fishing to big rainbows during the Hex hatch.) Perhaps the most famous river is Michigan's Au Sable, where the Hex emerges in a defined sequence across various sections of the river (water temperature being the key variable).

The amber to brown nymph resembles the Green Drake, which makes sense because both flies evolved to burrow into silt. They normally take about two years to mature, and (during that time) they contribute a lot to the diet of trout as they crawl out of the mud to shed their old skins as many as 30 times. For this reason, it is never a bad idea to prospect Hex habitat with a weighted nymph fished deep.

Duns have yellow-gray-brown bodies with maroon marks and gray wings with an olive cast. During the hatch, the nymphs rise to the surface where they struggle out of their shucks as they ride in the surface film. All of this commotion can attract big trout.

They usually emerge after dark, sometimes late at night. The huge size of the fly means you can see them in the moonlight, which can make for some very exciting fishing. Trout will begin working the surface sometime between dusk and midnight. Fish dry flies sizes #4–6, and further east even a #8.

Spinners appear 24 to 72 hours after the hatch. The female will lay on the water and deposit all of her eggs at once, after which she dies and remains in the current and floats away. This will attract the attention of trout, again at last light and into the night.

Blue-Winged Olive: Always There

(Latin Name: Baetis vagans)

Like a good second baseman who hits .250 and always seems to be in the right place, the Blue-Winged Olive doesn't get the headlines but is a player you can count on. The Blue-winged Olive is a valuable year-round food for trout. Actually, it would be more accurate to say Blue-Winged Olives (plural) because this family includes a bunch of flies ranging in size from #14–26. They hatch from March through November but can appear any time that flies are hatching. Often, there can be a hatch of more eye-catching and bigger flies going on at the same time. This is called a *compound hatch.* So, while you try to get the trout to take your entire selection of Hendrickson nymphs, spinners, emergers, and duns, the trout may be eating only the much smaller and unnoticed Blue-Winged Olive. Learn to look for these flies and fish them.

Nymphs are dark to light olive-brown. They inhabit runs and riffles with gravel bottoms and slow runs full of vegetation. Some species live in slow water only. Limestone-rich waters, like many spring creeks, often produce big hatches. Because the nymphs are strong and fast swimmers, they can provoke aggressive takes from trout. You will often see the sides of trout flashing just under the surface as they pick off these nymphs.

Duns have olive-brown bodies and light to dark-gray wings. In summer, hatches come in the late afternoon, more so at dusk. In fall, they occur in the late morning and late afternoon. Emergence slows down when the water temperature goes over 60°F. Duns have trouble thawing early and late in the season and have trouble with turbulent water, all of which makes them good trout targets because they will float for long periods, making it easy for trout to pick them off. But if you remember what I said about mayflies coming off in the pleasant part of the day, you can often forget it with Blue Wings. It can happen, but just as often it is the most miserable cold, sleety trout fishing weather of the year. So what, if the trout are cooperating!

The spinner is light to dark gray, its wings pearly with dark-brown spots on the front edge. It can appear anywhere from hours to several days after a hatch. After mating, females land on and crawl down rocks or plants sticking in the water. They slip into the water (on the downstream side of these obstructions) to lay their eggs.

In general, the Baetis is a good go-to fly when you can see that something is happening and nothing else works.

Now that you know its habits and things like where to look for spinners, you will, if you pay close attention, begin to see Blue-Winged Olives quite often.

There is one very special Blue-Winged Olive that is not a Baetis at all. Most often known as the Pseudo, short for its Latin name of *Pseudocleon,* it is extremely petite — it's the smallest fly that I fish. What it lacks in size, however, it makes up for in numbers. And this is a critical factor for the trout. While a larger fly may be more of a mouthful, the trout is often more concerned with the total amount of floating meat on the water, and that can often mean that you need to use a tiny fly.

Fishing Pseudos requires a sharp eye and lots of patience. Also, strong nerves are required. These little flies abound where trout grow the largest, such as the Missouri River just below Three Forks, Montana. In this section, the mighty Missouri is the world's biggest spring creek. Slow flowing, nice and cool, and with an amazingly rich food chain (near the top of which are rainbow trout as fat as footballs).

Isonychia: Fast and Furious

(Latin name: Isonychia bicolor)

If you walk along the banks of any Catskill stream in the summertime, you will notice that streamside rocks are covered with chestnut colored nymph cases. These are the shucks of the Isonychia, a swift swimming nymph that triggers some of the most reckless feeding on New England and midwestern U.S. streams.

When the nymphs are ready to hatch, they move in large numbers into the shallows and begin climbing onto rocks late in the afternoon. It happens all of a sudden, and (when it does) the trout seem to turn on. It is a real no-brainer to fish. You tie on a traditional wet fly like the LeadWing Coachman or a more impressionistic modern fly like the Zug Bug and cast to the shore. Let the current swing your fly around, and (somewhere in that arc) a fish will hit.

In July, on New York's Esopus Creek, you can be fishing along with no action at all and then, as the direct sun leaves the stream, the Isos start moving; and you can catch 20 trout in an hour. For flat-out action, it doesn't get more intense than this.

A century with a fly rod

I was on assignment for *The New York Times,* looking for new trout waters in central Montana. Doug McClelland, who teaches business law at Montana State University, had taken me to try some private waters on a few ranches near White Sulphur Springs. These little fished-for fish were perfect. A nice grasshopper pattern could yield a half dozen 15-inch fish in an area no bigger than my living room (and because I live in New York City where real estate is mega-expensive, my living room isn't all that gigantic). A couple of hours of that, and we all felt like hotshot fishermen. We decided to hit the evening hatch on the Missouri on our way home.

Where to fish wasn't a problem. We drove until we saw *riseforms,* the tell-tale disturbances in the water that trout make when they take a fly on or near the surface. We waded into the river, nearly chest-high, and positioned ourselves between an island and some grass beds. There were at least a half dozen pods of excellent fish dimpling the surface with the most seductive slurps. They were gorging themselves so much that I half expected to hear a trout belch like he had just chugged a Budweiser. The guy in the fly shop told us to try Caddis flies, which I did

and got a number of looks but all of them refusals. Next, I tried a general purpose attractor pattern, the Parachute Adams, which is a favorite in those parts because it has a little white tuft sticking up that makes it easy to see. I resisted putting on a Pseudo imitation because they are so small and can only be fished on very light tippet.

Finally, I gave in and tied on a Blue-Winged Olive. After a dozen casts or so, I hooked a super strong rainbow. When he leaped clear of the water, he looked to be a good three pounds with big shoulders. I lowered my rod when he landed and tightened up to try and pull him from the weed beds. But there was no turning the fish, and he popped off. In the next half hour, loud curses from my fishing partners indicated similar experiences. When we compared notes, we had all gone to Blue-Winged Olives on very light tippet and we had all lost fish. So there we were, three seasoned anglers with nearly a century of fly rodding among us, and our score for the evening that had started out with such cockiness was three lost fish.

The lesson: Sometimes, no matter what you do, the fish win.

Dry flies have never produced as well for me on this hatch, but that is to be expected when the nymphs all leave the water *before* they unzip their nymph cases and become grown up mayflies.

The spinner, which is quite large (#10–12) is imitated by a fly whose name alone endears it to anglers if not fish. The White Gloved Howdy, so called because of its big white wings, is the traditional fly of choice for the spinner fall. I have never caught a fish when the spinners are happening, but I have only begun to understand spinners in the last few years. Keep your eyes open and you may learn how to solve this stage of the hatch before I do. Maybe part of the problem is that I never see the spinners until very late in the year, and by that time, I am starting to think more about shooting grouse and woodcock than about catching trout.

Chapter 7
Tying Flies

You don't need to tie your own flies in order to enjoy fly fishing any more than you have to be a cook in order to enjoy a great meal. However, I cook and I tie flies. In both cases, I think that I can more fully enjoy, understand, and appreciate the activity at hand — whether it's eating dinner or catching fish — because I understand more of the process. And when you consider that flies cost a lot more when you buy them ready-made, learning to tie your own flies will save you lots of money.

How Many Flies Do I Need?

Millions of pages have been written about flies. Every fly rodder has an opinion, a favorite fly, and a neat little trick. And although I have no doubt that every situation has a *best* fly; you can spend years learning these situations, and *I* would much rather spend my time fishing. If you want to learn a great deal about a great number of flies, don't take this as a warning not to learn. Your continuing study can pay off. Still, as the years go by, I find that I catch more fish with a smaller selection of flies. I really believe that a well-presented fly that gives the *impression* of the real thing is often just as effective as a fly that *duplicates* whatever it is that the fish are eating. And sometimes, the best strategy is to go against the hatch and give the fish something that stands out from the crowd. The flies discussed in this chapter will make a good basic trout arsenal. I will deal with flies for bass and for saltwater later. As far as trout fishing goes, if you pack these flies in a variety of sizes and if you have good presentation, you can pretty much catch any trout that comes your way.

Tools of the Trade

Fly tying is a pretty low-tech operation. If you *want* to spend a lot of money on gear, I suppose that you could; but in the end, the fish are not going to know if your vise was snazzy titanium or boring old stainless steel. You can actually get started with a basic set of tools and some very good materials, shown in Figure 7-1, for less than $100.

With the following tools you can tie 95 percent of all the fly patterns in the world.

The vise squad

You use a vise, shown in Figure 7-2, to hold your hook in one place. This tool frees up your hands to handle materials as needed. You don't absolutely need a vise. Lee Wulff could tie the smallest and neatest flies just using his hands. I remember sitting in his sun room up on the Upper Beaverkill late one winter afternoon and watching him tie a size #28 dry fly with no vise. I could barely see the fly, much less think about duplicating Lee's tying feat. Lee Wulff was a one-in-a-million angler, make that one-in-a-billion, and I'm not. My guess is you're probably closer to my skill potential than Lee's, so get yourself a vise. If you move your fly-tying station a lot, a C-clamp vise will attach to any tabletop and will bring the business end of the vise very close to your body. I prefer the pedestal-mount vise because I can put it wherever I find a convenient free spot on a table (which takes some doing with two daughters). Some vises come with a little spring coiled around the vise for holding materials that need to be tied in and then left for a later step in the fly tying process.

Bobbin basics

The bobbin holds your thread. You can wind some thread around the hook and then leave the bobbin hanging and it keeps tension on the thread, which keeps the whole fly together until you are ready to finish it off.

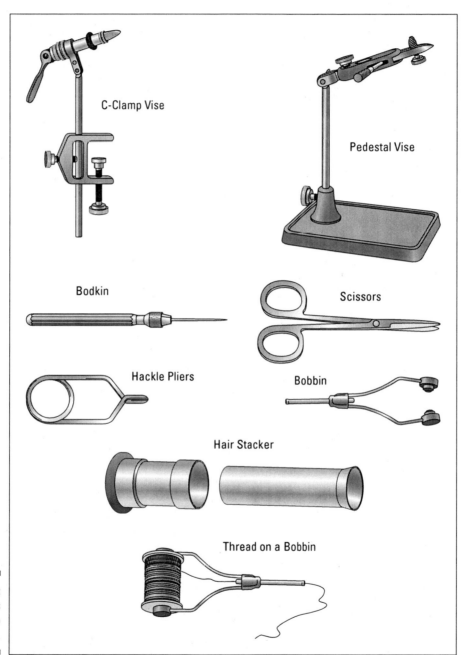

C-Clamp Vise

Pedestal Vise

Bodkin

Scissors

Hackle Pliers

Bobbin

Hair Stacker

Thread on a Bobbin

Figure 7-1:
The tools
you need to
tie flies.

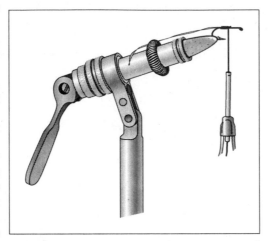

Figure 7-2:
A materials clip keeps certain things ready but not in the way, and it is a basic rule of fly tying that *everything* tends to get in the way.

Don't point your bodkin when you talk to me

This gets my "Word I Never Heard Of And Then Once I Did I Figured I Would Never Use Anyway" Award. It sounds like something out of Mary Poppins. A *bodkin* is a good, Old English word. For the fly tier, it means a needle on a stick. You use it to help finish knots, to tease fur and hair from underneath thread, to apply glue, or to lacquer the head of the fly both neatly and delicately. I have a bodkin to help me thread my bobbin. (Now there's a sentence I never thought I would grow up to write!) It is a wire loop that you use to pass the thread through the hole in the bobbin.

Hackle pliers

Many flies require you to wrap a feather around a hook or to wind some other material that is equally hard to manage. A pair of hackle pliers is the tool for this job. Also, after you have wound something on, it can be left hanging and maintain nice, steady pressure on the material, keeping whatever material you are working with in place until you need to do more with it. Like many of the tools described here, hackle pliers serve as a third or fourth hand without forcing you to have to put up with the person who is usually attached to a third or fourth hand.

Don't use it for anything else

Use your scissors for cutting thread, fur, and feathers. If you need to cut through metal or anything else that could dull the blades, use a different pair. Don't use your fly scissors to cut your nails, open letters, or make little cutout dolls of trout. If you keep the scissors for the basic fly-tying materials, you will always be able to make that short and sharp cut that means a good, neat fly.

A good pair of scissors

You need a *sharp, pointy* pair of scissors. Your 5-year-old kid's scrapbook scissors won't do the job. Usually, the drugstore has a good pointy pair for not a lot of money. You want a short pair because this will let you work close in to the fly. Make sure that your fingers fit comfortably through the holes of the scissors handles before you buy them.

Hey, where's the top to my lipstick!?

It is very handy to have a little tool that will let you stack hair, like deer hair, so that all the ends are neat. It is also pretty near impossible to do this without a *stacker,* which is nothing more than a short tube, closed at one end, that can hold a bunch of hair. You can buy a stacker from a fly-tying supply catalogue, or you can use an old top to a lipstick. If you choose the latter because it is cheaper, make sure that the lipstick wearer knows about this or you will face major flack.

Three Basic Fly Types

Until fly fishing grew so rapidly in the last few years to include patterns for all kinds of non-trouty and non-salmony fish, there were only three kinds of flies: dry, wet, and streamer. Now, you have flies that look like nothing a trout or salmon would eat. Still, the basic lingo of what goes into a fly and what the different parts of a fly are called comes from the lore of trout and salmon fishing in which you find the original kinds of flies.

High and dry

For most trout anglers, most of the time, the dry fly is the preferred method of taking trout. However, a dry fly (shown in Figure 7-3) is not always the most effective method, and it doesn't always pull up the biggest fish (although there are times when it does both). I think that this preference exists because of the thrill of anticipation experienced when watching the fly floating down the stream, knowing that a trout may take it at any moment. And if and when the trout takes your fly, it engenders one of angling's great feelings (just as the plug fisherman gets a happy jolt when watching a largemouth slam a popping plug).

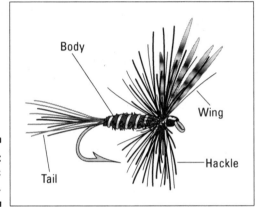

Figure 7-3:
The classic
dry fly.

The traditional dry fly has the following features:

- ✔ The tail is as long as the body.

- ✔ The tail is usually made of stiff fibers from the *hackle* (neck feathers) of a rooster. The hackle is what allows the traditional fly to float high and dry — just like a real mayfly.

- ✔ The body is made of fur that is wound around the hook with silk thread.

- ✔ The wing is often made from the soft body feathers of a wood duck.

Not every dry fly is tied to imitate a mayfly, and not every dry-fly mayfly imitation has all of the parts shown in Figure 7-3. For example, I often use the Compara-dun on flat, clear water. This mayfly imitation has no hackle, but it floats just fine. In most of the world, most of the time, however, when people talk about a dry fly, they are talking about the classic mayfly.

At the end of the hatch, as described in Chapter 5, you usually get a spinner fall, and for the next few hours, you may have excellent dry-fly-fishing of a special kind. That's when you use a special kind of dry fly that imitates the spinner. This imitation typically has less-bushy hackle and wings that lay flat rather than stand upright.

Wets came first

Wet flies are called *wet flies* because they get wetter than dry flies; they sink beneath the surface. (You probably could have figured that out without the aid of this book.) I believe that the original artificial flies were wets. True dry flies aren't mentioned in fishing literature until many years after Izaak Walton wrote *The Compleat Angler* in the 17th Century. Does that mean that trout anglers didn't fish dry in the old days? Absolutely not. They just cast their wet flies and allowed them to drift in the same way that today's dry-fly angler does.

The classic wet fly (see Figure 7-4) has the same parts as the dry fly, but the wing is attached differently — it lays flat. Instead of riding high and dry, a wet fly lays down on the water. Also, the hackle is softer *(webby)* so that a wet fly rides in or under the film.

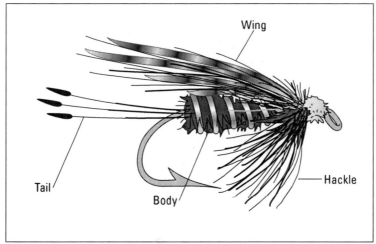

Figure 7-4:
An old-time
wet fly.

Nymphs: New kids on the block

Back in the old days, wet flies served for everything: duns, emergers, nymphs, and spinners. Gradually, anglers grew more specialized in their choice of flies. The dry fly came along and spawned a whole school of fishing and fly-tying techniques. Next, anglers looked for a more effective nymph imitation than the traditional wet fly, and the modern artificial nymph was born. An artificial nymph usually looks more like a natural nymph than a wet fly does. The wing is gone and is replaced by a wing case and nubby fur that often imitates the gills that run along the side of a nymph's body (as shown in Figure 7-5). Fished free-floating, or with the purposeful action of a live nymph rising to the surface and hatching into a dry fly, the artificial nymph is a versatile fly that often scores when nothing else does. Remember, even during a blizzard-like hatch, more nymphs are in the water than drys are on the surface, and trout frequently continue to feed on nymphs through the hatch.

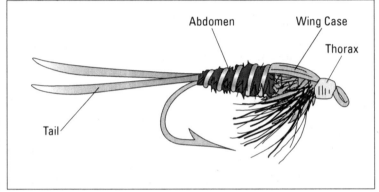

Figure 7-5:
A typical
nymph.

Of all trout flies, the nymph pattern looks most like the natural product (at least to the human eye). The wing case, thorax, abdomen, and tail all correspond to a stream-borne nymph.

Streamers: More than a mouthful

Trout, especially large trout, like to eat small fish. Whether the fish is one of their own kind or just a forage fish, such as a minnow, sculpin, or alewife herring, is not that important. To a trout, a bait fish (compared to a dry fly) provides much more meat on the hook — make that meat on the fin. Anglers have long known this, and their attempts to imitate this favored food source resulted in the *streamer fly*.

If you take a feather and hold it sideways, it has the rough outline of a fish. For this reason, many streamer patterns started out as a pair of feathers tied lengthwise along the shaft of a hook. And many fish were caught, and continue to be caught, by such simple streamers. Some more-developed streamers have hackle feathers wound around the head of the hook to give the fly some lifelike motion in the water. In addition to feathers, *bucktail* has long been used as streamer material. (Although it has always been a mystery to me why the hairs from a deer's rear end attract fish. You never see a trout nibbling at a deer's backside.) I think that deer hair (like much of the fur and hair of land-dwelling animals) works so well on flies and other lures because it behaves like *living* material. Marabou feathers also work well when attached to streamers as do a whole range of synthetic materials that shine, sparkle, and wave seductively, as shown in Figure 7-6.

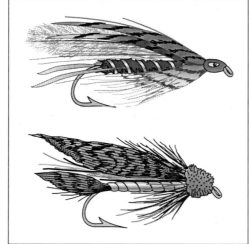

Figure 7-6:
Streamers
old (top)
and
new(ish)
(bottom).

The Gray Ghost, shown at the top in Figure 7-6, is a classic feather-based streamer first tied by Carrie Stevens (one of the Mothers of American Fly Fishing) in the Rangeley Lakes region of Maine in 1924. Decades later, Don Gapen revolutionized streamer fishing with his deer-hair sculpin imitation, the Muddler Minnow, which is at the bottom in Figure 7-6.

Tying Your First Fly and Then Some

If you already know how to tie, you might want to skip my step-by-step instructions, although I would urge you to look over the recipe for these flies and the ones that follow. You might find something that will simplify your tying, which even though it may be enjoyable, isn't as much fun as fishing.

And finally, for those of you who don't have the time or inclination to tie your own flies, you can buy most of these ties from commercial tiers.

The Woolly Bugger

When you can only have one fly, many fly rodders will tell you that the Woolly Bugger (see Figure 7-7) is the one fly to have. With its simple body and a long, supple feather tail, this fly ranked number one on a survey that I did on the Internet, probably because it catches fish everywhere. I will never forget a day on a slough full of enormous rainbow trout in Argentina. Nothing was hatching, and there was no visible sign of fish. I tied on a Woolly Bugger and stripped it in 6 inches at a time (that is, I retrieved it in short pulls). I caught fish after fish, up to an unbelievable 11 pounds. When one fish struck, I pulled back to set the hook with such violence that the hook pulled out of the trout's mouth, and my momentum carried the fly over my head and into the water about 20 feet in back of me where another 5- or 6-pound rainbow took the Woolly Bugger on my backcast! This was the ultimate case of using the right fly at the right time. Depending on what size of Woolly Bugger you use, it can be taken for a stonefly, a leech, a minnow, or a worm. Is it a nymph or a streamer? I'm not sure, probably a little of both. The Woolly Bugger can be found in sizes 4, 6, 8, and 10.

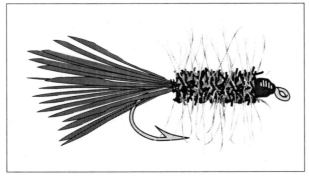

Figure 7-7:
The Woolly
Bugger.

After you know how to tie flies, all you need to do is look at a recipe and you can probably take it from there. The recipe is a standard format that most tiers recognize and follow.

Here are the vital stats for your first fly:

Hook	Mustad 9672 or 79580
Size	4–10
Thread	Black, fine diameter
Body	Olive chenille

Hackle	Grizzly saddle hackle
Underbody	Lead wire, .020 inch diameter
Tail	Black marabou

Note: All of these instructions (which are shown in Figures 7-8 and 7-9) are for right-handed fly tiers. Lefties, my apologies, but I am sure that you are used to making these corrections for righty writers.

1. The Jam knot: Hold the end of the thread in your left hand *behind* the hook. Holding the bobbin in your right hand, begin to wrap thread over the thread in your left hand. This will jam the thread down against itself. In this and almost every other operation you do in fly tying, you wrap clockwise — over the hook and away from your body.

2. After five or six wraps (or turns), let the thread in the bobbin hang down. The weight of the bobbin will provide enough tension to hold the Jam knot together. Take your scissors and trim the open, or *tag,* end of the thread.

3. Continue winding the thread until you reach the beginning of the bend of the hook. This will give you a nice foundation of thread that will provide some traction for the rest of the materials as you wind them on.

4. Take a fluffy piece of marabou. Wet the tip of your thumb and forefinger with your tongue, and then stroke the end of the marabou feather so that the fibers clump together. Now, hold the feather as shown (with the fibers that will form the tail being about as long as your hook), secure the fibers to the hook with a few wraps of thread, and trim the feather just forward of these wraps.

5. Take about 6 inches of lead wire and, starting right in front of the trimmed end of the marabou feather, cover the main part of the shank of the hook. Using your bodkin, smear a few drops of head cement or clear lacquer on the lead and let it dry. This will give you a nice, smooth underbody on which you can wrap the rest of the material. Alternatively you can just let it dry to tackiness so that the next bunch of materials are bound to the body by the cement.

6. Take a 6-inch piece of chenille (a fly-tying material that looks like limp pipe cleaner) and strip the fuzz from the end of the chenille. Now, you can easily tie in the chenille at the bend of the shank. After tying in the chenille, wrap the thread forward two or three turns.

7. Holding a piece of saddle hackle (the kind that has flimsy, not stiff, fibers), stroke the fibers forward so that they stand out from the center quill.

8. Tie in the exposed quill and wrap forward eight or nine turns to secure the feather pretty firmly. These turns should be tight wraps, but don't put too much tension on the thread. If you do, you will either break the thread or spin the feather around. Trim the tag end of the feather, and wrap the thread forward.

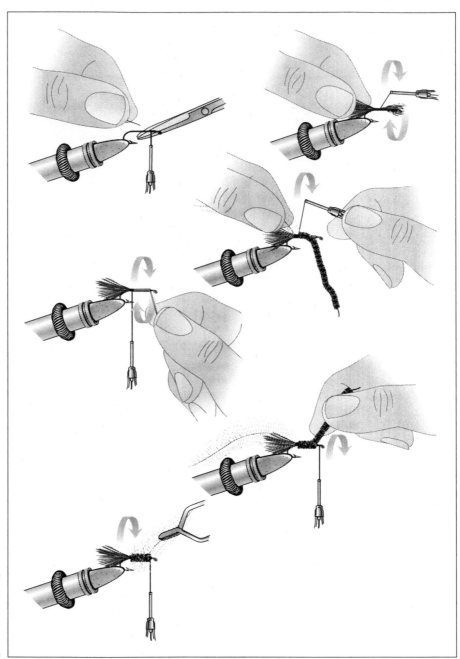

Figure 7-8:
Tying a
Woolly
Bugger.

9. Wrap the chenille forward. The first wrap should be behind the feather, and the second wrap should be in front of it. To tie off the chenille, hold the chenille in your right hand and work the bobbin with your left hand. Trim the tag. This kind of wrapping lets you work with bulky material without having a big buildup at the head. You probably have figured out by now that you will have to let the bobbin hang down for a few seconds while you switch from the right hand to the left hand for winding. That's what the bobbin's for — it maintains tension even when you are not tying.

10. Take the hackle in your hackle pliers and wind it forward as shown. Notice how the barbules of the feather stand out at a right angle from the hook. This technique of winding hackle along the length of the body of the fly is called *palmering*. Trim the end of the feather, and build up a nice head of thread with 10 or 15 wraps, leaving a little space behind the eye for the finishing knot.

11. You are now ready to *whip finish* your fly. As shown in Figure 7-9, make a loop using your hand, and snug this open loop against the shank of the hook. Y is the thread behind the loop. Wind this thread over the X part of the thread for six or seven wraps, and then (as shown in the close-up) use your bodkin to create a firm and tight final knot. Pull tight, and trim. Apply head cement, and let dry.

12. Take your fly out of the vise and run around the house screaming, "Hey, everybody, look what I made!"

Congratulations — you have made your first fly! And what's more, you have just mastered about 90 percent of the techniques that you will need to tie any fly. It's all in the way you wrap things. Now, I don't want to make this seem easier than it is. Like everything else in angling, the touch of the individual is so important. My main piece of advice is don't think of these instructions as a shop manual for a piece of machinery. Flies are made of organic materials. They are not metal. Tying in a piece of material is like carving meat or slicing fish. You have to get a feel for what you're doing and adjust your technique accordingly. Maybe this explains why whenever I meet a chef who ties flies, he or she is usually a very neat and artistic tier.

One of the most important little tricks I have learned in tying is called the *pinch wrap,* or at least that is what I call it. You use it when you are tying in bucktail, elk hair, or anything else that will have a tendency to fan out and spin if you don't take proper precautions.

You pinch the strands of material together between your thumb and forefinger and then sneak a loose loop over it. You have to hold the material tightly yet get that thread all the way around it. Then (and only then), you pull down firmly while continuing to pinch the material. Repeat this process three or four times and you will have a neatly tied-in clump.

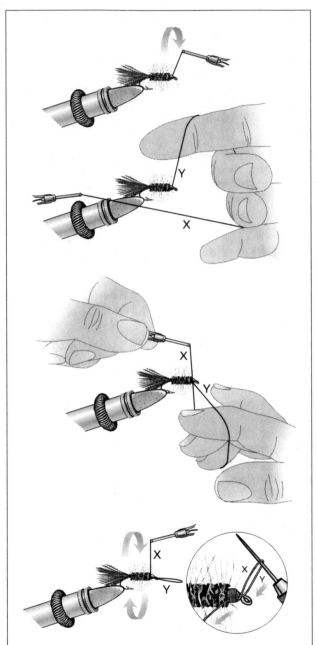

Figure 7-9:
Finishing up
the Woolly
Bugger.

The Gold Ribbed Hare's Ear

In a little fly survey I did on the Internet, this old, reliable fly as well as the Woolly Bugger were so far ahead of the rest of the field that they seemed to be running in first and second place with nothing else even on the same racetrack. The Gold Ribbed Hare's Ear, shown in Figure 7-10, is a general, impressionistic nymph that picks up flash from gold wire coiled around its body. The fur used to tie this fly is, as its name suggests, from the ear of a hare. It is gold, brown, white, and black in color, and its texture is stubby and filled with many short hairs (also known as guard hairs) that stick out at all kinds of angles. To a hairdresser (no pun intended), these short hairs would be thought of as unsightly split ends. To a fish, this unkempt look is very buglike. Drop this fly in a glass of water and you will see little bubbles form because of the unruly nature of the fur. This is exactly the kind of bubble a living insect might give off as it rises to the surface and shucks its nymphcase. In recent years, some anglers have been fishing the Gold Ribbed Hare's Ear with the addition of a shiny metallic bead head that gives it both a jigging action and some more flash.

Figure 7-10:
The Gold Ribbed Hare's Ear.

Hook	Mustad 3906B or the equivalent
Size	8–16
Thread	Brown, 6/0 waxed
Tail	Hare's ear-guard hairs
Thorax	Hare's ear fur
Abdomen	Hare's ear fur
Rib	Flat gold tinsel
Weight	Medium lead wire
Legs	Dubbing picked from thorax
Wing case	Oak turkey wing (quill)

Figure 7-11 shows you how to tie a Gold Ribbed Hare's Ear.

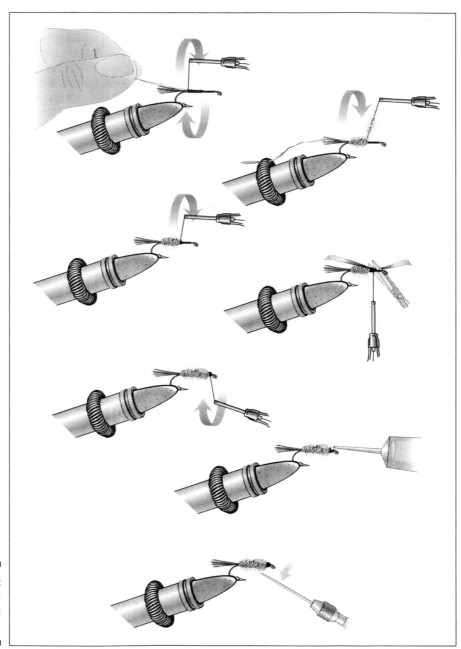

1. Using the Jam knot, start your thread and wind back to the bend in the hook. Take the hare's ear fur and pull out about a dozen of the stiffer bristles (often referred to as *guard hairs*). Tie in as a tail and continue to wind forward about halfway down the shank.

2. Cut a 5-inch strip of tinsel, snipping the end on the bias so that you have a nice, defined point to tie in. Wind thread over the tinsel to bend. Secure the tinsel in your materials clip so that it stays out of the way.

3. You are now ready to *dub* fur onto the thread. Wax the thread and then take a little bit of fur between your thumb and forefinger and press the thread forward with your thumb as it rubs over your forefinger. The fur will stick to the thread. Continue until you have a 3-inch length of dubbed thread, and wind forward to the midpoint of the hook, each turn slightly overlapping the previous one. When you reach the midpoint, remove any remaining fur from the thread.

4. Now, wind the tinsel forward in a loose spiral. The end result will be evenly spaced, alternating bands of fur and tinsel. Tie off the tinsel, snip, and cover with a few more turns of thread.

5. Take your turkey wing and snip a section about $1/4$-inch wide or just a smidge wider. Place your snipping on top of the hook with the cut end facing forward and the shiny side facing up. Tie on the feather (or *quill section*) by loosely wrapping once and then holding the feather in place as you apply pressure while pulling *up* to tighten the feather. If you pull down on this first wrap, you will pull the feather over the top and onto the side or bottom of the hook. Wrap four times, and snip the end of the feather.

6. Thickly dub fur onto 2 inches of thread, and wind a nice fat abdomen ending about $1/8$ inch from the eye.

7. Pull the quill section over to form a wing case, and (once again) wrap loosely and pull up to tighten. Build up a thread head. Whip finish, and apply head cement.

8. When the head is dry, take your bodkin and pick out (or tease) some guard hairs out of the abdomen to simulate legs.

The Variant

A Variant is a dry fly with no wings (see Figure 7-12). Instead, you rely on the hackle to give the impression of the buzzing appearance of insect wings, flapping at great speeds and breaking up the light that shines through them. In his later years, Lee Wulff fished for trout almost exclusively with variants. And the great Art Flick, who wrote *The Streamside Guide* (in my opinion the best and most useful trout-fishing book ever), was a major fan of variants. When variants are tied the way that Flick tied them (with oversize hackle and a slim body made from the center quill of a hackle feather), they are the most delicate of dry flies. For some reason, I have always thought of these classic variants as the fly fishing version of the simple but beautiful designs of the Shakers, who lived just one mountain range over from the Catskill Mountains where Wulff and Flick fished. Variants come in sizes 8–18.

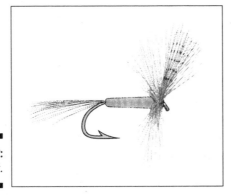

Figure 7-12: The Variant.

The truth about hackles

Many flies, as you saw in our anatomy of the basic flies, have a part called the hackle. It is made from the neck feathers of a bird, usually a rooster or hen of specially bred representatives of the good old barnyard chicken family. Some of the terms used to describe the parts of the hackle are also used to describe other things in fishing. You just have to remember the context in which you are using these words.

✔ **Quill:** The stiff spine running up the center of the feather.

✔ **Fluffy stuff:** That squiggly stuff at the base of the hackle feather (pretty obvious).

✔ **Web:** The part of the barb structure where the barbules (also called fibers) are held together by interconnecting pieces. "Web" hackle isn't stiff, wets easily, and is not the part you want to use on dry flies, although it can work well for wet flies, nymphs, and emergers.

✔ **Barbs:** Also called barbules or fibers. The stiff fibers that provide the best dry-fly support come from the tip of the hackle.

Hook	Mustad 94840
Size	14–16
Thread	Yellow
Tail	Ginger
Body	Stripped ginger hackle quill
Hackle	Ginger and grizzly saddle hackle one or two sizes larger than you would use for a standard dry fly (in other words use hackles for sizes 10 or 12 here)

The following steps walk you through the creation of a Variant (see Figure 7-13).

1. Strip all the barbs, fluff, and web from a hackle feather, and soak the quill in water to soften it up.

2. Jam knot your thread at the middle of the hook and wind to the rear.

3. Gather a bunch of long, stiff hackle barbules and tie them in at the tail.

4. Remove the quill from the water and tie it in at the narrow end. Wind the quill forward to slightly beyond the midpoint of the shank.

5. Tie in two oversized hackles, about a size or two bigger than a normal dry-fly hackle for the hook size you are using. If you don't have a hackle gauge, get one from your local store or in any fly-tying catalog. They are cheap and indispensable for beginning fly tiers to help them pick the right size hackle for the fly.

6. Wind the hackles forward. Tie them off. Whip finish, and cement.

The Light Hendrickson

This fly, shown in Figure 7-14, is what is known as a classic Catskill dry fly. When tied correctly, it is very sparse. It's the way all dry flies were tied up until the last few decades. In terms of pure fish-catching, newer techniques seem to score more consistently, although there are many times when these American originals do just fine. And the techniques involved in tying them are central to so much else that goes on in fly tying. Besides, they're just gorgeous.

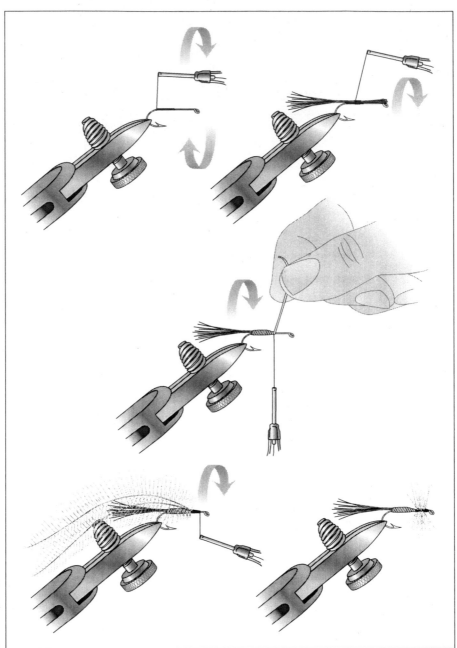

Figure 7-13:
Tying the
Variant.

Figure 7-14:
The Light
Hendrickson.

Hook	Mustad 94840
Size	14 – 16
Thread	Yellow or primrose
Wing	Lemon wood duck, upright and divided
Tail	Dun hackle fibers
Body	Light- or buff-colored fur
Hackle	Medium dun

Follow these steps and see Figure 7-15 to tie a Light Hendrickson.

1. Jam knot the thread in the middle of the hook. Wind the thread to the end and tie in about a half dozen stiff hackle feathers. Wind forward about three-quarters of the way up the hook shank.

2. Take a wood duck flank feather, and cut a V as shown. Then gather the feather barbules together in a bunch so that all the ends are even. Snip off a bunch that is just a bit longer than the hook shank.

3. Tie in the feathers. By now you should know how to tie them in so that they stay securely on top.

4. Now, you are ready to stand the wing clump upright like a real wing. Pull the clump up and make a thread lump in front of the wing to prop it up, as shown.

    Note: It is very important here, and in every step of the dry fly, not to use too many turns of thread. You will get a sturdy fly but also a lumpy one that will sink.

5. Divide the clump, and use the figure-8 wrap, as shown, to create two upright wings.

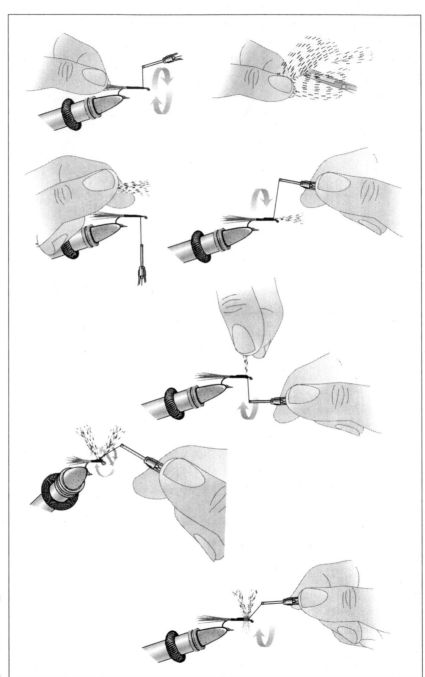

Figure 7-15:
Tying a
Light
Hendrickson.

A fish-eye view

You may want to try dropping a fly into a tall glass of water and watch it descend. As it does, you may see a few little air bubbles escape from the fly. This escaping-air-bubble effect looks incredibly lifelike to a fish. While I'm on the subject, looking at all these flies you tie in a glass of water is worthwhile. When you do, you can see how the hackle dimples the water on a classic dry fly and how a Compara-dun lays in the film. If you can trap a natural insect and float it next to your fly, you will get an interesting lesson in what features of the fly stand out from the vantage point of a fish.

---

6. Select two hackles of the right size for the hook, and wind them in, as shown.

7. Whip finish, and cement.

The Ausable Wulff

This member of the Wulff series of flies, shown in Figure 7-16, is named after the most famous angler of this century, Lee Wulff, who was born in Alaska in 1896. One day, in the 1930s, Lee became quite upset when a friend of his was fired from his job just a few weeks from retirement. Wulff, who was a commercial artist at the time, told his boss what to do with his job. "I never wanted to compete for money again," Lee later said. He spent that summer camping out on the Esopus Creek in the Catskills. One night, during a hatch of the mayfly known as the Dark Hendrickson, he tied a fly using a bushy deer hair wing instead of the less-buoyant wood duck feathers of the standard Hendrickson pattern. The new fly, the Gray Wulff, worked well in the high and roily water, and a new style of dry fly was invented. The Ausable Wulff, a variation on the same theme, is lighter in color than the Gray Wulff, and I find it to be an excellent *prospecting fly* (one you use to search the water when no fish are rising). It works especially well in riffly pocket water. I usually carry an assortment of these Wulffs in sizes 12, 14, and 16.

Hook	Mustad 94840 or equivalent
Size	8–14
Thread	Fluorescent Orange
Wing	White calf tail
Tail	Woodchuck tail fibers
Body	Tan fur
Hackle	Brown and grizzly mixed

Figure 7-16:
The
Ausable
Wulff.

This is not a hard fly to tie. In fact, if you have tied a Light Hendrickson, you've already done it. The trick is learning to tie with calf's tail, which is not as well behaved and easy to line up as hackle fibers. The same techniques of hair handling wash for elk hair, deer hair, woodchuck, and so on.

The steps are exactly the same as for the Light Hendrickson, except for preparing the calf tail or other animal hair for the wing and tail of the fly.

1. Clip off a clump of hair, a little more than a wing's worth. Using a small comb (like the kind they sell with beard trimmers or for mustaches), comb out all the fuzz and smaller hairs.

2. Even the hair out in a stacker. The top of a lipstick case or a .30-06 shell casing works equally well; so does a stacking tube that you can buy at a fly-tying supply shop. After this is done, tie in as you did for the wood duck in the Light Hendrickson. All the other steps are the same.

The Griffith's Gnat

This little, all-purpose fly, invented by John Griffith, the founder of Trout Unlimited, is the one I go to when there is small stuff on the water. The hook of the Griffith's Gnat is wrapped with a body of peacock *herl* (fibers of peacock eye) and a palmered, small hackle from a grizzly rooster (which has multicolored feathers of white, black, and gray). To the fish, I think that all those neck fibers sticking out must make the Griffith's Gnat look like a buzzing little bug (see Figure 7-17). I've used this fly for gnats, tricos, midges, and ants. It is one of those flies that fish often take even though they may be bigger than the natural insect on the water. Sizes 16–22 are available. One word of tying advice: This is a small fly, so be very sparse in your use of thread.

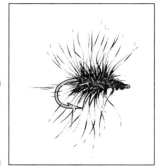

Figure 7-17:
The Griffith's Gnat.

Hook	Orvis 1637
Size	18–22
Thread	Black
Body	Peacock herl
Hackle	Grizzly palmered

Check out Figure 7-18 to tie a Griffith's Gnat.

1. Jam knot the thread in the middle of the hook. Wind back to the shank, and tie in one grizzly hackle tip and three or four pieces of peacock herl (the iridescent barbules that you find on a peacock tail feather). Wind the thread forward.

2. Gently twist the peacock herl strands together very carefully because they break easily. Wind forward, and tie off.

3. Palmer the grizzly hackle through the body of the hook. Tie off, whip finish, and cement.

The Compara-dun

Al Caucci and Bob Nastasi, two buddies who fish the very challenging waters of the West Branch of the Delaware, devised these no-hackle, deer-wing flies so that they would float flush in the surface film. I have found that Compara-duns (see Figure 7-19) really score well with highly selective fish. I especially like them when the little, yellow mayflies (known as Pale Morning Duns) are hatching, which they do with great frequency on the blue-ribbon waters of the Rocky Mountains. The Compara-spinners, also no-hackle flies with *spent deer hair wings* (that is, wings that lie flat and to the side, like outriggers) are the best spinners I know. Size varies depending upon what's happening, insect-wise, on the water.

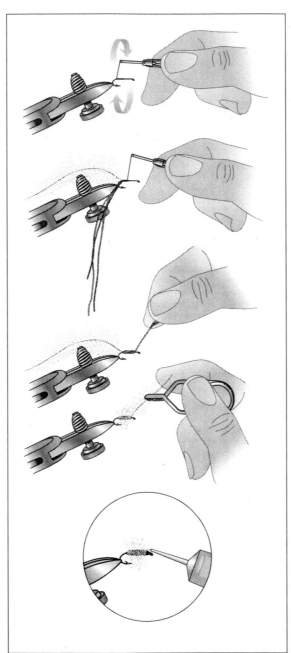

Figure 7-18:
Tying a
Griffith's
Gnat.

Figure 7-19:
The
Compara-
dun.

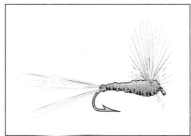

Hook	Mustad 94840
Size	8–16
Thread	Tan
Wing	Light tan elk or deer body hair
Tail	Light tan elk or deer hair
Body	Amber dubbing

These steps and Figure 7-20 can help you tie a Compara-dun.

1. Jam knot the thread and cover the middle of the shank. Cut and stack deer hair as you do for the Ausable Wulff.

2. Tie hair on with a couple of pinch wraps and then, after second wrap, pull down firmly. This will fan the deer hair out 180 degrees. Continue to wind to rear of hook and trim ends of deer hair.

3. Wind thread forward and stand wing upright as you do for the Ausable Wulff, and wind thread to rear of hook.

4. As shown, tie on a small ball of dubbed fur and then tie in deer or elk hair tail fiber. Hold the fibers together as you wrap toward the dubbing ball and just before you reach it, release the hairs and continue winding. This will fan out the tail fibers.

5. Dub more fur and wind forward to just behind the wing. Wind bare thread to just in front of the wing and dub on more fur to build up the thorax, as shown. Whip finish and cement.

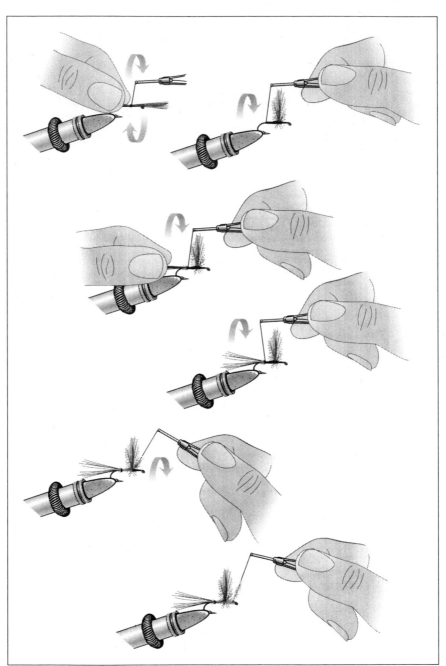

Figure 7-20:
Tying a
Compara-
dun.

The Elk Hair Caddis

Although elk hair gives this fly extra buoyancy, it still has a sleek and delicate profile (see Figure 7-21). The Elk Hair Caddis is a very good prospecting fly when you see a few splashy caddis rises. I think that the palmered hackle breaks up the light just the way a skittering caddis will as it darts about the surface. I usually carry sizes 14, 16, and 18.

Figure 7-21:
The Elk Hair Caddis.

Hook	Mustad 94833 or 94840
Size	10–20
Thread	Brown
Body	Olive fur
Hackle	Ginger grizzly palmered over body
Wing	Light elk hair

Figure 7-22 shows what's detailed in the following steps:

1. Jam knot the thread. Wrap to the shank. Tie in the hackle.

2. Dub fur and wind forward. Wind the hackle forward and tie in, but *do not clip.*

3. Clip a V-shape in the top of the hackle so that the wing can lay in there after you tie it on.

4. Stack a clump of elk hair, and tie in where the palmered hackle ends. This will form your wing.

5. Finish winding the hackle in front of the hair wing, nice and compactly. Whip finish and cement.

Figure 7-22:
Tying an Elk
Hair Caddis.

Final destination

The Elk Hair Caddis fly illustrates a good point. You don't always tie something in just before you use it. In this case, the grizzly hackle was tied in first but it actually was involved in the middle and very last steps of tying the fly. You need to think about where the thread is going to be when you need to use a material. Because the thread was in the front of the fly and the hackle was at the rear when you needed to use the hackle, it made sense to tie the hackle in when the thread was at the rear of the hook. Like knots, all flies have a logic to the way in which they go together. After you begin to understand this logic and the ways in which different materials are used, you will begin to make up flies that fit the water you fish and the little quirks of your local game fish. That's part of the real fun of fly tying: figuring something out all on your own that will catch a nice fish!

The Black-Nosed Dace

This fly is the first "match-the-hatch" streamer that I know of in modern American trout fishing. Like so much else in our sport, we are indebted to the late Art Flick, "The Great Simplifier," who studied trout fishing really hard and then explained it so simply for the rest of us. This is a bucktail fly that imitates a common minnow in the Catskills, but I have used it all over the world and continue to score with it even when there are no Dace swimming around. I guess it just looks like something universally good to eat (see Figure 7-23).

Figure 7-23: The Black-Nosed Dace.

Hook	Mustad 3665A
Size	6–8
Thread	Black
Wing	Three layers: white bucktail bottom, skunk tail or black bear hair middle, brown bucktail top
Body	Silver tinsel
Tag	Red yarn

See Figure 7-24 to tie a Black-Nosed Dace.

1. Start your thread, and tie in a shot length of red yarn. This will be a tag at the back of the fly that seems to get the attention of fish.

2. Clip the yarn, and wrap it forward. Tie in tinsel. Cut it on the bias where you begin to wrap the thread to secure the tinsel. Wind the tinsel to the back of the fly and then forward. Overlap the wraps of the tinsel to keep it smooth and tight (but don't worry if it's not perfect).

3. Tie off the tinsel, trim, and build up a base of thread at the head to accommodate the bucktail layers to come.

4. Tie in a clean, evened-up clump of white hair. Keep it sparse. People have a tendency to tie too much hair on this fly, which makes for a big, soggy mess instead of a streamlined thing that looks alive in the water. Secure the white bucktail with a number of wraps, making a thread base for the next clump.

5. Repeat Step 4 for black and then brown bucktail. Build up the head. Whip finish and cement.

The Clouser's Minnow

This fly is another great invention of an observant angler. Let me say that a little more strongly. The Clouser's Minnow, shown in Figure 7-25 and invented by Pennsylvania smallmouth master, Bob Clouser, is the greatest fly invented in the last 20 years. Though it was originally tied for smallmouth bass, I have caught largemouth bass, stripers, trout, bonefish, and almost (but not quite) my first permit on a Clouser's Minnow. In the way that all people like French-fried potatoes, I think that all fish like the Clouser's Minnow. It is a simple streamer with lead eyes that allows you to give it a jigging retrieve. Because it rides upside down, it is good at avoiding snags. I carry the Clouser's Minnow in sizes 2, 4, 6, and 8.

Figure 7-24:
Tying a
Black-
Nosed
Dace.

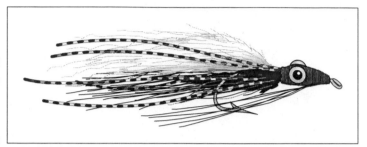

Figure 7-25: The Clouser's Minnow.

Hook	Mustad 9672
Size	2–6
Thread	Black
Head	Dumbbell eyes
Lower wing	White bucktail or synthetic
Highlight	Krystal Flash (an iridescent synthetic that really shimmers in a way that gets the attention of most fish)
Upper wing	Green bucktail

Figure 7-26 and the following steps show you how to tie a Clouser's Minnow.

1. Lay a foundation of thread, as shown, and tie in the lead eyes. Use figure-8 wraps to secure the dumbbell, holding it in position. Apply cement to the thread and let dry.

2. Even out a sparse clump of white bucktail and tie in. Next, secure white bucktail at the rear of the lead eyes and then bring thread underneath so that you can tie in the next material in front of the eyes.

3. For convenience, turn the hook upside down and tie in some Krystal Flash (or peacock herl will do as a substitute).

4. Even up your green bucktail tie in, build up head, whip finish, and cement.

So Which Fly Do I Use?

During any hatch, the trout may be keyed in on one phase of the mayfly's life cycle. If you can figure out what the trout are taking, you have a fighting chance to "match the hatch." This match-the-hatch principle is one of fly fishing's deeply held articles of faith: You try to give the trout a fly that looks like the food that it is currently eating. Just as mayflies have different stages of life, different artificial flies represent each of those stages.

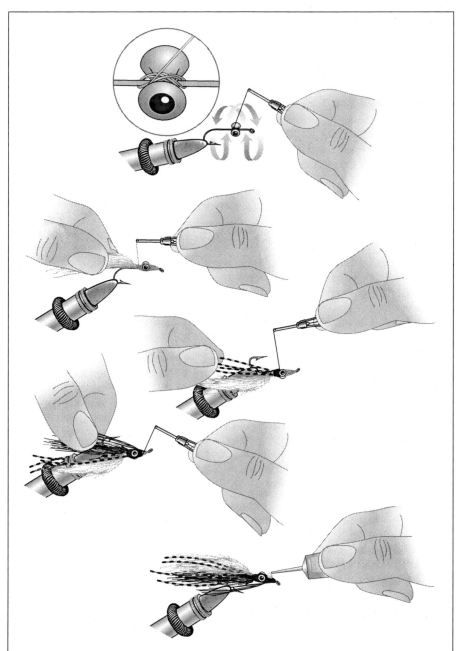

Figure 7-26:
Tying a
Clouser's
Minnow.

For many years, I preferred the nymph to the dry fly. In part, this preference was because (in those days) I fished on a free-stone Catskill stream with not much surface feeding. Nymphs seemed to work more. Of course, part of the reason they worked more is because I used them more. Which leads to an obvious tip, but one which bears repeating.

Use the flies and methods that you find you are most comfortable with. If you have no confidence in a certain lure, fly, bait, or technique, you will not catch many fish. On the other hand, sometimes the "wrong" fly, fished with style and confidence, takes the fish. Or (put another way) it isn't always *what* you fish with, but the *way* that you fish with it that counts.

The opposite point of view

Okay, got that? The "not what you fish with, but how you fish with it" rule *is* a pretty good rule to follow, except when it *isn't* a good rule to follow. I know this statement sounds a little arbitrary, but let me try to explain because I think that your fishing can improve if you understand the exception to this rule. Although many anglers fish the dry fly or nothing, I used to fish with a dry fly only when I saw activity on the water. Back then, my theory was this: "Trout spend a great deal of time eating, so if I do not see them eating on top, they must be eating down below. I'll stick with nymphs or streamers." Well, that self-advice sounded pretty practical, so I congratulated myself on what a clear-headed angler I was.

Then I started fishing with Ben. Ben is one of those fishermen who can *sense* what the fish want and how to give it to them. Many times we would go out fishing together. Seeing no surface activity, I would put on a nymph or wet fly, and Ben would tie on a little dry fly. Sure enough, Ben would score fish after fish, and I would flail the water. I learned then and there

that my so-called clear-headedness was just an excuse to not try something new. So although the rule that you do best with the methods you know and believe in is true, don't get set in your ways — keep learning new techniques.

Not surprisingly, after I started to fish a dry fly a little more, I became much more attuned to the many subtle ways in which a fish takes a dry fly. In other words, in the old days, I didn't fish dries much because I didn't see any feeding activity on the surface. It turned out that I wasn't seeing that feeding activity because I wasn't looking for the right signs.

And this advice doesn't apply only to fly fishermen. For example, I took the same prejudice to surf casting. If I didn't see any surface action, I fished deep. But only after I saw a veteran surf jockey pull in striper after striper with a topwater plug did I realize that part of what makes a good angler is the ability to *entice* fish, even if you don't see a great deal of feeding activity going on.

Chapter 8
Great Rivers for Trout

In This Chapter

▶ The Battenkill

▶ The Delaware

▶ The Letort

▶ The White River

▶ The Madison

▶ The Yellowstone

▶ The Green River

▶ The San Juan

▶ The Deschutes

▶ Hat Creek

*F*or the trout fly rodder, great fishing most often means fishing in rivers and streams, moving water. There are a few lakes that offer great trout fishing, but by and large, most trout fishing is done in rivers and streams, and trout fishing techniques are developed for rivers and streams. I could have included more rivers on this list and still have kept up the angling quality, but in the interests of keeping it simple, here are ten great rivers around America. They represent every kind of water and all the major hatches discussed in Chapter 6.

Note: In all of the hatch tables in this chapter, I have included the common name of the flies as they are known locally. To me, a Pale Morning Dun and a Pale Evening Dun are the same fly, but if the locals have two different names that is what I am giving you. That way, the guy in the tackle shop won't think you are totally clueless. By the way, a note of thanks to a fellow angler Jason Heilig whose Internet site, Flyfishing America (http://www.angelfire.com/co/flyfishingamerica), contains hatching information on many great rivers.

The Battenkill: Vermont

Years ago, I had a book called *The Shooter's Encyclopedia* or something like that. There was a picture of an old delivery truck with oversized tires in the middle of a field somewhere in the southern U.S. The caption explained that the rig was a quail wagon that rich sports used to ride out to their shooting fields back in the 1920s. "What does all this have to do with fishing?" you ask. Well, the photo credit that caught my eye said, "Lee Wulff, Shushan, New York."

Now, if you don't know who Lee Wulff was, let me introduce you to the greatest American fly fisherman of this century. He invented the Wulff series of dry flies and the fishing vest. He could tie tiny flies without a vise and he could cast far and fine, subduing fish on the lightest tackle. Lee lived in Shushan for a while because Shushan is on the Battenkill and the Battenkill, in addition to being home water for the Orvis company, is a beautiful and classic northeastern trout stream. It's shown in Figure 8-1. In recent years, it has received a lot of pressure, and fishing isn't what it was 50 years ago, but then, neither am I. It is still gorgeous, holds big fish, and surrenders them to the dedicated angler.

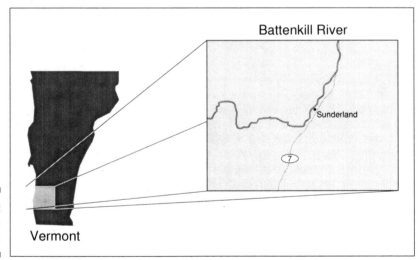

Figure 8-1:
The
Battenkill.

It is a typical free-stone stream and is 90 percent wadeable. There are some ledges here and there, some good-sized rocks, but not very much pocket water (even in the upper reaches). There aren't many tributaries that feed the Battenkill, but there is lots of ground water so the river stays cool and the fish have a good environment through the summer. A good deal of natural cover has been lost to agriculture and recreational stress from canoeing — canoe trippers remove fallen trees and limbs from along the banks to allow passage and take away much of the cover trout would have. If you want good fishing, don't mess with Mother Nature! Leave the river as you found it.

Roads on either side of the river offer easy access. As of this writing, there is a daily "in possession" limit of six browns or six rainbows (or a combination of the two) but no catch-and-release requirements. In a special area near West Arlington, Vermont, fish 10- to 14-inches long must be returned and a three-fish-per-day limit is enforced. The Vermont side of the river has no stocked fish and contains a good population of wild brown and brook trout. As the river flows into New York, the first 4.2 miles are restricted to artificial lures — flies, spinners, and so on — and there is a three fish-per day-limit.

Battenkill veterans suspect that due to recreational stress, bigger fish have been moving upstream to deeper water with undercut banks — reaches of the river where there isn't much canoeing pressure. Recreational stress, by the way, doesn't always mean fishing pressure. It can also mean that canoers, tubers, and the like drive the fish as crazy as I would feel if the people upstairs from my apartment threw non-stop parties every weekend. I would move.

The major hatch is the Hendrickson — it is the biggest and marks the official start of the season. Cahills, Sulfurs, and Caddis are also big hatches, and in the dog days of summer, I have had nice Trico spinner fishing. Summer, if the weather cooperates, you can fish a big Trico hatch. As the season moves along, there is a lot of small stuff in the surface film and small Blue-Winged Olives or Griffith gnats produce. There are also lots of Sculpin in the Battenkill, so muddler patterns work, especially early in the season or after a rain.

For Battenkill information:

Orvis Manchester
Route 7A
Manchester, VT 05254
802-362-3750; fax 802-362-3525

For license and regulations information:

Vermont Department of Fish & Wildlife
103 South Main Building
10 South Waterbury, VT 05671-0501
802-241-3700

Battenkill Hatches	
Common Name of Fly	*Dates of Emergence*
Blue-Winged Olive	May 25 – into October
Hendrickson	April 20 – May 20
Pale Evening Dun	May 15 – June 20
Yellow Quill	June 2 – June 25
Cream Variant	June 20 – August 10
Trico	July 15 – September 14

The Delaware: New York and Pennsylvania

The most beautiful water I have ever seen is on the Delaware just below the juncture with the Lackawaxen (see Figure 8-2). In the spring, when the shad are in, the fly rodder has a chance for smallmouth, trout, and shad in this one place. There are big swirly green patches of water flowing over huge rocks. On the western (Pennsylvania) shore, there is a modest home where Zane Grey, who wrote in order to have time and money to fish, lived for more than ten years. It is one of those places in this world that seems to stop you and ask you to look while whispering "Fish here" into your ear.

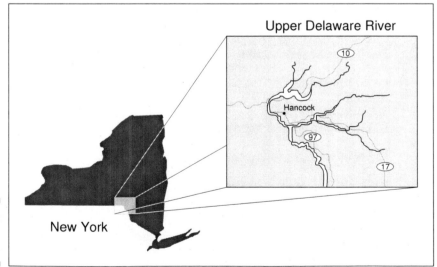

Figure 8-2:
The
Delaware.

In the last 20 years or so, the Upper Delaware River, between Hancock and Calicoon, New York, and its tributaries, the East and West Branch, have become the most prized waters of the Northeast. It is a *cold-water bottom release fishery,* which means that it is fed by cold water from the bottom of reservoirs. This means, at least in theory, a steady flow and uniform temperatures exist within these waters. The steady flow part is in the hands of the New York City reservoir bureaucracy, so like so many things in my home town, it is often a mess. Still, this stream has the best and most dependable hatches of Mayflies all day, and all season, long. In that respect, the Delaware is unique in the Northeast. With its long pools and wide bends, it is, in many parts, a wonderful and easy river to float. Remember, however, that a lot of those inviting pools are not trouty from head to tail. They are trouty at the head and the tail. The large calm stretches in the midpool are not productive for the fly rodder.

It is a very wadeable river, but beware of drop-offs in those same long pools. You may have to do some driving to get from one access point to another, but the boatless angler can still fish a lot of productive water.

There is a good mix of wild browns and rainbows, and they are challenging fish. Lots of insect life mean lots of practice in developing selectivity. The good news is that the fish are usually looking up and taking flies. The other part of the story is that these are among the most challenging fish I know. And if I can be casting to trout that I see rising and have them continue to rise as I carefully continue to cast and change flies, I am a happy camper, or at least an interested one.

Two tribs of the East Branch of the Delaware, the Beaverkill and its tributary, the Willowemoch, are the last of the great free-flowing Catskill trout streams, where America's fly fishing pioneers developed the sport in the last century. Both are still well managed for fly fishing and have made remarkable comebacks since the bad old days of the early 1960s, when they were just put-and-take fisheries with dinky trout. Still, developers and industry keep threatening the river, and it takes constant vigilance on the part of anglers to preserve these waters.

Rules vary by section — there are catch-and-release sections as well as trophy sections.

For more information about the Upper Delaware:

Al Caucci's Delaware River Club
HC 1
Box 1290
Starlight, PA 18461
800-6-MAYFLY
http://www.mayfly.com

For license and regulations information:

New York State Division of Fish and Wildlife
50 Wolf Road
Albany, NY 12233-4750
518-457-5690

Delaware Hatches	
Common Name of Fly	*Dates of Emergence*
Blue-Winged Olive	April 15 – October 30
Pseudo	April 15 – October 30
Cahill	May 15 – July 15 (although cahill-ish flies can come off into September)
Pale Evening Dun	May 15 – July 20
Trico	May 1 – October 7
Isonychia	May 15 – July 15, August 30 – October 15
Stone fly	June 1 – August 31
Flying Ants	June 1 – November 1

The Letort: Pennsylvania

The Letort is a classic limestone river. Silver Creek in Idaho, the Fall River in California, and Nelson's Spring Creek in Montana are all of this class of stream and require similar tactics. Stealth and delicacy count for so much on any spring creek. The fish are there. They are big. And they are tough. I chose the Letort because it is a historically great stream. Theodore Gordon, the Godfather of American fly fishing, lived here as a young boy, and Vincent Marinaro, who had so much to do with teaching us all how to fish with patterns that imitate landlubber bugs (like ants and beetles), was also schooled on the Letort. If you want to learn how to deal with frustration, you will not find a better teacher than this placid mid-Pennsylvania stream, whose location is shown in Figure 8-3.

The Letort, over the course of nine miles, is fed by spring creeks that keep the water temperature fairly stable. It has a slow current and is deep and weedy in places. It is not floatable, and is about 20 to 25 feet wide. Access to the Letort is possible by car, but along the banks, on foot, access is difficult because of heavily foliage. In late spring and summer, lots of weeds choke the marshy banks as the river rises with rains. In many spots, you can wade only one side of the Letort — it's not easy to cross, and because there are very silty sections along the bank, you use up much effort just fishing one side. Because of all of these factors, you really have to think through each cast *before* you make it. Where is the backcast going to go? How long a float will you get? Can you let the fly get past your fish a good distance before picking up your line and spooking a nice fish? These are questions that you should ask yourself in any situation, but the Letort forces them on you if you expect to catch anything.

Most of the fish in the Letort are very wary wild brown trout, but there are a few rainbows. The average fish is usually 13 to 15 inches long, which is really great. There have been some problems with runoffs and chemicals in the last few years that have hurt insect life in the stream, but the river appears to have turned the corner on that threat. The Letort seems to be coming back quite well. Fishing here, as elsewhere, tends to suffer most from the too-many-fishermen syndrome. Because the water is so clear and placid, if some bozo walks along a stream bank and whips the stream to a froth with a lot of sloppy casts, you'd be much better off finding a patch of stream that no one has been on because once Letort fish are disturbed, they get as neurotic as Woody Allen, and about as likely to take a fly.

This is one of the rivers where terrestrials (land insects such as ants and beetles as well as grasshoppers) can make up a large part of the trout's diet), so much so, that the great Vincent Marinaro basically invented the modern way of imitating and fishing terrestrials on the Letort. So bring some of these patterns along.

Nearly all the Letort is fishable water, and there are a number of places where you can approach it. The primary river access is at Bonnie Brook Road. Marinaro's Meadow and the Barnyard Stretch offer access as well. The Heritage Area offers a mile and a half of classic water, and there is some access near the late, great Charlie Fox's house.

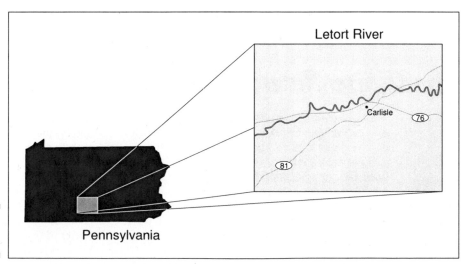

Figure 8-3:
The Letort.

Fishing on the Letort is all no-kill fly fishing only, and only barbless hooks may be used. You can fish from an hour before sunrise to an hour after sundown.

The next five years will determine the future of the Letort, as a large tract of land in the Heritage Area is up for development. My advice: Fish it now, and then stay involved with the fight to preserve it.

For more information about the Letort:

Falling Spring Outfitters, Inc.
P.O. Box 35
Scotland, PA 17254
717-263-7811

For license and regulations information:

Pennsylvania Fish and Boat Commission
P.O. Box 67000
Harrisburg, PA 17106
717-657-4518

Letort Hatches	
Common Name of Fly	*Dates of Emergence*
Blue-Winged Olive	April 1 – May 10 and September 20 – October 31
Pale Evening Dun	May 1 – June 20
Trico	July 1 – October 31
Ants, Beetles, Hoppers	July 1 – September 30
Freshwater Shrimp	January 1 – December 31

The White River: Arkansas

When you say Arkansas, trout fishing is not the first word that comes to mind. And when you say the White River, remember, there was once a time that it meant great float fishing for smallmouth bass. But with the impoundment of the White, a great *tailwater* fishery (bottom release of cold water from the base of a dam) has created one of the half dozen best trout fisheries in the U.S. Low water can be found pretty much over the entire 70-mile stretch of trout water. The White is also fishable in high water, and while it is wadeable in most places, it is also floatable all the time. The river has a textbook riffle pool kind of character that provides a selection of the kinds of waters that should satisfy any angler. Access to the river is very good all along State Highway 412 (see Figure 8-4).

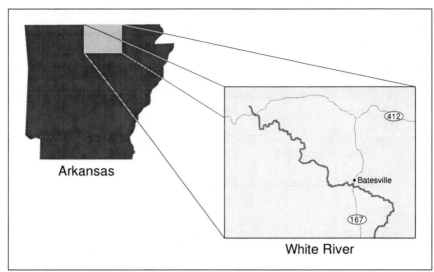

Figure 8-4:
The White
River.

The White River is known for trophy-sized trout and many record fish have been taken here. There are more rainbows than browns, but enough of both. There are good wild browns in the upper reaches. As is the case on many rivers, during the fall spawning run, a good number of trophy browns are taken each year. If you like fishing for brookies and cutthroats, the White has them, too. From November 1 through January 30, certain parts of the river are closed to allow fish to spawn without being disturbed.

There are two main catch-and-release sections — immediately below Beaver Dam and in Rim Shoals. Outside of catch-and-release areas, taking fish is governed by state regulations. In Arkansas, you can take up to six fish per day, but no more than two browns and two cutthroats at least 16 inches long.

For more information on the White River:

Blue Ribbon Fly Shop
1343 Highway 5 South
Mountain Home, AR 72653
870-425-0447

For license and regulations information:

Arkansas Game and Fish
#2 Natural Resources Drive
Little Rock, AR 72205
501-223-6351

White River Hatches	
Common Name of Fly	*Dates of Emergence*
Caddis	March 15 – May 20; small Caddis all summer
Light Cahill	May 12 – July 20
Sulfur	May 15 – July 20
Pale Morning Dun	Early spring, sporadic through summer
Blue-Winged Olive	Early spring, fall
Midges	Small, sporadic hatches all year

The Madison: Montana

In the 50 years since World War II, the Madison (shown in Figure 8-5) has been the most famous and probably most fished, big fish river in the country. Since 1991, the Madison River, like many of our blue ribbon trout waters, has been the victim of whirling disease. Actually, the river didn't get sick, but a lot of fish did, mostly, but not exclusively, rainbows. Whirling disease is a fatal infection that was introduced into the wild by criminally idiotic stream stocking with contaminated fish. In the last two years, the mighty Madison has appeared to have turned the corner, which is a blessed thing, because the Madison is a great river.

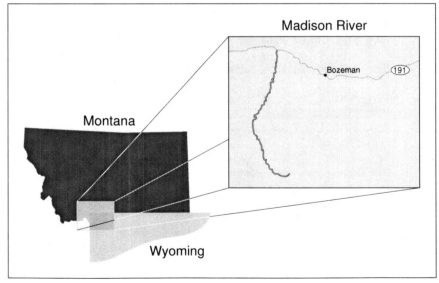

Figure 8-5:
The
Madison.

The stream bed is mostly round river rock, and the river itself is not so much a riffle pool kind of stream as it is a 50-mile riffle. The current is not overpowering, and the entire river is floatable and wadeable with lots of public access. Be careful when you wade on the slick bottoms. Stream cleats, or at least studded boots, are not a bad idea. In addition to great browns and rainbows, there are native populations of cutthroats and grayling. All the fish are wild. Rainbows, cutthroats, and grayling must be released, but browns may be kept in certain sections.

The Salmon Fly hatch on this river is one of Troutdom's great experiences. Later in the season, Hoppers have the same effect, bringing up big trout to dry flies.

The Madison flows into the Missouri at Three Forks, Montana. About an hour's drive downstream, you reach the section of the stream below Holter Dam, near the town of Craig. This cold water release fishery is, in the opinion of many anglers whose opinion I respect (including myself), the best piece of trout water in the U.S. at this time. You need to be a pretty fair fly rodder to do any good on it, but, tough as it is, it is worth the effort. The fish are mind-blowing.

For more information about the Madison:

The Tackle Shop Outfitters
127 Main Street
Box 625
Ennis, MT 59720
800-808-2832

For license and regulations information:

Montana Department of Fish, Wildlife, and Parks
1420 East 6th St.
Helena, MT 59620
406-499-3186

For Yellowstone Park license and regulations information:

Yellowstone National Park Fishing Permit Office
P.O. Box 168
Yellowstone National Park, Wyoming 82190
307-344-2107

Madison Hatches	
Common Name of Fly	*Dates of Emergence*
Grannom Caddis	April 15 – May 30
Pale Morning Dun	May 20 – July 20
Caddis (various)	June 1 – July 30
Salmon Fly	June 20 – July 20
Pseudo	April 10 – May 10 and September 1 – October 31
Hoppers	August 1 – September 15

The Yellowstone: Wyoming and Montana

The Yellowstone, shown in Figure 8-6, is good everywhere and has just about every kind of trout fishing you would care to try. Up in Yellowstone Park, its tributaries, the Lamar, Soda Butte Creek, and Slough Creek are meadow stream gems that are easy to wade and not too big to test the skills of reasonable casters. Way up at the source of the main stem, where it drops out of Yellowstone Lake, the Yellowstone is a strong river with a steady and powerful current that requires good wading skills. All of the fish in this upper stretch are native cutthroat trout. It is prettier than any place on earth, and when you throw in the bonus of good fishing, you realize that it is not always necessary to die to get to heaven.

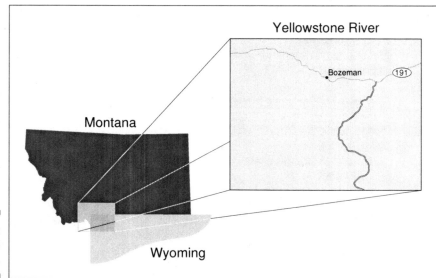

Figure 8-6:
The
Yellowstone.

Don't be a butthead!

If you happen to be in a boat and are fishing your way downriver, please give the wading angler a wide berth. It may have taken him or her a half hour to walk down to that particular spot in the stream. If you crowd it or fish over it, you will definitely spoil it for the wading angler. You have a whole river to fish. Stop casting for a few minutes until you pass.

As it leaves the park, the Yellowstone is a wide, swift-flowing, free-stone river, whose sheer size can daunt you, but it doesn't have to be that tough. You need to do what the fish do, break up the river into a lot of smaller environments, or little rivers, side channels, mid-river islands, submerged rocks, and dead falls, all of which create eddies, currents, and the general structure that makes for great habitat. Fish each little area, and ignore the rest of the river around you. The Yellowstone cutthroat is a cooperative trout. Give him a proper cast, and he will rise to your fly. The brown trout is, as he is everywhere, a lot more wary, but the water is fast enough that even the brown needs to be a highly opportunistic feeder and will often rise to a well presented fly even if it is not the so-called right fly.

There is very good access to the water throughout Montana along Route 89 and I-90. The bottom is mostly round rocks and is very slippery. Add to that the power of the current and you have a recipe for easy falling. Be careful and take it slow and don't try to wade past your comfort zone. Take my word for it, there are trout everywhere in this river. There are lots of riffles and runs, which make for lots of fishable pocket waters. There is good wading access, and floating the river has become popular to the point of being a pain in the butt.

There is a no-kill rule for cutthroats on the river and its tributaries, and though you may take one brown or rainbow over 18-inches long per day, most anglers are pure catch-and-release on this river. It is such a nice river with such great fishing that I have to second that motion. With the amount of pressure that there is on the Yellowstone these days, if every one of us kept fish, it would go from being a great fishery to an okay fishery. We already have enough okay fisheries: Help save the Yellowstone for the next generation of anglers. There is no stocking in the Yellowstone, which means that any fish you catch is a born-in-the-stream, wild fish.

The Caddis Fly hatch is the biggest of the season, and in years when the flow is right, the Mother's Day hatch is a first-rate, early-season fishing hatch. Like the Madison, the Yellowstone has a major Salmon Fly hatch, and the Western Green Drake is making a comeback after losses to pesticides.

For more information about the Yellowstone:

Dan Baily's Fly Shop
P.O. Box 1019
Livingston, MT 59047
406-222-1673

The Yellowstone Angler
P.O. Box 660
Livingston, MT 59047
406-222-7130

For license and regulations information:

Montana Department of Fish, Wildlife, and Parks
1420 East 6th Street
Helena, MT, 59620
406-499-3186

Yellowstone Hatches	
Common Name of Fly	*Dates of Emergence*
Pseudo	April 20 – June 10 and August 15 – September 30
Little Blue-Winged Olive	April 10 – May 10
Black Caddis	May 1 – May 30
Salmon Fly	June 15 – July 15
Mahogany Dun	September 1 – September 20
Hoppers	August 1 – September 15
Western Green Drake	Sporadic through summer

The Green River: Utah

The Green River (see Figure 8-7) has edged its way into national trout fishing consciousness in the last few years, with good reason. It is a Class-A Rocky Mountain stream. The Green River presents every type of fishable water — runs, riffles, and pools. I have not fished the Green, so I can't report on it first hand, but so many good anglers say such good things about it that I think it isn't too boneheaded to include it right up there with the great streams of the nation.

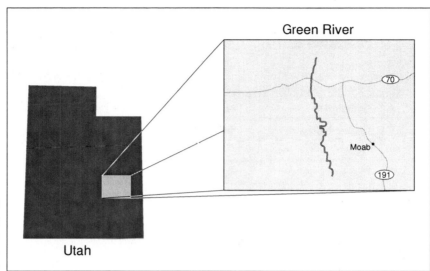

Figure 8-7:
The Green
River.

The river is very wadeable. The bottom varies from gravel to mossy rocks, big rocks to boulders. It is also easily floatable.

The trout population is made up of mostly browns and rainbows, but there are a few cutthroat. The daily limit is two fish under 13 inches, one over 20; trout between 13 and 20 inches must be let go. The river is open year round, 24 hours per day.

For more information on the Green River:

Spinner Fall Fly Shop
1450 Foothill Dr.
Salt Lake City, UT 84108
800-979-3474

For license and regulations information:

Utah Division of Wildlife Resources
1596 West North Temple
Salt Lake City, UT 84116
801-538-4700

Green River Hatches	
Common Name of Fly	*Dates of Emergence*
Pseudo	March 1 – April 30 and September 15 – October 31
Pale Morning Dun	May 15 – July 30
Salmon Fly	May 1 – May 30
Caddis (various)	May 1 – July 30
Trico	July 15 – October 31
October Caddis	September 15 – October 31

The San Juan: New Mexico

Like many of the best public waters, the San Juan is a cold tailwater fishery. It has a number of easily fished side channels and deep runs as well as a number of spring creeks in its valley. It is wadeable along the banks and shallow sections, but be careful of sudden drop-offs. It is floatable, with frequent drift boat access. The entire river, whose map is shown in Figure 8-8, is accessible on foot, and there are a number of access points along the first quarter mile, which is the high-quality water section.

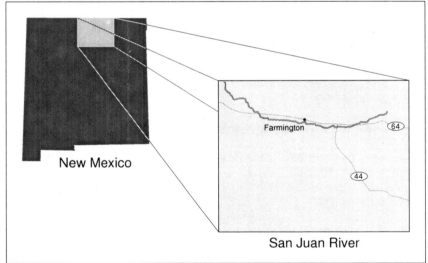

Figure 8-8:
The San
Juan.

New Mexico

San Juan River

The section of very high-quality water is a catch-and-release area. The rest of the river has a daily limit of one trout that is 20-inches long or longer, but as with our other blue ribbon streams, the move to catch and release is helping to preserve an outstanding fishery. The trout mix is mostly rainbows with a fair amount of browns and some cutthroat. Some of the rainbows are stocked. The browns in the lower sections are wild, as are the *cutbows* which are rainbow-cutthroat hybrids. The average size for most fish is a memorable 16 inches. This high average size is probably explained by a consistent year-round level of food.

The famous San Juan worm, which imitates a sort of skinny earthworm, is a year-round pattern. Leech and scud imitations work well. The San Juan is known as a nymphing river — you can cast nymph patterns all year, but dry flies and streamers produce, too, especially in the fall.

For more information about the San Juan:

Abe's Motel & Fly Shop, Inc.
P.O. Box 6428
San Juan River, NM 87419
505-632-2194

For license and regulations information:

New Mexico Game and Fish Department
Villagara Building
Santa Fe, NM 87503
505-827-7911

San Juan Hatches	
Common Name of Fly	*Dates of Emergence*
Little Blue-Winged Olive	March 1 – October 31
Grey Caddis	May 1 – June 30
Midges	January 1 – December 31
Pale Morning Dun	July 10 – September 15
Hoppers	August 1 – August 30

The Deschutes: Oregon

The Deschutes River, shown in Figure 8-9, contains two main game fish: the Deschutes redside, a purely wild rainbow trout, and the steelhead. The redside can be caught all through the lower 100 miles of the river. The steelhead are mostly summer run, catchable May to October with August and September usually being the best months.

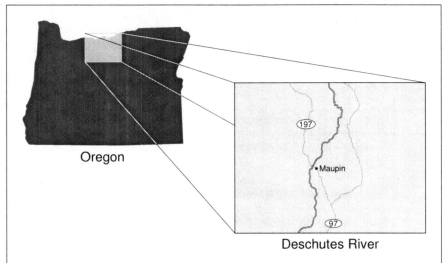

Figure 8-9:
The
Deschutes.

Oregon

Deschutes River

It is a beautiful, brawling river typical of the well watered Northwestern rivers, yet not so big that the beginner-to-intermediate fisherman can't do well on it.

The bottom varies from rocks to gravel to silty gravel. There are many riffles. In fact, there is just about every type of water imaginable — such as big eddies with sandy bottoms or gravel bottoms, grassy banks, and some bouldery pocket water.

The Deschutes is reasonably accessible by foot and is wadeable near the bank, but you can't wade across because of the strong current. The Deschutes is listed as a federal navigable river and is floatable.

Regulations allow only artificials, lures, and flies. The daily limit is two trout between 10 and 13 inches.

For more information about the Deschutes:

Gorge Fly Shop
201 Oak St.
Hood River, OR 97031
541-386-6977

The Fly Box
1293 Northeast 3rd Street
Bend, OR 97701
541-388-3330

For license and regulations information:

Oregon Department of Fish and Wildlife
Box 59
Portland, OR 97850
503-229-5551

Deschutes Hatches	
Common Name of Fly	*Dates of Emergence*
Little Blue-Winged Olive	March 1 – April 30 and September 15 – October 31
Pale Morning Dun	May 15 – July 30
Salmon Fly	May 1 – May 30
Caddis (various)	May 1 – July 30
Trico	July 15 – October 31
October Caddis	September 15 – October 31

Hat Creek: California

Dirty Harry sometimes fishes this river. That's right, Clint Eastwood himself is a Hat Creek angler. I can just picture him as a big trout rises to his Green Drake: "Go ahead, eat my dry."

Hat Creek, shown in Figure 8-10, is a big spring creek with only three miles of really good fishing, but if you can catch fish here, you are becoming a master of the game. The nearby Fall River which is only accessible to float fishing is also a spectacular trout stream. Hat Creek is not floatable, but you can wade its side waters just about anywhere. On the upper-half of the good water, the bottom is mostly gravel and there is much aquatic vegetation. The lower half is rubble and begins to drop more steeply over the rocks. Big tule reeds and a mucky bottom mean that there are some good fishing spots where you cannot wade out very far, and at the same time, your backcast is liable to catch in the reeds near the shore. Like I said, it ain't easy, but it is a kind of water that you will run into throughout the West, and you need to learn how to handle it.

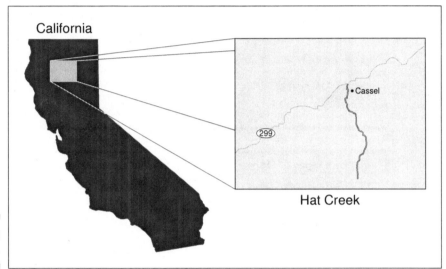

Figure 8-10:
Hat Creek.

The water is pretty accessible. You can reach most places on the lower half by car, and you can drive to several access points on the upper section.

The fish population is mostly made up of rainbows, but there are some browns. There is no stocking of the Hat Creek; sometimes stocked fish find their way into the creek from other stocked waters. An average fish on the Hat Creek is between 10 and 14 inches. There are big fish in there, but it takes a good angler to catch them. You can keep two fish over 18 inches daily.

For more information about Hat Creek:

The Fly Shop
4140 Churn Creek Road
Redding, CA 96002
916-222-3555

For license and regulations information:

California Department of Fish and Game
1416 Ninth Street
Sacramento, CA 95814
916-445-3531

Hat Creek Hatches	
Common Name of Fly	*Dates of Emergence*
Blue-Winged Olive	May 25 – August 2
Pale Morning Dun	May 1 – June 30
Pale Evening Dun	June 1 – July 15
Green Drake	May 1 – June 30
Trico	June 1 – October 31
October Caddis	June 1 – July 30 and October 1 – October 30
Salmon Fly	April 1 – May 30

Chapter 9
Freshwater Fish

*W*here you live and the common fish in your local waters have a great deal to do with the choice of fish that you fish for (although some fly rodders routinely travel thousands of miles to go after the fish they love). Through the 50 or so generations that people have fished for sport (rather than necessity), they have sought out fish that offer a bit of a challenge to catch. How well the fish fights is another big consideration. Whether or not they taste good also counts. And personal preference also plays a role. Some people find that one fish is just more fun to catch than another. I may have left your favorite fish off the following list, and if I did that, I apologize. Still, I think that most anglers would agree that the fish covered in this chapter are pretty much those at the very top of the anglers' hit parade.

The Trout

If the number of words written about a fish is any indication of popularity, then the trout is the runaway winner. A great deal of what has been written about trout, however, is just a bunch of hot air. Still, the fish is clearly a supreme game fish that is at least the equal of any other sport fish. In the old days, an angler was judged by how many trout he or she brought home. These days, thanks largely to the influence of American anglers, catch-and-release is more the rule. If you kill the occasional trout, however, don't let anyone make you feel guilty about it. They are delicious fish. On the other hand, if you kill every trout that you catch, you are being more greedy than wise. Trout are usually the main predator in their environment, standing at the top of the food chain in many rivers and streams. Top predators are, of necessity, rarer than animals lower down the chain. A little bit of pressure can alter the quality of angling in a stream very quickly. So enjoy yourself, enjoy your meal, but remember that the fish you return to the stream will ensure the natural balance that provides for good angling.

The champ: Brown trout

The brown trout is a fish designed for the angler. It often feeds on the surface. It rises to a properly presented fly. It fights like the dickens. Another reason for the brown trout's popularity is that it is the primary predator fish in English streams, where so much of our angling lore and technique originated. The brown didn't acquire a reputation as a "gentleman's fish" because it had particularly good manners and went to the right school. The simple fact of the matter is that rich English gentlemen, with time on their hands, embraced the earliest forms of fly fishing and popularized it everywhere. Because their local fish was the brown trout, it became the fish of choice for sportsmen there and in the New World. If the English sportsmen had started out in Georgia instead of England, you'd find a lot of flowery literature about largemouth bass.

The brown trout is a cold-water fish that lives in lakes and streams and is most active when the water temperature is in the 60°F range. A temperature much above 80°F is liable to kill brown trout. As shown in Figure 9-1, the brown trout is covered with spots everywhere but its tail. The majority of the spots are deep brown, like coffee beans, with a light yellow halo. You also find a few red and yellow spots here and there on its creamy-brown skin.

Brown trout are long-lived animals and can reach weights up to 40 pounds, but most stream-bred fish average less than a pound each. Common wisdom has it that a few wise browns in every stream usually reach weights of 10 pounds or more. I've never caught one that big.

Fly line world record

Randolph Harrison caught a 29-pound, 12-ounce brown on the Rio Grande, in Tierra del Fuego, Argentina, on January 19, 1992.

Figure 9-1:
The brown trout is one of the wiliest and most rewarding fish taken on rod and reel. Its instinct to dash for cover when hooked adds up to a great fight for the angler.

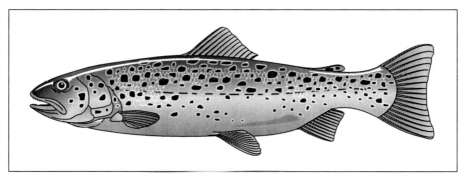

Who was Izaak Walton anyway?

Without question, the most famous book ever written about angling is *The Compleat Angler* published by Izaak Walton in 1653. Since that time, it has been through over 300 editions and is probably the most widely read (or at least widely owned) book after the *Bible* and the *Koran*. Because *The Compleat Angler* is an all-around handbook for fishing in England, people not familiar with Walton have the idea that the book is only for fly fishing snobs.

It isn't.

Izaak Walton was primarily a bait fisherman who came late to the fly. He was a self-made businessman who retired in his 50s and wrote the book that would earn him immortality at age 60. His prose is so strong and true that most people today can read his book with much less difficulty than they can read Shakespeare, for example.

Much of the best advice in the book was actually written by Charles Cotton, a young man of leisure who was an amazing fly rodder. It was Cotton, not Walton, who wrote "to fish fine and far off, is the first and principle rule for Trout angling." In other words, use a light leader and keep your distance from the fish so you don't spook it. This advice is as valuable today as it was three-and-a-half centuries ago when Walton and Cotton filled their days fishing and talking.

Not quite cricket, but so what?

Brown trout are very wary, and they are also creatures of habit. If you know their habits, and the habits of the anglers who fish for them, you may have an advantage that you can exploit. This advantage worked for me on my first visit to the Test, one of the historic English trout streams. I visited during the time of year when a large fly, which the English call The Mayfly, hatches. Whereas Americans call all the up-winged aquatic insects mayflies, the English reserve the name for this humongous hatch. It is a big fly and makes a fat target. Trout are supposed to be so easy to catch when this hatch is on that English anglers call this time of year "Duffers Fortnight" because, during this hatching period, *anybody* can catch a trout.

"Anybody" didn't include me that day. Three or four hours of casting didn't yield even one rise. On a hunch, I cut off my dry fly and tied on a little nymph. I walked upstream and crossed over an old wooden bridge. I then walked downstream through thick undergrowth on the unfished side of the river. (With the angler facing upstream, most English trout streams have the left bank cleared so that a right-handed caster can present a fly upstream without hanging up the backcast in pesky branches and grass.) I cast my little nymph about 6 feet into the current, which was as long a cast as I could manage in those close quarters. I let the fly swing into the bank, and a trout took on my first cast. After a hellacious fight, I landed him. He weighed 6¼ pounds and was the big trout of the season on that river.

To catch him, all I did was present a different fly in a novel way. By using the least-favored bank and breaking the gentlemen's code that requires an angler to cast upstream only, I proved that although the trout of the Test may have been well educated when it came to mayfly imitations presented by a right-handed caster on the left bank, anything that looked like food and that came from a different direction had a much better chance of interesting a good fish.

The moral of the story: Try something different if you have a feeling that it may work. (No law says that you have to fish the way that everybody else does.)

High jumpers: Rainbow trout

Guess what? A couple of years ago scientists decided that the rainbow trout isn't a trout after all. This fish looks like a trout and behaves like a trout. It feeds like a trout and eats flies like a trout. Probably because of those characteristics, those same Englishmen who gave us the lore of the brown trout decided to call the rainbow a trout.

I passed many years firm in my belief that the rainbow was a trout. Now that the rainbow has been reclassified as a smaller cousin of the Pacific salmon family, I haven't noticed my angling pleasure diminishing any.

Rainbows coexist nicely with brown trout in many streams. While the brown prefers the slower water and calmer pools, you can depend on finding the rainbow in the more oxygen-rich and swift-running riffles. This scenario is what you would expect from a fish that predominates in the streams of the Rocky Mountains, where it is a primary predator.

If you ask a hundred anglers to name the most memorable thing about the fight of a rainbow, you may well have 100 answers singling out the rainbow's leaping ability: Although the brown, when hooked, usually *sounds* (dives to the bottom) and makes for cover, the rainbow's instinct is to leap and run and leap some more. These acrobatics are thrilling, and on light tackle, they demand a sensitive touch.

As shown in Figure 9-2, the rainbow may have spots over the whole body (although in many rivers and lakes, the larger rainbows are more often an overall silver). A much more reliable sign of "rainbowness" is the pink band or line that runs along the flank of the fish from shoulder to tail. But even this marking is not always 100 percent foolproof because some stream-borne rainbows have a faded, almost invisible band, the same kind that you find on browns and brookies.

Fly line world record

A 28-pound rainbow was caught by Chuck Stephens on the Skeena River, in British Columbia, Canada, on October 20, 1985.

Figure 9-2:
The rainbow trout is the leapingest trout and also one of the hardiest, which has helped fish and game departments plant them anywhere that has cool running water.

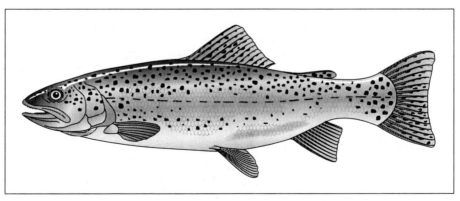

Steelhead — a salty rainbow

Almost all species of trout — given the chance — drop downstream to the ocean where they usually grow to much greater size than trout that are confined to streams and lakes. Sea-run brookies and browns (those that forage in the ocean and return to spawn in freshwater) also appear in North America, but the main target for anglers of sea-run trout is the steelhead, which is nothing more than a rainbow that has gone to sea. The steelhead have usually lost the distinctive coloration of the freshwater rainbow (although they still have the pink lateral line). As their name suggests, steelheads have a bright metallic coloration.

Sentimental favorite: Brookies

Like the rainbow, the brook trout, or *brookie,* isn't a trout. The brook trout is actually a char, which makes it a relative of the lake trout (not a real trout either), the Dolly Varden, and the Arctic char. It is the animal that fills the trout niche in the cooler streams of the northeastern U.S., east of the Allegheny Mountains. It is the original, native trout of this area. It has had to compete with the brown introduced from Europe in the late 1800s, and the rainbow introduced from the west around the same time.

Brookies like cooler water and cannot stand the higher temperatures that the brown and the rainbow can tolerate. Before Europeans cleared the great hardwood forests of the northeastern U.S., most streams had the shade and pure water that brook trout need. I think that the fact that the brookie is found only in wilderness areas explains part of the fondness that anglers have for him: He is a sign of pure water and a healthy ecology.

With the clearing of the forests and the coming of brown trout and rainbow trout, the brookie often retreated to the less-accessible headwaters of many streams. As explained by the principle of "smaller fish in smaller water," many people, whose only brook trout experience is on these smaller waters, have assumed that the brook trout is typically smaller than the rainbow or the brown. This is not true. In the old days on Long Island, for example, many brook trout ranged from 4 pounds to 10 pounds.

Although it is much-praised for its great beauty, the brookie is regarded by many anglers as an empty-headed glamour puss. I have to say that I agree in most cases. Of course, very wary, hard-to-catch-brookies do exist, but by and large, most of them are prettier than they are smart.

As shown in Figure 9-3, the brook trout has many red spots that are surrounded by a blue halo. The fins have a telltale black and white tip. The belly and fins have an orange cast that can be quite brilliant and almost crimson in spawning season. The tail of the brook trout is more squared off than that of the brown and rainbow, hence the nickname *squaretail.*

Figure 9-3:
The brook trout, originally a native of the east coast of North America, is universally admired for its gorgeous coloring.

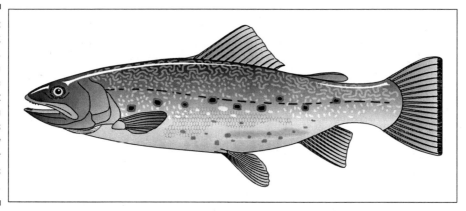

Fly line world record

A 10-pound, 7-ounce brookie was caught on the Assinica Broadback River, in Quebec, Canada, by James Francis McGarry on September 5, 1982.

The trout and Dan'l Webster

Back in 1828, Long Island had a number of gin-clear trout streams full of big, beautiful brookies, many of them fat from their summer diet of bait fish out in the Great South Bay. Daniel Webster and his fishing buddy, Martin Van Buren, often fished the Connetquot River, being particularly fond of the spot below the mill pond of local miller and innkeeper Sam Carmans.

A local rumor told of a great trout feeding in the mill race, and Webster, Van Buren, and Van Buren's slave, Apaius Enos, spent the better part of a day trying to entice the brookie (who could be seen feeding steadily), but they couldn't interest the fish. The next morning, somewhat the worse for a night spent dipping into Sam Carmans' rum barrel, Webster and Van Buren went to church, having left instructions with the slave to come and get them if that trout began to feed.

The trout appeared and Apaius carried out his orders. Webster and Van Buren tiptoed out of church as inconspicuously as they could, but everyone knew what was up — pretty soon the preacher was left preaching to an empty church. At the pond, Webster took up his rod — which was nicknamed "Killall" — and after two casts, hooked the fish. A memorable battle took place until, finally, Webster led the brookie to the slave's net. Screaming, "We have you now, Sir!" Apaius scooped up the fish. It was weighed on Carmans' scale which, if anything, gave short weight, and a figure of 9 pounds, 4 ounces was recorded. (The exact weight that the trout is held to have been is somewhere in the 10-pound range.) The brookie was packed on ice, and the next morning, Webster caught the first stagecoach for Delmonico's, the great restaurant of old New York. There, chef Charlie Ranhofer served it poached in white wine and showered with slivered almonds. Webster was awarded the world record and held the title for nearly a century.

The cutthroat

You may think of the cutthroat — which is really a cousin to the rainbow (see Figure 9-4) — as the Rocky Mountain version of the brook trout. In many undisturbed waters, just like the brookie, the cutthroat is the native fish. After ranching, logging, and the introduction of other game fish takes place, the cutthroat often retreats to unpressured headwaters. As with the brook trout, the cutthroat has the reputation of having less intelligence than the brown trout. Apart from the fact that I don't know how one can administer an intelligence test to a brown or a cutthroat, I don't agree. Cutthroats (sometimes called *cuts*) can be extremely selective. They do not have the bulldog, head-shaking determination of the brown nor the leaping instinct of the rainbow, but in all of Troutdom you won't see anything like the surface take of the cutthroat: He comes up, sips the fly, and shows you his whole body before descending with the fly. All you need to do is come tight to the fish and you're on.

Figure 9-4:
The cutthroat trout is most easily identified by the red and orange slashes around the lower jaw and gills.

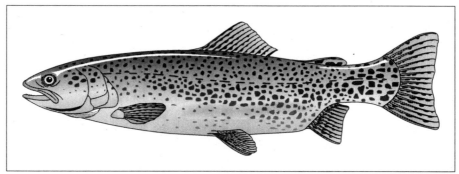

The cutthroat is the native trout in the drainage of the Yellowstone River, where it is protected by a complete no-kill policy in all of the flowing water in Yellowstone Park. To fish them at the outlet of Yellowstone Lake is one of the great angling experiences in North America.

Fly line world record

A 14-pound, 1-ounce cutthroat was taken from Pyramid Lake, in Reno, Nevada, by Donald R. Williamson on April 4, 1982.

Lakers: Big Macks

Widely known as Mackinaws or gray trout, the lake trout (or *laker*) is the largest char. The Mackinaw requires colder water than any other freshwater game fish, optimally about 50°F; it will die at 65°F.

Right after ice-out in the spring and right before spawning in the autumn, lakers may be taken in shallow water. And this is the time to fish for them with a fly rod. Bait fish imitations score best.

Unlike all the other trout (true trout as well as rainbows and chars), the laker spawns in lakes, not streams. This fact is much on the minds of biologists in Yellowstone Park, where some lamebrains dumped a few lakers in Yellowstone Lake a few years ago. Prior to that, this lake held the last pure strain of cutthroats in the Rockies. The lakers began to prey on cutthroat fry. This situation was bad enough, but because lakers don't run up the rivers as the cuts do, and because so many cuts had been eaten by the lakers, about 20 percent of the upriver food supply of the grizzly bear, osprey, and eagle had been removed from the ecosystem. This is a prime case of messing with Mother Nature. I don't blame the fish, however. In fact, I like lakers. I do blame idiotic people, though, who think that dumping any fish in any old place will improve the fishing.

As shown in Figure 9-5, the laker, like the brookie, is heavily spotted. Its body is usually a medium to dark green with white spots. It has a forked tail, in contrast to the square tail of the brookie.

Fly line world record

James Boyer pulled a 27-pound, 8-ounce laker out of Nueltin Lake, Alonsa, Canada, on June 24, 1994.

Figure 9-5:
The lake trout resembles a giant brookie with a forked tail.

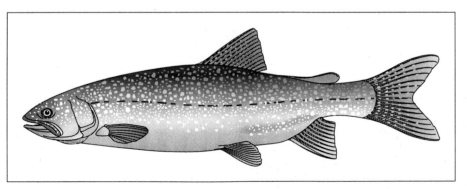

Pacific Salmon

Pacific salmon come upstream to spawn just as Atlantic salmon do. The Pacific salmon's flesh is pink, just like the flesh of an Atlantic. They even taste the same. But the six species of Pacific salmon are completely different animals than the Atlantic salmon, which is the only *true* salmon. The Pacifics are the much larger, mostly ocean-going cousins of the rainbow trout.

Some years ago, Pacific salmon were introduced into the Great Lakes to help control the spread of the alewife herring. The alewives were so plentiful and the salmon fed so well on them that the Great Lakes now hold the greatest fishery for both the coho and chinook salmon sport-fisher. This situation, however, though good food angling, shouldn't allow you to forget the alarming drops of these great game fish in their home range. After all, the Pacific Ocean holds a great deal more water for these fish. In the Pacific, they range from Taiwan north across the Bering Strait and down to San Diego. Overfishing in their natural range has dangerously depleted them, as has the construction of dams.

Shallow-water and stream fly casters have the most luck as the fish gather at stream mouths just before spawning. Fishing when the salmon are still *bright,* or fresh from the ocean or lake, can be great sport with these brawny, athletic fish. After they have been in the stream for any length of time, I find that landing even a 30-pound fish is about as much fun as lugging a duffel bag full of books up a steep staircase. Little egg sac imitations that look like rainbow trout spawn will often take salmon. In lakes you usually must fish deep with big streamers. Trolling is often the only way to hook them and this is not a method that I consider to be fly fishing, although you will catch them on a fly rod this way. Once hooked, the fish gives a great fight on fly tackle.

Pacific salmon like cold water, about 55°F. They move with currents and tides to maintain themselves in that *thermocline,* a big word meaning a region in a body of water with a specific temperature. A cold front may bring salmon close to shore. A wind may drive the cold water and the fish further offshore. When looking for them in a lake, you absolutely must use a thermometer to check water temperature.

As with many saltwater fish, or as with fish that spend a good amount of time in saltwater (the term for fish that live in both fresh and saltwater is *anadromous*), the chinook and coho like flashy, bright-colored flies.

Figure 9-6 shows the coho and chinook salmon. The usually smaller coho has black spots only on the upper part of its tail, although the chinook's tail is spotted on both top and bottom. The chinook's dorsal fin is spotted; the coho's isn't. The gum in the lower jaw of the coho is grayish, but the same gum in the chinook is black.

Figure 9-6:
For many freshwater fly rodders the coho (top) and chinook (bottom) salmon are by far their largest quarry.

Fly line world records

A 21-pound coho was caught by Gary R. Dubiel on the Karluk River, in Kodiak, Alaska, on September 6, 1988.

On November 13, 1987, Bill Rhoads took a 63-pound chinook on the Trask River, in Oregon.

Look before you eat

Few fish are as delicious as the Pacific salmon (which is one of the reasons they are so heavily harvested by commercial fishermen). In many areas, however, particularly in the Great Lakes, fish can pick up some toxic pollutants. The presence of toxic pollutants doesn't make Pacific salmon less fun to catch, but eating fish from these waters is not a good idea. Always check the local health advisories before you take a fish for a meal.

Atlantic Salmon

The Atlantic salmon is regarded by many as the aristocrat of fishes. Perhaps it has this reputation because you have to be an aristocrat to be able to afford a few days on one of the choice salmon rivers. Not surprisingly, you have to rent a guide to fish such a river. Don't hold any of this against the salmon — he had very little to do with all the tradition surrounding him.

The salmon is a cousin to the brown trout but spends most of its time at sea (although a salmon's infancy is passed in a river and it is to that river that it returns to spawn). The Atlantic salmon (shown in Figure 9-7) does not die after spawning once, so you may return a salmon to the stream after catching it and be confident that it may well return to create even more fish the following year. Returning salmon to the stream is a good practice because the Atlantic salmon is a very pressured animal. Perhaps if we conserve our salmon harvest now, they will return to the numbers they had back in George Washington's day, when they were so plentiful that farmers used them for fertilizer!

Many of the traditional salmon flies are combinations of blue, yellow, red, orange, and black feathers on big black hooks with turned-up eyes. Why do they work when they really don't imitate anything in the river? I have no answer. But because anglers have been catching them this way for years, there must be something that triggers a response from the salmon. Don't try to reinvent the wheel here. Do hire a guide. It is pricey, but you are not going to have too many opportunities in your life to fish for these fish, so spend a couple of bucks to give yourself a fighting chance.

Figure 9-7:
The Atlantic salmon. Despite the efforts of fisheries biologists, transplanting this magnificent game fish to the Pacific has proved impossible.

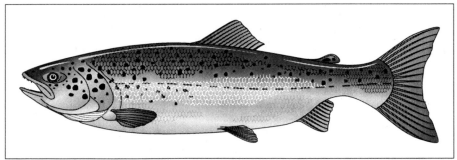

If plenty of action is what you crave, salmon fishing is not for you: Just one fish a day is a very good average on most streams. And by the way, the landlocked salmon is a just a freshwater Atlantic salmon that has been cut off from the sea for some thousands of years. Other than that, it is genetically identical to the oceangoing fish.

Fly line world record

Mort Seaman caught a 51-pound Atlantic salmon on the Alta River, Norway, on July 7, 1994.

The Basses

The trout may win the number-of-pages-written-about-them contest, but if the number of anglers counts for anything, then the basses (largemouth and smallmouth) are certainly the most popular game fish in America. The largemouth and smallmouth are not, however, true basses. That distinction belongs to the bass of Europe who had first dibs on the name. The American basses belong to the sunfish family. When you stop to consider this situation, though, the largemouth and smallmouth don't know or care what they are called; and the American basses, also known as the black basses, are pretty amazing game fish.

Largemouth

To my mind, no experience in angling is as thrilling as the moment that a largemouth bass takes a popper cast ever so smartly to the cover along the water's edge. There you are, on a still summer day. Things couldn't be quieter. A few dragonflies buzz around a lily pad. A frog or two basks in the heat. You cast to the lily pad. You let it rest for a few seconds, and then you twitch it. You twitch it again. A rough ripple that rocks the popper is followed by an onrush of water, out of which emerges a ferocious largemouth that engulfs the plug. The instant it feels the hook, it begins to shake its head and jump or dive or both. An experience like this never ceases to thrill me, and it never ceases to take me by surprise. I am almost 100 percent a popping-bug fisherman when it comes to largemouth.

The largemouth bass, originally a native of the Mississippi drainage and the southeastern U.S., was early recognized as a prime game fish and has since been transplanted all over. Lakes, rivers, streams, and brackish coastal water all have populations of largemouth. They are most catchable when the water is in the 65°F to 75°F range.

As shown in Figure 9-8, the jaw of the largemouth extends farther back than the eye. (This jaw length is not true of the smallmouth.) The largemouth is usually dark gray to dark green in color with a dark band along the lateral line. The dorsal fin is divided into two distinct portions: hard spines in front and softer ones in the rear. The largemouth is also known as the bucket-mouth because of its large mouth, which appears even larger when it attacks your popper. Imagine taking a bath one Saturday night when suddenly the tub turns into a fish mouth and swallows you whole. That's the image I have of a largemouth devouring a popping bug.

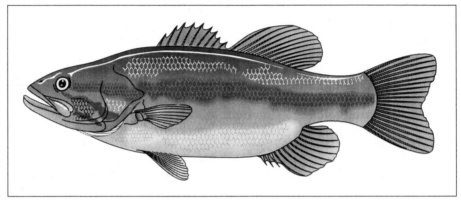

Figure 9-8:
The largemouth bass, the most sought-after game fish in America.

Fly line world record

Ned Sparks Sewell caught a 13-pound, 9-ounce largemouth on Lake Morena, in San Diego, California, on April 4, 1984.

Smallmouth: The gamest fish

In what is perhaps the most-quoted phrase in angling literature, retired Civil War surgeon James Alexander Henshall said of the smallmouth bass: "Inch for inch and pound for pound, the gamest fish that swims." This opinion set off a century of debate. Some said trout were the gamest fish; others awarded that honor to salmon. Bonefish, permit, snook, and tarpon all had their partisans, but no one ever said that Henshall was out to lunch for the high opinion in which he held the smallmouth, known affectionately as the *bronzeback*.

How to pick up a bass

Trying to pick up a bass by grabbing its body is about as easy as trying to diaper an angry baby. The little suckers can *really* squirm. Even worse than babies, bass have spiny fins that can deliver nasty pricks. With a bass (and with many other soft-mouthed fish), however, you can nearly immobilize it if you grab it by the lower lip, holding it between thumb and forefinger as shown here. While picking up your catch by grasping the lower lip between thumb and forefinger works very well with bass, it has been reported that this technique doesn't work as well in singles bars.

Like its largemouth cousin, the smallmouth is a native of the Mississippi drainage, which makes him a true heartland (or maybe "heartwater") fish. Where the largemouth likes slow or still water with lots of food-holding weeds, the smallmouth prefers clean, rocky bottoms and swifter water, ideally in the 65°F to 68°F range. Lake-dwelling smallmouth often school up, which means that if you catch one, you can catch a bunch. In rivers and streams, they are more solitary.

Like the largemouth, the smallmouth is a pretty opportunistic feeder, but given a choice, he likes crayfish and hellgrammites. That may explain why I do so well with black Woolly Buggers and small Clouser's Minnows.

As shown in Figure 9-9, the smallmouth has a series of dark vertical bands along its flanks. The dorsal fin is one continuous fin (as opposed to the separate spiny and soft parts on a largemouth's fin). Note that the smallmouth's upper jaw does *not* extend backward beyond the eye.

Figure 9-9:
The mouth of the smallmouth isn't *that* small, but its upper jaw is shorter than the largemouth's, which is why the smallmouth is called the smallmouth.

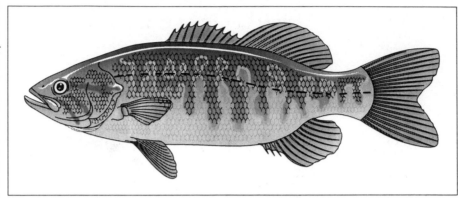

Fly line world record

A 6-pound, 4-ounce smallmouth was caught by Pamela Kinsey McClelland on Pine Lake, in Michigan, on August 12, 1995.

What's in a name?

Question: How many people have both an element and a fish named after them?

Answer: One. His name was Deodat Dolomieu, and it happened in 1802. Dolomieu was a famous man-about-town in Paris as well as a mineralogist. The mineral dolomite was named after him. Dolomite is a favorite rock of anglers because its high limestone content makes for streams rich in food (which means big fish).

A naturalist named Lacepede also lived in Paris at that time. Someone had sent him a strange-looking 12-inch fish for classification. It was a smallmouth from Louisiana, which was still ruled by France in those days. This smallmouth had a gap in its dorsal fin, probably from a run-in with a pike or a beaver. Lacepede had never seen a smallmouth before, leading to his assumption that all smallmouth had teeny fins. So he called the new fish *Micropterus* which means "small fin" in Latin. Then he needed a second half for its Latin name, but nothing came to mind. Because Dolomieu was coming to dinner that night, Lacepede, at a loss for anything better to call the newly classified fish, decided to name it after his friend, which is why the smallmouth bass is known to scientists as *Micropterus dolomieu*.

Pike ("And the Winner of the Mean and Ugly Contest Is . . .")

For flat-out ugly looks, nothing in freshwater rivals the looks of a pike, pickerel, or muskellunge. A long, greeny fish with big eyes, a pointed snout, and rows of stiletto teeth, the average pike looks like what you might get if you crossed a snake, a crocodile, and a shark.

Northern pike

The most popular member of the pike family is usually known, simply, as *the* pike. It is also called a *northern* and is a native of the Great Lakes and its cooler tributaries.

Pike are clearly designed to attack and devour. One observer called them "machines for the assimilation of other organisms." All forms of bait fish and game fish, birds, muskrats, frogs, snakes, snails, leeches, and anything else it finds within striking distance can (at one time or another) find its way into a pike's belly.

You are liable to find pike in weedy shallows where they wait for prey to ambush. As stealthy as a lion in wait or as swift as a springing panther, pike stalk and pursue their prey, most actively at water temperatures in the mid-60s in the morning and during the day. They are not very active after dark.

When the pike strikes, strike him back quickly, and get ready for a hellacious struggle that may include some wild writhing on the surface. Most often you take them with the same surface poppers and big streamers that work for bass.

As shown in Figure 9-10, the pike is a sleek and ferocious-looking predator.

Fly line world record
Barry D. Reynolds caught a 33-pound, 8-ounce pike on Nejanilini Lake, in Manitoba, Canada, on July 14, 1994.

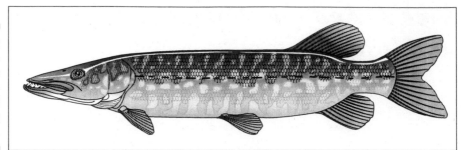

Figure 9-10:
The northern pike, a well-designed killing machine.

Pike popping in the key of G

I was in Canada fishing for giant brookies and I am going to let you in on a secret. Even though writers can go on for days about what a purely great fish the brookie is, after you have caught 100 of the big boys, you realize that you should be hooking every one you cast to: They are just not that hard to hook.

It was while we were casting around near the outflow of one lake into another that I cast a popping bug to a lily pad, just like you would do for a largemouth bass. I had no good reason for this departure from North Country fishing orthodoxy other than whenever I see a lily pad, I feel an uncontrollable urge to cast a popping bug. I did and pulled it off the lily pad, continuing to pop my bug for a good 15 feet.

Moving at warp speed, a 6-pound pike engulfed my fly and gave me a great fight until he bit through my leader. The good part of the experience was that I caught a pike on a popper. The bad news was that I only had a few poppers with me. (If I had been a well-organized angler I would have had none;

they would have been filed in my bass box.) Worse, pike fishing calls for wire leaders, and I had none. Who fishes for trout with a wire leader?

I was 80 miles from the nearest road in the midst of a trackless northern forest. It wasn't as if a tackle shop was right around the corner. Then I remembered that our Eskimo guide played guitar and that the high E string on a guitar was probably thin enough to work as a leader.

Ray, our guide, was no fool. He knew that he had me over a barrel and extorted a carton of cigarettes (this was back in my smoking days) and my only bottle of whiskey. I reasoned that I could always drink and smoke if those were my chosen vices, but how often would I get the chance to catch a really big pike on a fly?

We made the cigs-booze-guitar-string trade and the next day I hooked, fought, and landed an 18-pound pike on a 6-weight fly rod.

Talk about sharp!

When landing a pike, be extremely careful of its sharp teeth. They are about the nastiest thing in freshwater fishing. (This advice goes for the pike's cousins, the muskie and pickerel, too.) As shown in Figure 9-11, the safest way to land a pike is to grab the fish by the eye sockets (the socket, *not* the eye!).

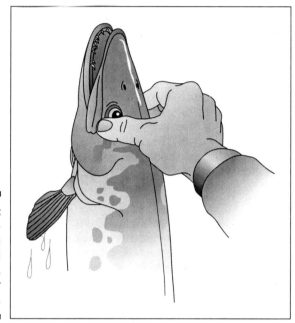

Figure 9-11: The finger-preserving way to land a pike, muskie, or pickerel.

Muskellunge

The muskie is a northern fish, found in the upper parts of the Mississippi drainage, the St. Lawrence River, all over New England, and through most of Canada. If you are the kind of person who likes the odds in the state lottery, you should enjoy fishing for muskellunge. Your chances of winning the lottery and catching a muskie are roughly equal. (Actually, that is a bit of an exaggeration, but not by much.) The old-timers say that when fishing for muskellunge, it takes 10,000 casts for every strike. And then when you do get a muskie on, its teeth are so sharp, it can be so big, and its fight can be so dogged, that it takes brawn and skill to land one. If you manage to land a muskie, you have a real trophy.

Like the pike, the muskie likes to hang out in likely ambush spots: weed beds, deep holes, drop-offs, and over sunken islands. Although it spends the majority of its time in the depths, it appears to do most of its feeding in shallower water (at less than 15 feet). Optimum water temperature for muskies is in the low 60s.

The muskie is an opportunistic predator and is completely unpredictable, so my advice to the beginning muskie fisherman is to get a guide or a local expert to take you until you get the hang of it. Muskies take big bass flies that move actively and will chase them for a long distance. So when casting for muskie, you usually make longer casts to places where you think they are — strip steadily and be ready for a mad, slashing strike late in the retrieve. The fight that a muskie provides is tenacious and forceful. I recommend that you have an 8 to 9-weight rod.

Figure 9-12 shows that a muskellunge's appearance is quite similar to that of a pike. You can't always be sure which is which unless you get pretty close to the fish, in which case you can see that the muskie, in contrast to the pike, has no scales on its lower cheek and gill covers. Its markings tend to look like dark bars or spots, but northern pike usually have lighter-colored spots that are shaped like beans.

Fly line world record

An 18-pound, 9-ounce muskie was caught by Russell W. Fischer on Pike Lake, in Lac de Flambeau, Wisconsin, on June 28, 1989. That overall record was nearly edged on June 18, 1995, by Rick Kustich's 18-pound, 8-ounce muskie caught on the Niagara River in New York. (Don't you just hate it when you catch a fish that hasn't been snacking enough?)

Figure 9-12:
Muskies are typically bigger than northern pike, but they both have the same murderous mouth.

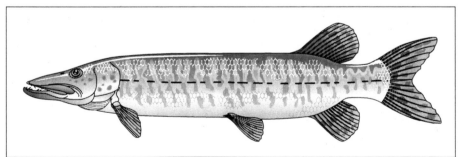

Pickerel

Though smaller than the pike and the muskie, the pickerel is (in every other way) as pugnacious and predatory as its larger cousins. If you're ever fishing a shallow bass pond on a day when nothing is happening, look for the arrowhead-shaped wake of a feeding pickerel. Whether the pickerel is cruising or sprinting from its lair in a weed bed, I think you will agree that it is exciting to watch a well-equipped predator going about its deadly work.

The pickerel is to angling what the toy is to a box of Cracker Jack. The toy isn't the reason you buy the treat, but it's a nice surprise when you get a good one. Many a bassless day has been saved by the voracious appetite of the pickerel. Just about any fly that will take a bass will also take a pickerel.

Figure 9-13 illustrates a chain pickerel, whose dark green side markings appear to line up like the links in a chain.

Figure 9-13:
The chain pickerel looks like a miniature pike, but these two predators do not commonly coexist in the same waters.

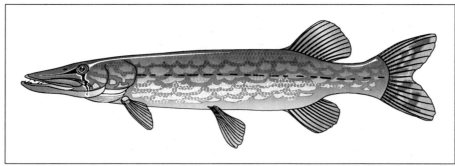

Fly line world record

A 4-pound, 5-ounce pickerel was caught by Donna Wilmert in the Mingo National Wildlife Refuge, Missouri, on October 21, 1995.

Panfish

I know what you're thinking: Fly fishing for trout is the old classic part; fly fishing for tarpon, salmon, and bonefish is the new classic part; and fly fishing for bass is the unclassic-but-fun part. Panfish, if you think about them at all, you probably toss off as something for kids with cane poles and worms. Wrong. Panfish are extremely sporty on a light fly rod.

Panfish is really a catchall category that includes a whole range of fish, including most of the sunfish (except the largemouth and smallmouth bass) as well as crappie. The reason panfish are called panfish is they fit in a frying pan. This fact tells you something — namely, that panfish are good to eat. They are also found just about anywhere, in most kinds of water all across the country. Ounce for ounce they fight as hard as anything out there, so if you match them with the right size line and rod, you'll do fine.

Extra small poppers are made to cast to sunfish. They also take small nymphs and grub-like imitations. You can also tie a dropper nymph to the bend of the hook of a popper or streamer to attract panfish as you cast for bass.

Figure 9-14 shows some of the more popular panfish, which are described here:

- **Bluegill:** Sometimes known as the *bream*. It has a blue edge to the breast area and a dark ear flap and is probably the most-caught sport fish in America. Fly line record: 2 pounds, 12 ounces, caught by Curtis Ray Holmes, Jr., in Guilford County, North Carolina, on November 4, 1984.

- **White crappie:** A very widespread fish all over North America. It thrives in silty and slow-moving water and has flourished in the impoundments that have been created in the south since World War II. The white crappie is the only sunfish with six spines on the dorsal fin. Fly line record: 2 pounds, 8 ounces, caught in Amelia County, Virginia, by Adam S. Plotkin, on September 6, 1986.

- **Black crappie:** Prefers somewhat clearer water than the white crappie. Because of its mottled skin (the white crappie is more barred), a regional name in some parts of the south is also *calico bass*. Fly line record: 2 pounds, 13 ounces, caught by T. Carter Hubard in Custis Millpond, Virginia, on April 4, 1994.

- **Perch:** Both white and yellow perch are completely delicious fish. French chefs steam them in parchment and call the process *en papillote*. In Door County, Wisconsin, the old-time commercial fishermen would get the same effect by wrapping their perch in wet newspapers along with some onions, salt, and pepper and throwing them on the housing of their overworked diesel engines. Because these fishermen cooked on the domes of their engines, they were called "domers." Fly line records: a 2-pound white perch was caught by David Goodman, in Nantucket, Massachusetts, on July 21, 1991; a 1-pound, 6-ounce yellow perch was caught on February 5, 1995, on the North River, in Currituck, North Carolina, by Thomas F. Elkins.

- **Rock bass:** Sometimes called *redeye,* this small, bronze-colored bass looks like a chubby, stunted smallmouth and is often found in largemouth bass waters. It'll take good-sized streamers and Woolly Buggers. No fly line records exist for the rock bass (according to the IGFA's *1997 World Record Game Fishes*).

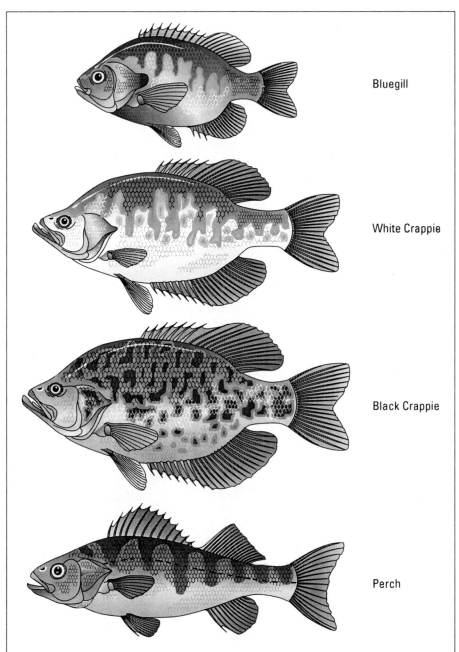

Bluegill

White Crappie

Black Crappie

Perch

Figure 9-14:
Four
popular
panfish.

Catfish

Unless you are the mother of one, catfish are generally conceded to be pretty ugly. But because most catfish feed at night, I suppose their looks aren't much of a drawback. Counting bullheads, more than 20 species of catfish are found in the U.S., and they are very popular because of their catchability, their accessibility, and especially because of their wonderful taste (which just goes to show that bottom feeders aren't all that awful). People usually eat crispy fried catfish the way they eat potato chips — until the last one is gone.

Because catfish are nocturnal feeders, they rely on touch, taste, and smell to identify food. They are active in warm water and may be taken with water temperatures in the high 80s. Cast a weighted streamer, maybe with some fish scent on it, and retrieve slowly. This is not a tweedy fly rod method, but catfish are not a tweedy fly rod kind of fish. Marabou Leeches and weighted Woolly Buggers also score.

Figure 9-15 clearly shows the difference between proper catfish and bull-heads. Notice that both have long whiskers or *barbels*.

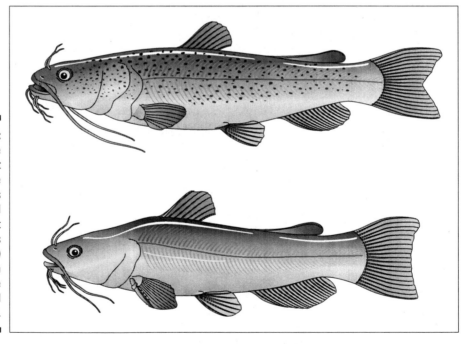

Figure 9-15:
The channel cat (top), a true catfish, has a forked tail, but bullheads (bottom) have a more rounded tail.

Prickly whiskers

When you handle a catfish, it "locks" its pectoral and dorsal fins together. The projecting spines are very sharp and carry a painful toxin. A good deal of fishing lore, some of it true, is about people suffering terrible stabs from the spines of big catfish. Though not fatal, a spine wound can be nasty and painful. If you are pricked while handling a catfish, treat the wound immediately with a disinfectant, as swift action often nullifies the poison. Apply a bandage. Your revenge on the catfish is that you get to eat him.

Fly line world records

A 30-pound, 2-ounce channel catfish was caught on the Red River, in Manitoba, Canada, on May 13, 1992, by Kastaway Kulis.

Richard E. Fahler, Jr. caught a 2-pound, 8-ounce brown bullhead in Kebert Pond, Pennsylvania, on May 12, 1992.

Fly line records for both the black and yellow bullhead are open.

Shad

The shad, which is a large member of the herring family, lives most of its life at sea and returns to the river of its birth to spawn and die. This anadromous trait is not its only similarity to the more-aristocratic salmon. The shad does not feed after it enters a river; but again like the salmon, it can be induced to strike a brightly colored fly. Nobody knows why they do this. I have read that they do it out of anger, or perhaps because they are reminded of food that they ate in the stream as a baby. Some brightly colored shad flies are expressly designed to provoke a shad, and I have also scored on a Clouser's.

I have fished for the smaller hickory shad in Florida in March. When hickory shad are in the rivers, thousands of white pelicans come in from the Atlantic to feast on their carcasses. In the northern part of the United States, the main river systems for shad anglers are the Delaware, Susquehanna, and Connecticut, where you can take them from a boat or while wading.

When playing a shad, remember that its mouth is very soft. Give it room to run. If you try to *horse* the fish (muscle it in), you will surely pull your lure or fly out. If you let it run, it will reward you with a number of beautiful leaps, just like a salmon.

Both the American and the hickory shad have the large scales and deeply forked tails characteristic of the herring family, as shown in Figure 9-16. The hickory shad is generally smaller, and its lower lip extends out past the upper lip.

Fly line world record

A 7-pound, 4-ounce American shad was caught by Rod Neubert on the Feather River, in California, on June 30, 1983.

Figure 9-16: American shad (top) and hickory shad (bottom).

Chapter 10
The Beautiful Black Bass

*I*f you took a survey of anglers — including bait fishermen, spinners, canepolers — there is no question in my mind that the result, in two simple words, would be "Bass rules!" In the old days, in my part of the country, they were called black bass, and I have always been partial to that name. In the southern U.S., I have heard them called green trout. Whatever. Flat out, bass are the all-American fish. But fly fishing for bass has always been an afterthought, something you did if there were no trout around. Why? Among the European dukes and counts who traditionally made up the lion's share of 19th Century fly rodders, there were no bass. Largemouth and smallmouth, two incredible game fish, were not on the European radar screen. In traditional fly fishing, trout and salmon were *the* quarry. Everything else was thought of as a *coarse* fish. Some fly rodders and trout enthusiasts in this country still view the bass with disdain. They don't know what they are missing. There are few thrills in fishing that equal a largemouth inhaling a popping bug or the tail-walking acrobatics of a smallmouth.

Smallmouth and Largemouth

When you get right down to it, the smallmouth bass and largemouth bass are very similar, but very different animals — if that makes any sense. Kind of like the kids in a family. At first they look similar, but some key differences exist.

I talk about some of the things that distinguish these fish in Chapter 9, but there is one more factor that has a big effect on the way you fish. Smallmouth are more like trout in the kind of water they like: fast-moving streams and rivers with good riffles, lots of rocks, and gravelly bottoms. They need a good amount of oxygen and don't like warm water. Largemouth, on the other hand, like still water, and they do fine with very sluggish current. Warm water makes them happy, and a little bit of off-color water doesn't really bother them, nor does salt, as largemouth are often caught in brackish water.

To have success with a fly rod, you need to study the fish to find out where smallmouth and largemouth like to hang out in their respective waters and how to fish for them. For smallmouth, streamers and nymphs fished in riffles, runs, and seams between fast and slow water often do the trick. Minnow and crawfish imitations can be fished along the bottom, bouncing them off rocks. Sometimes you can just let a streamer, such as a Woolly Bugger, hang in the current off a rocky bottom and a smallmouth will pound it. In the right conditions, smallmouth will devour popping bugs, and when they do, it is pure heaven.

For whatever reason, largemouth often come to the surface more readily. Poppers are always my first choice. I also go through my collection of surface flies that imitate frogs, mice, or wounded fish. These almost always take bass. Next, I go subsurface with a big black Woolly Bugger or Marabou Leech.

As with every fish, at issue is not what the angler likes to use. The heart of the matter is what a bass wants to eat. To learn that, study the water.

Mainstays of the Bass Diet

What's for lunch? Everything. There is no Weight Watchers program in Bassdom. Bass can eat good-sized bait and, like all predators, are opportunistic. As long as you cast an imitation of something they like in the right place, and present it properly, you have a fighting chance.

More often than not, the bass are eating one or more of the following critters.

Mayflies: Not just for trout anymore

Yes, we know mayflies well as trout bait, but smallmouth in big streams and rivers also like these tasty bugs. Hatches of larger flies, or heavy hatches of smaller species, attract the most fish.

The rules are the same as for trout: Try to match the hatch. When big flies are splashing on the surface, use a big imitation. On smooth, still pools where bass are sipping down little mayflies, tie on and delicately cast a similarly small imitation, just as you would fish for a trout. And, as with trout, it's always a good idea to catch a natural fly and try to match it, although hatch matching isn't as critical with bass as it is with trout. You may also fish nymphs and wets.

For a full selection of mayflies, see Chapter 6.

Wrong fly, right place

One year I visited Michigan's Upper Peninsula and the waters that Hemingway made famous in trout writing's greatest short story, "Big Two-Hearted River." It was after Hex time and a 90°F heat wave hung over the Great Lakes, generally discouraging the trout. One night, my host, Ted Bogden, suggested that we try our luck on nearby Dead Lake. We fished the shore with Muddlers (see Chapter 6) and tried some imitations of the small flies that occasionally provoked a rise.

We weren't doing much good. About 9:30 p.m., there was still a fair amount of daylight and I noticed activity at mid-lake. We approached very quietly and watched nice fish feeding on big fat Hexes. None of us had any imitations, but I did have a big old Green Drake that I had used on the Hat Creek in Northern California. The color was wrong but the size was right

and I figured, from the trout's point of view, it would just be a dark silhouette against the lighter sky. I tied it on and cast it out. It was so big that it caused ripples on the calm surface of the lake when it landed, just the kind of thing a newly hatched Hex might do.

Then it happened. A good fish took, not a trout, but a gorgeous 19-inch smallmouth. He broke water and shook off huge droplets as he twisted in the air. There were three others just like him who surrendered to my fly before it fell apart. It was the wrong fly and the wrong fish, but it was great fishing. This story also says something in favor of keeping a few weird, out-of-place flies in your fly box because you can study flies as much as you want and become a real expert, but you still can't be sure what Nature is going to throw at you next.

Damselflies: Big and crunchy

Both largemouth and smallmouth will eat damselflies, but smallmouth seem to take them more readily. These insects are active in the spring and summer months. Adult damselflies, which look like a svelte version of the dragonfly (see Figure 10-1), come in a variety of colors — red-brown, blue, green, black — so find a pattern that matches a natural, usually in a size #6 or #8. Cast along grassy areas, under tree boughs, around downed, protruding trees and brush along the bank. Twitch the fly on the surface.

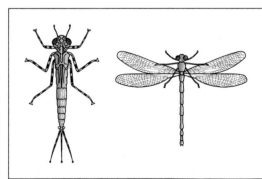

Figure 10-1: The damselfly and nymph.

Dragonflies: Bassing's B-1 Bomber

Largemouth and smallmouth bass take their share of dragonflies, both nymphs and adults (see Figure 10-2). If you see them on the wing, chances are that you will find some on the water as well. These are larger flies so carry them in a variety of colors, sizes #4 to #8. If you don't have the right color, don't worry — the silhouette is usually the trigger. You can cast an imitation just about anywhere you see an adult flying in the spring and summer. If you score with the dry, you can also try nymph patterns over silty bottoms and near grass beds and swim them with a quick, darting action.

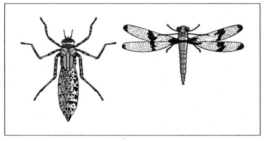

Figure 10-2:
The dragonfly and nymph.

Crickets and grasshoppers: Always good, by Jiminy

These bugs will always attract bass. A grasshopper is shown in Figure 10-3. As the summer rolls on, the bugs get bigger and attract bigger bass. When lots of hoppers are on the water, bass will cruise weedy, grassy banks waiting for some unlucky hopper to fall in or be blown onto the water. Use an imitation pattern in size #6 to #10, and fish them tight against the bank. Often a messed-up cast that overshoots the bank will bring up a bass as you pull your hopper off the bank. There is something about an imitation that falls naturally just like a live bug that seems to turn bass on.

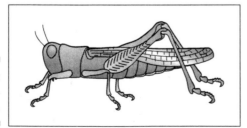

Figure 10-3:
A grass-hopper.

Hellgrammites: Darn good

Hellgrammites are the larvae of the Dobson fly — they look like a WWF version of the stonefly nymph (see Figure 10-4). They thrive in large numbers in smallmouth waters and grow to a length of 3 inches, which explains why smallmouth are so partial to them. By the way, I owe all you hellgrammites (and hellgrammite anglers) an apology. In *Fishing For Dummies,* I kind of dumped on hellgrammites as bait, never having had much luck with them. This caused a number of computer-savvy angling friends to flame me something fierce. They pointed out that the leech and Woolly Bugger patterns that I had been fishing for years are often taken for hellgrammites by bass. Which goes to show you that you can even learn something when you are wrong, provided you go public with it and can take the heat.

Hellgrammites are most active in spring, summer, and early fall, and are a good go-to bait when nothing else seems to work for the smallmouth. The best spots to fish them are in riffles with pea-sized to golf-ball-sized rocks. Smallmouth will often hang at the head of the pool and dart into the riffle when hellgies are active. If you don't have a hellgrammite pattern, try a big nymph pattern or small Woolly Bugger.

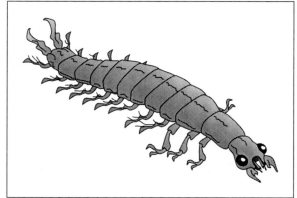

Figure 10-4:
The hellgrammite.

Leeches: Finally something good about these slimers!

I know the mere mention of leeches brings up visions of that scene in *The African Queen* when poor Humphrey Bogart quivers and groans because leeches have latched onto him. But these awful little wormy creatures, one of which is shown in Figure 10-5, are a great all-around bass and trout bait (and they are also hellaciously good for walleye). They are active spring through fall, after dark or under cloudy conditions. Most leeches are black, brown, or green, and swim with a snaky motion. Use a Woolly Bugger or a Marabou leech in sizes #4 to #8.

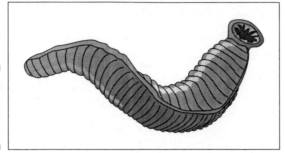

Figure 10-5:
The
common
leech.

Crayfish: If you don't eat them yourself

Crayfish, those little freshwater lobsters (see Figure 10-6), are a staple of smallmouth. Crayfish creep along the bottom but can tuck their tail and shoot backwards in a burst of speed when threatened. Sink a crayfish imitation — a small Clouser's in brown and red can be effective — sizes #4 to #6, on the bottom, letting it bounce, and then lift it with a long, even strip and a slight raising of the rod tip. The first strip should be crisp because, when a crayfish starts, it accelerates quickly and this action is what catches the attention of bass.

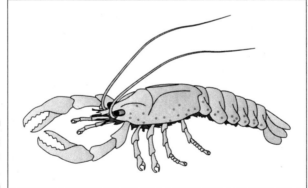

Figure 10-6:
The
crayfish.

Frogs: The bass cookie

Frogs are great bait. To a fish, they're as irresistible as a chocolate chip cookie is to a kid. Frogs are mostly active at dusk and at night. The bullfrog, the green frog, and the leopard frog are the most common species and are imitated by pretty much the same artificial patterns, differing only in size. Bass take them usually when they first enter the water and bob on the surface, their long legs dangling below. This is, no doubt, a big bummer for the frog. (Getting eaten is an all-around bummer for just about every species, really.)

I don't tie frog flies. They take a lot of material, and mine always look like big hair balls instead of frogs. Maybe you can do better. Whether you buy, borrow, or tie this fly, try an imitation of spun deer hair or cork that has feather or latex legs — ones that hang down below the surface and have some action when you twitch the fly. Fish tight against lily pads, logs, and fallen trees, giving the fly frog-like twitches. The strike of a bass will be explosive. Be ready, which means mind your slack because it will defeat you every time.

Sculpins: Little big head

Sculpin are flat-headed brown bait fish — imagine a toad with fins and a tail. They need well-oxygenated water just like smallmouth. Sculpin hang on the bottom and hold under rocks. If you don't have a specific fly imitation, a Muddler Minnow works well, sizes #4 to #8.

Shiners: A classic bait

Shiners are often found in large numbers in bass waters. They are about 3 or 4 inches long usually, have a dark back and silver sides, and look like the classic minnow-type fish (see Figure 10-7). They school in the shallows and bass come in out of the deeper water to pick them off. Sometimes you will see shiners leap out of the water to avoid a pursuing bass. The Clouser's, in sizes #4 to #8, works well, as will any streamer that is mostly white. Also try a white Marabou Muddler. When you see shiners splash on the surface, cast a streamer a few yards in front of the leaping fish and begin your retrieve immediately while your fly is on the same level as the fleeing bait fish. During spawning time, bass will positively assault shiners (probably because shiners prey heavily on bass fry — revenge). This can be a great time for catching bass, but *please* release everything you catch during this time, which is so crucial for the future of the bass.

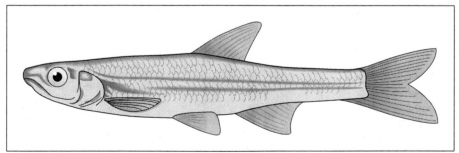

Figure 10-7:
The shiner.

Mice: A bonus

Bass will eat mice that plop in the water (bass can eat ducklings, too). You hardly ever actually see it happen, so this one is the last of my bass bait — an extra. Have a mouse fly in your box just for that rare occasion when you suspect a mega-bass is in the neighborhood. Mice, not being aquatic animals, usually enter the water when they fall off a log, a rock, or a stream bank. Their panicky dog paddle is a bass attention-getter. Fish a size #4 or #6 deer hair mouse pattern along the bank (see the pattern explained later in this chapter). Retrieve kind of jerkily. The strike should be pretty strong.

Great Bass Destinations

Bass are everywhere, so you may very well have good bass fishing right down the road from your house. For those of you who have the urge to fish farther afield, I have put together a list of places around North America that have given me some of my best bass memories (see Figure 10-8). They are also a complete cross section of bass habitat. Many of the most famous bass fishing spots don't appear on this list simply because their typically deep water isn't very productive, or fun, for the fly caster (and to my way of thinking, fishing sinking lines all day, while more fun than bagging groceries, isn't that terrific a pastime).

Figure 10-8:
Great
places
to catch
bass.

The Everglades: Overlooked but not overrated

My choice over the more-famous Lake Okeechobee, the sawgrass prairies crisscrossed by canals that extend through Palm Beach, Broward, and Dade Counties, are very little fished compared to the crowds in the Keys and along the coast. You can get way back in the Seminole or Miccosukee Lakes and have days when the largemouth attack your fly from dawn 'til dusk.

The best guide — he pretty much invented this kind of fishing — is Jack Allen of Fort Lauderdale, Florida, 305-764-6115.

For more information:

Florida Game and Freshwater Fish Commission
620 South Meridian St.
Tallahassee, FL 32399-1600
904-488-1960

The St. Johns: Fishing with eagles

The St. Johns River, which for much of its length is a series of lakes connected by flowages, has always been one of the premier largemouth fisheries in America. It has also been pounded mercilessly. With the return of some of its upper reaches to free-flowing river in north central Florida, some remarkable fly rodding is available in newly drowned forests. In the area around Welaka, where the panfishing is more furious than anything I have ever seen, you can hope for an 8- or 9-pound bass on a fly. Big poppers on lily pads and streamers that imitate the big shiners in these waters yield trophies every year. Part of the reason is the fish just seem to grow bigger in north Florida. I remember fishing there one year and catching bass on one cast, hickory shad on another cast, and flounder on subsequent casts. I once watched a manatee come cruising through to add to the show. Topping it off one day, I saw an osprey swoop down and pick up a big pumpkinseed (a local name for a large sunfish), and as it lumbered skyward, an eagle came screaming down from on high, its talons extended. The osprey, who was no dumbbell, let go of its fish, and the eagle swiped it out of free-fall and headed back to its nest. Not a bad sideshow for an afternoon's fishing.

For more information:

Downstream Outfitters
4000-4 St. Johns Ave.
Jacksonville, FL 32205
904-389-6252

Acres of bass

One fine spring day, I took my eldest daughter, Lucy, fly rodding in the Big Cypress Reservation with Jack Allen. The chalky banks and slow-moving water of the Everglades canals are very like the limestone-rich streams of the Ozarks where Jack grew up, and Everglades largemouth respond to popping bugs as pleasingly as midwestern smallmouth: a fierce, fast, loud take and a leap into the air.

The air was still pleasantly cool as we ran off 10 miles of canal. As always on an Everglades morning, it seemed that every bird in creation took wing just ahead of us: black and white stilts, herons, egrets, ibises, coots, and directly overhead, a pair of roseate spoonbills, hot pink in the slanting light of the morning sun, and way up high, a pair of storks. Hundreds of alligators, alerted by our engines, abandoned their sunny mudbanks and plunged into the canal ahead of us.

Lucy took in the scenery. It was all new to her, and it was very beautiful. "Daddy, pass me a sandwich," she asked. I unwrapped a peanut butter, honey, and banana sandwich (a recipe I learned from Jack) and gave her half.

Jack cut his engines. Our wake washed up against the coral banks. As the noise subsided, I heard the wonderful slurping splat of feeding bass, punctuated by the smooching sound of feeding bluegill. Jack handed me a fly rod. I cast. A bass attacked the fly. I brought him to the boat and released him. I cast again. Another bass. And again. Another bass.

I traded places with Lucy. She waved the fly rod. Her cast was a little sloppy, but she got the bug in there and she stripped well with her left hand. A bass rose. Lucy struck and missed. Jack corrected her as he used to correct me.

I'd say it took him a good ten years before I was cured of the neurotically compulsive rod-waving of the trout fisherman and learned the slower, lazier cast of the bass angler (casting with a drawl, if you will). But Lucy had no bad habits to unlearn and cooperative fish sparked her enthusiasm.

Jack offered Lucy a cane pole. Lucy got the hang of it quickly — kids always do. The cane pole is very much like the fly rod of Izaak Walton's time, before the invention of the reel. Something in its architecture suggests the roll cast to anyone who picks it up. Lucy soon mastered the roll cast. She followed this with steady flicking of the wrist as she panned right (another reflexive motion that the cane somehow communicates to the novice), imparting just the right motion to the popping bug. The bass rose every time.

We passed the afternoon taking turns among the three of us. Lucy's session with the cane pole gave her greater confidence with the fly rod. Hundreds of fish rose to our flies on a canal where I have enjoyed myself on other days with just a dozen takes. In one ten-minute period, Jack and I decided to get down to some serious bass fishing in order to arrive at a baseline for the day. Lucy insisted on unhooking our fish (she took great pride in holding the bass by the lower lip and extracting the fly). She may have slowed us some, but we still boated 31 bass in 10 minutes.

Jack did the mental arithmetic that yielded a projection of 2,000 bass in the course of a nonstop fishing day. We didn't try to make our projections, though. Instead we just took our time, floating down the canal, driven, like the puffy April clouds, by a fresh following breeze.

Also see the preceding Everglades section for the Florida Game and Freshwater Fish Commission.

Alabama's Lakes and the Coosa River: Statewide bassin'

Alabama, like much of the southeastern U.S., is full of lakes, many lakes, most public, some private, that offer primo largemouth fishing. Make a special note of national forests with fishable lakes because you can find yourself in some unforgettable scenery. You can travel and cast your way across the state. Oak Mountain Lake, outside Birmingham, is a classic bass spot. Fishing is all-year-round and done best from a float tube. Spring is most productive, but be sure to return spawning bass to the water. A local favorite fly at Oak Mountain is a dragonfly nymph. The Coosa River runs for about 175 miles through central Alabama, and just about the whole river and its four main impoundments are accessible and fishable for largemouth that travel wherever the bait go up and down river. Tailwaters behind dams offer good angling. Striped bass have been planted in this river system and and can be fly rodded.

For more information:

Heney & Mullins Co.
2738 Cahaba Rd.
Birmingham, AL 35223
205-802-7508

Alabama Fish and Game Division
64 North Union St.
Montgomery, AL 36130
334-242-3465

The Ozarks: U-pick-it

The limestone-rich rivers of the Missouri Ozarks are about the best float-fishing waters I know. They are full of native, wild smallmouth, and they are among the most easily floated rivers I know. The Black, Big, Current, Meramec, and Gasconade Rivers are all productive streams, and many canoe liveries on these rivers rent and pick up at convenient put-in and take-out points. With the opening of many big impoundments in the last few decades, more and more people trailer their big bass boats over to the new lakes to fish for largemouth, transplanted stripers, and whatever other mix the put-and-take fisheries folks have whipped up for the weekend crowd. Good. This means that in the right time of year, you can have the rivers all to yourself.

The best time to fish is weekdays in spring. Weekends and summer bring out a lot of non-fishing canoers who tip off the bass to lie low. But the extra bonus is the local people — friendly folk who hunt and fish a lot.

For more information:

Missouri Department of Conservation
P.O. Box 180
Jefferson City, MO 65102
573-751-4115

The Shenandoah and Potomac Rivers: A good connection

In eastern Virginia run the Shenandoah and Potomac Rivers, the home waters of famous Virginia fly tier Harry Murray, who has made his reputation tying smallmouth flies and fishing with them on these historic rivers. The Shenandoah can be divided into two sections — the North Fork and South Fork. The North Fork, according to Murray, affords the best smallmouth fishing. This section, reminiscent of a Catskill free-stone river, is a classic rock-bottom, riffle-pool-riffle river with a lot of feeder springs. Wading here is pretty easy. Down through the South Fork, the Shenandoah turns into a limestone-type water with lots of ledges and deeper sections. The Potomac is the same way, with a large volume of water. Wading here is possible but sometimes tricky. Both rivers have good access. The North and South Forks and Potomac are all floatable, but using a canoe for transport and then getting out to wade is always a good way to fish a bass river. The smallmouth season starts in mid-May on the North Fork and lasts until mid-October. On the Shenandoah's South Fork and on the Potomac, the smallmouth start up in early June and go until mid-October. In late July and into August, the wide, sun-lit Potomac warms too much for the smallmouth and they slack off. When this happens, move back up to the cool spring water of the North Fork of the Shenandoah.

For more information:

Murray's Fly Shop
121 Main St.
Edinburg, VA 22824
540-984-4212

Virginia Department of Game and Inland Fisheries
4010 West Broad St.
Richmond, VA 23230
804-367-1000

The Susquehanna River: Birthplace of Clouser's Minnow

The Susquehanna is the home water of Bob Clouser and Lefty Kreh, which is about as star-studded an endorsement as you will find in the world of bass on the fly rod. The Susquie is a rich limestone river that is very wide in places. It flows many miles through the rolling hills of central Pennsylvania. The waters above Harrisburg are a very good place to fish for smallmouth that inhabit the runs and riffles created by the river's rocky bottom. This is where a Clouser's Minnow was invented. The Letort River (see Chapter 8) is not very far away, and a good weekend of fishing for trout and smallmouth may be devised for these two rivers.

For more information:

Clouser's Fly Shop
101 Ulrich St.
Middletown, PA 17057
717-944-6541

Pennsylvania Fish and Boat Commission
P.O. Box 67000
Harrisburg, PA 17106
717-657-4518

The St. Lawrence River: A lotta water

Look at it this way: The Great Lakes empty into the St. Lawrence. It hosts all kinds of bait and all kinds of great habitat. People didn't really think of the St. Lawrence or any of our northern rivers as particularly great bass spots, certainly not the equal of those southern lakes where bass pros wearing red jump suits run around in big boats hooking largemouth on plastic worms. Then Bassmasters had one of their tournaments up there about 15 years ago, and people were stunned at the amount and size of the bass. Mucho. Tom Akstens, the premier Adirondack guide and tier, saves a couple of weeks in June each year to fish the upper New York State tributaries of the St. Lawrence. They are smaller, quite floatable in a canoe and, in many spots, wadeable. Perfect, easy-going, early summer fly rodding.

For fly fishing guiding and instruction:

Tom Akstens
P.O. Box 111
Bakers Mills, NY 12811
518-251-2217
akstens@aol.com

For more information:

New York State Division of Fish and Wildlife
50 Wolf Rd.
Albany, NY 12233
518-457-5690

Quetico Provincial Park: The boundary waters

For pure wilderness experience, the nearly 2,000 square miles along the Ontario-Minnesota border is as close to living a page out of Hiawatha as I can imagine. Lake after lake, connected by cypress black water and tannin copper streams and every other imaginable kind of stream, make this a complete smallmouth experience. In May and June, the bass are up on the spawning beds, and if you come with enough bug spray to get rid of the black flies (or alternatively, don't shower for two months before embarking on your trip), this area offers a magnificent 100-fish-a-day experience. These are prime canoe waters, so give paddling a thought. In fact, it is probably the best way to get around. The lakes and streams are pretty navigable all around, though there is a lot of cover in places.

For guide services:

Piragis Northwoods Company
105 North Central Ave.
Ely, MN 55731
800-223-6565

For more information:

Minnesota Department of Natural Resources
500 Lafayette Rd.
St. Paul, MN 55155
612-296-6157

Down East: Ayuppp, pretty fayah fishin'

The St. Croix River system of lakes and flowages can be the equal of Minnesota's Boundary Waters, especially in June. Black flies can make you pray for a swift and early death; if you wear one of those amazingly dweebish-looking head nets, you may be mistaken for someone impersonating a 1940s film star, but it keeps the flies away. While the rest of the world stands elbow to elbow on a trout stream, you can drink deeply of the solitude that enhances a great fishing experience.

For guide services:

Wilds of Maine Guide Service
6 Abby Rd.
Yarmouth, ME 04096
207-426-8138

Maine Outdoors
P.O. Box 401
Union, ME 04862
207-785-4496

For more information:

Maine Department of Inland Fisheries and Wildlife
Station 41
284 State St.
Augusta, ME 04333
207-287-4471

Any farm pond

Farm ponds may be simple and small, and they may not have great names like Shenandoah and St. Croix, but let me tell ya, farm ponds are *good*. Largemouth bass aren't the most pursued freshwater game fish just because of their spectacular fight, although that's probably the best reason we go after them. They are possibly the most *widespread* good-fighting fish around. Any of the tens of thousands of small ponds that dot farmland and rural areas all over the U.S. can provide great fishing. More than one state record fish has been hauled out of these little ponds. Such waters are easy to fly fish because they are small and are usually in the middle of a field, so you have a clear backcast. One of my favorite tactics on a little pond I fished in South Carolina was to cast a hopper so that it landed on a dock, then I'd jiggle it so it fell in the water, a seemingly natural occurrence that the big largemouth, lounging in the shade underneath, believed completely.

Great Bass Flies

The following sections describe the flies that bass love.

Marabou Leech: The prettiest bloodsucker

This fly, shown in Figure 10-9, squirms very nicely with a slow retrieve in slow or still water. The pattern is a cousin to the Woolly Bugger, but the

Bugger works better in moving water where its construction allows it to swim both like a leech and a hellgrammite.

Hook	Mustad 36890, sizes #8 to #6
Thread	Fluorescent orange
Weight	Two or three twists of lead wire on shank front
Tag	Four or five turns of the tying thread
Body	Black angora yarn or white angora yarn dyed orange
Wing	A black marabou feather, nearly three times the hook length

Figure 10-9:
The Marabou Leech.

Hornbeck Smallmouth fly: Switch-hitter

This versatile fly, shown in Figure 10-10, is based on a couple of Adirondack-style ties. You can fish it on the surface, using floatant, so it appears like a hopper or big fly, but it also works well as a streamer.

Hook	Mustad 9672, size #6 or #8
Thread	Brown
Body	Gray wool yarn
Ribbing	Medium mylar, gold
Tail	Fox squirrel tail
Wing	Mallard flank or dyed wood duck, tied flat on top of shank
Hackle	Webby cree saddle hackle

Secluded largemouth

While visiting some friends in Ithaca, New York, in the late summer one year, I asked if there was any fishing around. My friends, a young couple, said they had been looking at a property wedged between farmland and that a pond was there. That evening I went to check it out. At the end of an overgrown driveway was a broken down old cabin and a perfectly sized pond ringed by dogwoods, pines, and briars. I found an open place with room for my backcast, so I didn't have to wade into the middle. I began casting. I don't think the bass missed one opportunity — every cast of that popper yielded a 15-inch largemouth, good-sized fish for up there. The size and population of these fish suggested that no one ever fished this pond, or if they did, they were disciplined catch-and-release people. I tend to think this place was unknown and not fished, and therein is the pleasure of the secluded farm pond: You found it, no one else knows about it, and you tell no one.

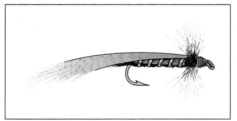

Figure 10-10:
The Hornbeck Smallmouth fly.

Hudson Duster: A little piece of licorice

This fly, shown in Figure 10-11, originated by Tom Akstens for the smallmouth of the Upper Hudson, is a general stonefly/hellgie imitation. The key thing about fishing it is that you get it down on the bottom and keep it bouncing. After tying this fly, pick out some of the thorax material to give it bugginess and movement in the water. Oh yes, the Hudson Dusters were a violent Irish street gang of Manhattan in the late 19th Century, so there is some poetic justice in watching them get mugged for a change, by a two-pound fish at that!

Hook	Mustad 9672, size #8 or #10
Thread	Black
Weight	Medium lead wire (seven to ten turns)
Tail	Clump of black marabou feather tip
Body	Black angora yarn
Thorax	Black Orvis "Fuzzy Leech" yarn
Wing case	Black goose quill

Figure 10-11:
The
Hudson
Duster.

Marabou Mickey: A great hybrid fly

Smallmouth love yellow. The tie, illustrated in Figure 10-12, is another Akstens original, based on the old Mickey Finn and a Marabou Black Ghost. A yellow Marabou Muddler is also a great pattern. I think the success of marabou has to do with its tendency to pulse as you pull it through the water. You'll see what I mean if you look closely at your streamer when you strip it in. It is a very "live look."

Hook	Mustad 9672, size #6 or #8 (#10 to 12 for bluegill)
Thread	Black
Weight	Lead wire, as long as the shank
Body	Black floss
Ribbing	Gold mylar tinsel
Wing	Yellow marabou
Tail	Red hackle fibers

Figure 10-12:
The
Marabou
Mickey.

The Hair Ball: The ugliest fly ever tied

Is it a mouse? A wad of mold? A coughed-up wad of cat fur? Who knows — just as long as the bass think it's something. You can use this fly (see Figure 10-13) in heavy cover and weeds because the thick body acts as a weed guard. This fly is so easy to tie that the only way to mess it up is to tie it neatly.

Hook	Mustad 9672, sizes #8 to #6 (wide gape)
Body	Deer body hair, brown, gray, or tan; spin onto the shank untrimmed except around the bend and point to allow the hook to strike cleanly

Figure 10-13:
The
Hair Ball.

Spin doctor

Learning to spin deer hair is an important skill to learn. If you don't tie flies and you look at a fly like a Muddler with clipped, spun deer hair, you probably think that it is for graduate fly tiers only. Actually, it isn't that hard.

1. Take a clump of deer hair and remove all the underhair and fuzz. Even up the ends by clipping with scissors. You will end up with a bunch of bristles all of the same uniform thickness. The thick bristles give the fly buoyancy and that is the chief virtue of deer hair.

2. Hold the clump at an angle to the hook and take one loose turn. Wind a second, tighter turn directly over that turn. Gently relax your grip on the clump. Take a third turn, applying more pressure on the clump, and fully release your grip. The deer hair should flare into a nice ball.

3. Trim the deer hair to the shape called for in the fly recipe. For the Hair Ball, the trimming requirements don't extend much beyond clearing the hook and the eye. For a Muddler Minnow or an Irresistible, two favorite spun deer hair flies, you have to trim a little more exactly. I have always used scissors for this, but if you are good with a single-edged razor, you will get a prettier fly. Once you get the hang of spinning, this fun technique will impress any greenhorn fly rodders looking over your tying bench.

Shenk's White Streamer

This is a simple tie (see Figure 10-14) originated by Pennsylvania tier Ed Shenk and first recommended to us by Harry Murray. I think its softness looks particularly juicy to a bass, but who knows? That's just one angler's opinion.

Hook	Mustad 9672, 4X long, #2 to #8
Thread	White
Tail	White marabou, same length as hook
Body	Thickly dubbed white rabbit or fox picked out and trimmed as shown
Weight	Lead wired

Figure 10-14:
Shenk's White Streamer.

Murray's Hellgrammite: Brother to the Bugger

This fly was developed by the well-known fly tier, Harry Murray, of Edinburg, Virginia, who was very generous with sharing his smallmouth knowledge for this book. This fly, shown in Figure 10-15, looks a lot like a Woolly Bugger but the materials act differently in the water, more like a swimming hellgrammite.

Hook	Mustad 9672, #4 to #10
Tail	Black ostrich herl
Body	Black chenille
Hackle	Dark, soft dun palmered over body
"Pinchers"	Black rubber band sections
Weight	Lead wire

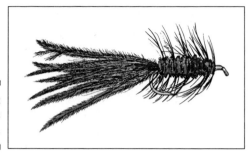

Figure 10-15:
Murray's
Hellgrammite.

Peck's Popper: My favorite

Jack Allen, my favorite bass guide, grew up fishing in the Ozarks back in the late 1930s and early 1940s. It was back then that a Tennessee building contractor and bass-a-holic named Ernest Peckinpaugh developed Peck's Popper (see Figure 10-16) and the tie has not changed since. I have caught thousands of bass using this bug. Jack likes the fly so much that he calls his johnboat "Father Peckinpaugh." You might want to try making your float out of a synthetic material which is more durable than the traditional cork. But here is the basic tie.

Hook	Kinked popper hook (don't panic — it's just a specialized hook that you can easily find in catalogs or at your local dealer)
Tail	Two pair of webby hackles, splayed
Collar	Stiffer hackle
Body	Cork face hollowed out and body tapered (optional paint eye, black pupil on white)
Legs	Rubber band segment threaded through body (you can use a needle to pull the rubber through the body)

Figure 10-16:
Peck's
Popper.

Clouser's Minnow: One of the best

This great fly was developed by Bob Clouser, a fly tier and smallmouth guide based in Middletown, Pennsylvana. The great acceptance of this fly, sometimes called Clouser's Deep Minnow, attests to its versatility. Lefty Kreh is reported to have said that it is the best streamer he has ever cast. See Chapter 7 for the tie recipe.

Chapter 11
Saltwater Fish

*P*eople have been fly rodding in the salt for more than 100 years, but not until just after World War II did it begin to catch on with a wider public. For the next 20 years, it was something that rich guys or pampered outdoor writers did to fill the time between the close of one year's trout season and next year's opening day. Yet in the last ten years or so, with the Great Fly Rod Boom that followed in the wake of Robert Redford's film, *A River Runs Through It,* a number of fly rodders have discovered the terrific sport in the saltwater close to home. This is true whether your home is in New York, Boston, Savannah, Miami, New Orleans, Houston, San Francisco, Seattle, or on up into British Columbia. (Take a look at the International Game Fish Association (IGFA) fly line records in this chapter — many of these records were set in the past eight years.)

This tremendous upsurge in interest gave birth to the first generation of full-time fly rod guides in many of these waters. Because their work takes them on the water so many more days than the average angler spends, and because their living depends on their clients' catching fish, the successful guides have had to develop and refine new flies and techniques in a nation-wide flowering of angling creativity. The only parallel I can think of is the work done on trout fishing flies and techniques by the great Catskill guides and tiers from the 1870s up through the 1970s. (This is roughly from the time railroad brakeman Roy Steenrod tied the first Hendricksen dry fly, through the innovations of Lee Wulff, and up to the Compara-dun series of Al Caucci and Bob Nastasi on the Delaware River.)

No slight intended against freshwater fish — trout are gorgeous, bass are exciting, and salmon are awe-inspiring. But pound for pound, the fight of a fish in the ocean is, in the opinion of most anglers, a great deal more fierce than the battle put up by any freshwater fish. Ocean fish are big and strong, and when they feel danger, or a hook, they run far and fast. For all of these reasons, ocean fly rodding is the big growth sector in our sport.

To walk along the shore with the surf crashing, flights of ducks cruising overhead on their way to winter quarters, pods of gulls wheeling and diving over acres of bait fish, and big schools of game fish showing in the breakers — that's a great feeling for the saltwater fly rodder.

One note of importance: Most saltwater fish have very tough, often toothy mouths and sharp gill covers *(rakers)*. You often have to embed the hook in their mouths to catch them. But a fearsome-mouthed, well-hooked fish presents a tough job for the angler who wants to release it. So before you go saltwater fly rodding, be sure that you have a full array of disgorgers, jaw grabbers, pliers, and rags with which to hold the fish. I'm no surgeon, but I've done well over the years with basic equipment for unhooking fish. I need my fingers to type.

Bluefish: Good and Tough

The bluefish is Fishdom's version of that guy in the bar who asks every newcomer, "Hey, buddy, are you looking at me?" and then, without waiting for an answer, throws a punch. The guy can be big or little, can win or lose a fight, but he keeps coming back for more. Fighting is in his nature.

When blues are around, they hit anything — live or artificial — but there are a number of flies that these bruisers can't pass up. Bluefish are excellent fish for newcomers because . . .

- ✔ They are very catchable — not real finicky about what fly pattern you offer them as long as the bait imitated by the fly is generally present, especially if that bait is schooling.

- ✔ They are strong fighters, so even the novice can begin to learn how it feels to handle saltwater fly equipment in a tough fight.

- ✔ If you catch one, you will probably catch more because they usually travel in groups.

- ✔ They are delicious when eaten fresh. In fact, if you want a good lesson in the difference between fresh fish and funky fish, eat a fillet of bluefish on the day that you catch it, and then leave one in the fridge for a few days. The fresh fish will taste light as a flounder. The refrigerated fish will have that oily taste that reminds me of last week's tuna salad.

Bluefish inhabit all of the world's oceans, spending a good half of the year in deep water. In the warmer months, when surf temperatures are between 55°F and 75°F, the blues follow bait fish into shallow coastal waters. When the bait runs up to the beach, the slaughter begins. During this kind of feeding frenzy, bluefish will take anything you throw at them, or so it seems.

If anchovies or shiners are around, use a Surf Candy or a Deceiver in sizes 4 to 2/0. Clouser's Minnow is also a good choice. For the same reason that anglers love the rise to a dry fly, I get a kick out of watching blues slam a popper.

Bluefish have very sharp teeth, so you need a heavy shock leader or a wire leader. They make wire that you can tie like tippet without too much crimping. To avoid the chance of a bite, pick up a blue as you would a pike: by squeezing it behind the eye sockets or grabbing it by the tail. Use pliers to unhook a blue.

Figure 11-1 shows a typical bluefish. They are kind of bluish on top when out of the water; but when you see them in the surf, they appear more coppery-green.

Figure 11-1:
The bluefish has extremely sharp teeth, a white belly, and (usually) a black blotch at the base of the pectoral fin.

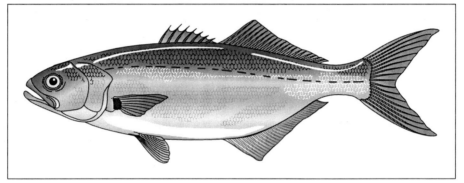

Fly line world record
Doug Hinson caught a 19-pound, 12-ounce bluefish off Nags Head, North Carolina, on November 2, 1987.

Weakfish and Sea Trout: Brothers in Angling

These are two different but closely related fish. Neither of them is a trout, but their torpedo shape and spotted skin (as shown in Figure 11-2) are similar to a trout's. (English colonists used the word *trout* to describe anything that looked like the English trout of their homeland, but I'll give

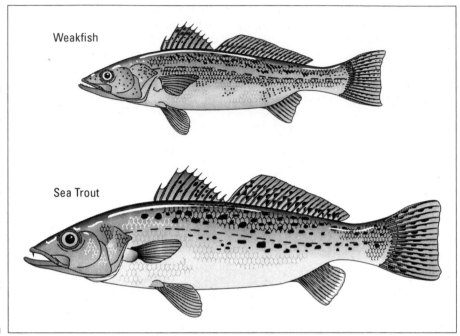

Figure 11-2:
Two closely related fish, the weakfish and the sea trout (or speckled trout) have telltale coffee-bean-like spots just like brown trout have.

Weakfish

Sea Trout

this one to them — weakies do resemble trout . . . sort of.) The weakfish is exclusively an Atlantic Seaboard fish, but the sea trout (or *speckled trout*) can be found from New England through the Gulf of Mexico. Weakfish and sea trout coexist, side by side, in the Mid-Atlantic states.

Although no one has ever been able to explain why, weakfish, like many other game animals, experience dramatic upticks and declines in population. Some scientists think that the weakfish/sea trout population fluctuation has to do with the availability of food in their deep water wintering grounds somewhere off the continental shelf.

Sea trout occupy grassy areas close to shore and eat menhaden, mullet, other small fish, and shrimp. Weakfish likewise eat small fish, worms, crabs, and shrimp, and they can be found over just about any kind of bottom — sand, grass, whatever. In the absence of any grass beds to hold shrimp, you need to fish tidal structures, looking for areas that are likely to carry bait fish in the moving tide.

Streamers in sizes 2 to 1/0 are good. Colors should be yellow, red and yellow, or red and white. Try a Lefty's Deceiver or a Clouser's Minnow (a small one so it can be taken for a shrimp). Any standard bonefish shrimp patterns will score. If you spot a school of fish, cast to the side and strip the fly evenly, not too fast, not too slow.

Even on Sunday

Spotted sea trout will also hit poppers (if they're in the mood), and they are magnificent to hook in this way. When I first started fly fishing in saltwater, outdoor writer Geoff Norman took me wading in the grassy flats near Pensacola, Florida. The lagoon was calm and quiet and our popping plugs hit the water sending out little rings like a falling twig might have made on the surface of a sheltered pond. Just like the old-time bass books said, I waited until the rings subsided, gave my plug a few burbling pops and enticed a 5-pound "speck" as the locals call it.

That first hookup seemed to call for an after-fishing beer, very cold, to offset the heat of a Gulf Coast afternoon. But it was Sunday and the liquor stores were closed near Geoff's house. No problem. We went to the Florabama, a store, as its name suggests, that straddles the state line. All you had to do was walk in the door on the Florida side — not the Alabama side — and you were legal.

Remember the weakfish's name and why it got it: The mouth is soft. Even though it requires steady pressure to keep the fish out of the weeds, you also need a light touch so that you don't pull the hook out. The fish does have some teeth that can nip you.

Fly line world records

A 14-pound, 2-ounce weakie was caught on the Delaware Bay, Delaware, by Norman W. Bartlett on June 5, 1987.

Sidney A. Freifeld caught a 12-pound, 7-ounce sea trout on the Indian River, in Sebastian, Florida, on March 5, 1984.

Striped Bass: A Silver Treasure

For the surf fisherman or fisherwoman, the striped bass (shown in Figure 11-3) is *the real thing*, the serious fish that makes your day. Rarely do you hear someone complain, "I was fishing for blues, but all I got was bass." The striper, like the trout in freshwater, offers a special challenge and a special satisfaction. Like the trout, the striper can sometimes be caught without a great deal of thought on the part of the angler; but true to form, the striper can also be maddeningly selective. You can hear and see them slashing all around, but no matter what you throw them, they do not take because they are keyed in on one particular bait that is all-but-invisible to the angler. Found from the Carolinas to Maine, and having been transplanted to the West Coast and a number of reservoirs all over America, stripers are a favorite game fish.

Figure 11-3:
The striped bass, as its name suggests, is easily identified by the thin black stripes that run the length of its body.

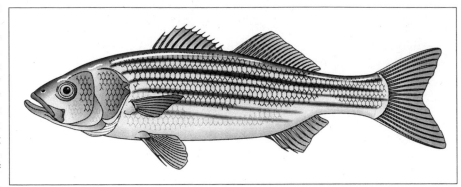

Schoolie (small) stripers can be caught on lighter rods. But the little guys aren't the only ones that run in schools. During the great migrations of spring and fall, stripers tend to travel in packs in which all the fish are of uniform size. (I have had days in early December off Montauk when they are all 30-inches long and gorging on herrings.)

Fly rodding for stripers has revolutionized fly fishing in the northeastern U.S. Now, instead of making the long drive to crowded trout streams, coastal fly rodders are finding great sport close to home with stripers, often major league fish in the 20- to 30-pound range.

A variety of big streamers in sizes 2/0 to 4/0 work. Deceivers, Finger Mullet, and other big imitations in red and yellow, red and white, or mostly white work the best. Clouser's Minnow, as always, is a great go-to fly. Late in the season, giant bunker flies can take really big fish. On white sandy bottoms, stripers will follow a crab imitation for a good distance before striking.

Even though you may score on subsurface flies, nothing is more thrilling than watching a striper rush to engulf a popper the way a blitzing linebacker blindsides an unsuspecting quarterback. Even if surface fishing sometimes means catching fewer fish, the thrill is well worth the price.

My main advice for fishing stripers is this: When you see no visible surface activity, fish them with the same kind calculations that you would use for freshwater trout or bass. Like the trout, the striper hangs on the edge of the current and looks for feeding opportunities. For that reason, tidal rips are often the first place to look. And like the freshwater bass, the striper likes to hang around sheltering structures, picking off bait fish. In this case, jetties and rocky shorelines can produce good striper action. This affinity for a rocky habitat no doubt accounts in part for the name *rockfish,* by which the striper is known in the waters south of New Jersey.

Fly line world record

Gary L. Dyer battled and caught a 64-pound, 8-ounce striper on July 28, 1973, on the Smith River in Oregon.

Redfish: A Cook's Tale

Thanks in part to the success of Louisiana Chef Paul Prudhomme's wildly popular recipe for blackened redfish, more people experience redfish on the plate rather than on the end of a fishing line. Prudhomme's recipe caught on so well that the redfish was nearly fished out on the Gulf Coast.

Little fly, big fish

Two summers ago, I grew quite frustrated with the striper fishing around New York. I would go out late at night, sometimes after midnight, and stripers would be boiling all around. You could hear them slashing furiously. In the darkness, the racket was nerve-wracking, seductive, and maddening. If I didn't know better I would have called it a striper mugging.

I thought that a popper would surely lure them on. No luck. Then a Clouser's. Again, strike out. I had seen sand eels in the shallows. I tied on a chartreuse Woolly Bugger. The stripers laughed at me. Well, if they didn't laugh, then they did the next worse thing — they ignored me. Then I tried a little red and sparkly fly tied to imitate the cinder worm that hatches on the big moon tides of the summer months. I couldn't see where I was casting so every time I heard a sound I quickly tried to sail a cast in the general direction. Within a half dozen casts I scored and kept on scoring all through the fast running part of the tide. The bass lined up as if they were in the feeding lane of a trout stream sipping happily through a hatch of mayflies.

My guide, Bob Roble, rigged me up with two flies, just like wet-fly fishermen used to do on trout streams in the old days. His reasoning was that with so much bait in the water, I might as well double my chances. When a good cast produced a tug that seemed to want to go in two directions at the same time, I realized that I was into a striper double header. It was all great fun, but the best part came last, at the end of the tide, just before dawn. The sky had begun to show the first faint blush of day and we had parked ourselves over the shallow outflow of a big back bay. Having been up all night, I didn't have a whole lot of enthusiasm left in me. Roble, who will not put up with a wuss on his boat, wasn't interested in my physical and mental state.

"Cast!" he commanded. The tide was fairly racing and my fly swept around quickly in the current when a striper hit it with full force. In the shallow water it couldn't dive, so just like a fish on the coral flats of the Keys, it made a beeline for deep water. It shook its head as it went, and I knew from the fight that this was a big fish. I hung on and fought for a good 10 minutes before we boated the fish just at sunup. He was 37 inches and shimmered with color in the dawn's early light.

Also known as the *channel bass* or *red drum,* this crustacean-loving game fish is caught from New Jersey to Houston, Texas. But it is on the grass beds of Florida and the Gulf of Mexico that the redfish (shown in Figure 11-4) becomes a super-challenging fly rod opponent — and the shallower the water, the more thrilling the fight.

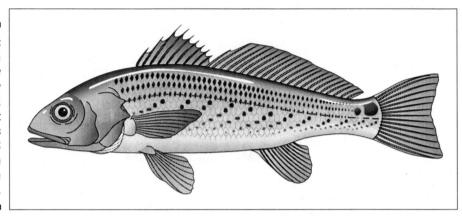

Figure 11-4: The redfish is easily identified by the black spot that resembles the CBS logo on the base of its tail.

New Orleans redfish guide Bubby Rodriguez has taken me out to the shallow salt marshes where the Barataria Bayou eases into the Gulf of Mexico and has put me on 10-pound fish in less than a foot of water. This is hold-your-breath, one-cast fishing. It is also very demanding. You need to put the fly right in front of the fish's nose (within 2 inches), and you have to avoid spooking him with your line at the same time.

Actually, you don't so much *spook* as you *turn off* the fish. Often, a bad cast gets a look from the fish; it stays within casting distance but ignores you once he has you "made," a term that cops use for having blown your cover.

The best fly for a red in Louisiana is a crab imitation, Del Brown's Crab or any similar pattern. Shrimp patterns also score consistently.

Fly line world record

A 43-pound redfish was caught on Banana River Lagoon, in Florida, by Greg Braunstein, on May 7, 1995.

Puffing for reds

With redfish and with sea trout, I have found that just because you don't *see* them on the grassy flats doesn't mean that they are not there. They could be following in the wake of a ray and picking up shellfish that the ray stirs up as it cruises. Look for tight puffs of turbid water that indicate a recently made cloud of mud. Cast into the trailing edge of the cloud and begin to retrieve line. I have caught many fish by this kind of blind casting. (Actually, it's not so much blind casting as it is blind hope!) One of the neatest things about such blind casting is that you don't always know what you may catch. You may think that you are casting to red fish, but you could very well end up with an 8-pound sea trout, which happened to me in the grass beds just south of Flamingo, Florida.

Fluke: Flat and Fun

No fly fishing organizations devote themselves to the mighty summer flounder, or fluke. And to tell you the truth, I have never gone out fishing with the fluke specifically in mind. But at the end of a day spent chasing stripers or hanging around waiting for the tide to turn, I have been known to drift over some fluke beds, and I have even caught a few fish with my fly rod. Tiny Clouser's Minnows do the trick. And, yes, it's cheating, but a little piece of fresh clam on the hook helps. This fish is not for purists, but fluke sure do taste good.

In addition to being catchable and delicious, the fluke is one of the great early-season fish. When the first warm days of spring make thinking about work harder and harder, nothing is more pleasant than giving winter the kiss-off by catching a bucketful of these flat fish.

The fluke's mouth and eyes are located on the left side of the fish, as shown in Figure 11-5. (The winter flounder, the fluke's close cousin, is right-eyed and right-mouthed.) The fluke is a little more spunky than the cold-weather flounder. And although fluke, too, are found mainly on the bottom, they sometimes surprise you by chasing your bait when you are after blues or weakfish. When they are really on the bite, jigging a small, weighted bonefish fly like a Crazy Charlie has worked for me.

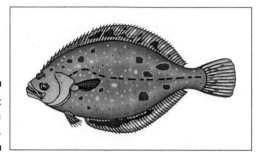

Figure 11-5:
Favorite
flatty: fluke.

Fly line world record

William N. Herold caught an 8-pound, 2-ounce fluke on October 27, 1991, off Greenwich, Connecticut.

Marlin: Fly Fishing's Mt. Everest

In traditional big game fishing, black and blue marlin are the most desired quarry. They are magnificent fish but are too big for all but the heaviest fly tackle. The IGFA does list a few records for these two brutes (those caught on the fly rod are welterweights of the species), but they are rarely sought by the saltwater fly rodder. Practically speaking, the most fly roddable marlin is the striped marlin, although anglers have had some success with the white marlin as well.

Striped marlin are found along the southern California coast all the way to Chile. Like all billfish (see Figure 11-6), they have a bill and a long, shark-like body. Marlin are distinguished by a dorsal fin far forward on their backs that ends in a long comb structure. Striped marlin are a dark purplish-blue on the backs, sky blue on their sides, and have pale blue or white stripes on their sides. An average fish is about 200 to 250 pounds.

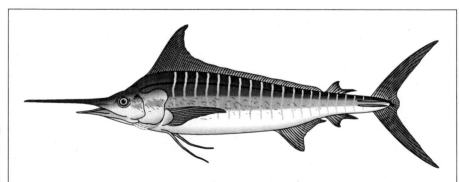

Figure 11-6:
The marlin.

Striped marlin spawn through the summer and are on the move during this period; you can also see them chasing surface bait at this time — your tip-off that it is time to pick up the fly rod.

White marlin are found only in the Atlantic, ranging from Brazil all the way up the East coast of North America. It is smaller than the striped marlin, weighing in at about 50 to 60 pounds. It has a greenish back, white body, and barred stripes very much like a striped marlin.

Getting marlin to the fly is the first step. With a powerful boat you will trail what are called *teasers,* sewn-up bonito bellies or big plastic squids tied without hooks. These splashing, flopping baits, cast in pairs, attract the marlin. At the precise moment of truth, your fishing partner or first mate will pull the teaser away from the marlin, forcing him to lunge after it. Cast your fly, a large streamer. It should provoke a strike.

Set the hook hard — strike the fish two or three times — and hold on. The captain must follow the running fish with the boat and stay close enough that you are able to slowly take back line. Slowly and surely you must gain back line, fight against the fish's runs and jumps, and get it close enough to be observed, sometimes tagged, and then cut the leader.

Once on, marlin run and leap, an action known as *greyhounding,* and they will take more line than anything you've ever seen. You have to load your reel effectively for these fish. Use a shock tippet no longer than 12 inches; the leader tippet itself should be 12-pound test at least 12 inches long to abide by regulations regarding record fish. The leader should be 6 to 9 feet of 60-pound mono. Your reel should be loaded with at least 10-weight line and have roughly 250 yards of 30-pound backing in addition to the fly line.

Fly line world records

Dean Butler took a 199-pound, 8-ounce striped marlin on April 20, 1996, off Newcastle, Australia.

A 104-pound, 6-ounce white marlin was caught by Bill Pate off Mohammedia, Morocco, on September 14, 1996.

Inshore Grand Slam Plus One

If you bought this book 50 years ago, the bonefish would have been the only fish in this chapter. Twenty years ago, the tarpon and permit would have been added along with the snook. These are good times in which to live and fish. In the same way that salmon and trout are at the top of the fly rod angler's hit parade, the saltwater fly rodder also has a short list of great fish:

the permit, bonefish, snook, and tarpon. (The traditional "Grand Slam" is taking a bonefish, a permit, and a tarpon all in one day — I added the snook because he deserves it and, hey, it's one more enjoyable fish to catch.)

No place on earth is more beautiful than a bonefish flat lit up by the sun. The water can be everything from gold to green to blue to black, and way off in the distance, the sight of the wagging tail of a bone or the fin of a placidly cruising tarpon is like sitting in a deer stand, watching a big buck make his way into range.

Bonefish: Gray lightning

If one fish is responsible for kicking off the saltwater fly-fishing craze, it is this silver-gray denizen of sandy and coral flats in the world's warm-water oceans. From the west coast of Africa to the Caribbean to the paradise of the South Pacific, the bonefish is among the wariest shallow-water fish and, like the trout, responds well to the right fly, properly presented. A sloppy presentation, on the other hand, will cause the bone to turn tail and run for deep water as fast as a cheetah.

The first trick to learn in fishing for bones is to see them. Initially, if you go with a guide (which is the *only* way for a newcomer to start bonefishing), you may feel that your guide is a liar or that you are going blind because the guide may constantly call out, "Bonefish at ten o'clock — forty feet out." And you will see nothing.

You will continue to see nothing for a long time, but trust me: Sooner or later the bones will materialize. Eventually, you will be able to see the telltale black tip of the tail (and then a silver-yellow-green outline) as they cruise. When you do, the trick is to cast 4 or 5 feet ahead on the same course on which the fish is moving. In other words, lead the bonefish as a shotgunner leads a duck or goose.

The preferred fly is a crab or shrimp imitation. A Crazy Charlie or even a little Clouser's are good patterns. Take a look at the local bait size and color when selecting the fly.

Can you eat bonefish? Only if you are absolutely starving. They aren't called bonefish for nothing. It's just as well: Any more pressure on these great fighters and the heavily fished flats of the Keys and the Bahamas would become the saltwater equivalent of an overfished trout stream.

With its big eye and down-turned mouth, as shown in Figure 11-7, the bonefish is well designed to find food on the flats. I can't get it out of my mind, though, that despite its valor as a game fish, the eye and mouth give the bone a goofy look (as in Goofy, the Disney character).

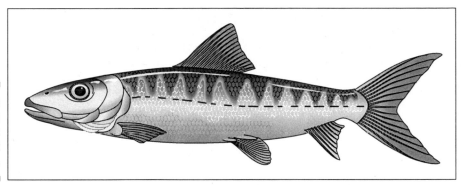

Figure 11-7:
The
bonefish:
gray ghost
of the flats.

Fly line world record

A 14-pound, 8-ounce bonefish was caught by Harry F. Weyher III on
March 30, 1996, off Islamorada, Florida.

Jingle bones

When the bonefish are feeding in shallow water, their tails often stick up in the air. This activity is known as *tailing,* and it is to the bonefish angler what a rising trout is to the freshwater fisherman. I remember one Christmas, shortly after I was married, my wife and I went to check out Christmas Island, an atoll about 1,500 miles due south of Honolulu. The fishing was spectacular, and on Christmas Day, we were invited to the feast and singing contest at the main longhouse in the village called Banana (honest, that was its name). Because we were two of the only six non-Micronesians on the atoll, we were honored guests. The food was great. The singing was great. After lunch, as they smoked hand-rolled cigarettes of highly prized tobacco, the village elders began to tell tales of courage and adventure on the high seas. Just as they were getting to the classic legends, my guide showed up and said, "The tide is moving out, and five miles of tailing fish are on the flat."

Right about there, I lost my interest in Tall Tales of the South Seas. We hightailed it to the flat. As promised, the shallow water held 10,000 (or maybe 10 million) bonefish, each with its tail waving in the pink-gold sun of the late afternoon. For the next three hours of the tide, we cast and caught, cast and caught. After you have been in and among tailing fish, catching one after another, you will understand the almost mystical awe that long-time bonefishers have for this fish in shallow water. One wrong move and you spook hundreds of fish. But if you take your time and fish carefully, you can catch them until you decide to give up, which is one of the most rare and satisfying feelings in all of fishing.

Permit: Wishful thinking

Only one fish may be harder to interest in a fly than a permit — a dead fish. Although permit eat (otherwise how would they grow?), this broad-sided pompano is the most finicky fish when it comes to taking a fly. I have tried and tried with no luck, so I can only imagine what the feeling must be to catch a permit on a fly. Please go catch one and write me all about it so I can fantasize.

In addition to being highly spookable, a feeding permit usually has its head down in the sand, looking for crabs. It concentrates on an area of just a few square feet. An angler's success in getting one to look up from feeding is like a parent's success when trying to get the attention of a teenager watching MTV: impossible.

Permit are found in the same kinds of water and under the same conditions as bonefish. Blistering as the bonefish may be in its initial run, the permit is its equal and then some. Add to this the fact that when a permit turns its body broadside to you, it can really put up some resistance. The result is a fish that many anglers classify as the hardest fight for its size.

For these fish use Crazy Charlies and Del Brown's Crab. The whole game is sight casting. Some fish want the fly put right on their nose. Others need to be led by a foot. You don't know which category a particular permit falls into until your cast lands. Half the time you will guess wrong, and even on the times when you are right, the slightest heavy-handedness in your cast can send Mr. Permit to deep water.

Often, the first things you see on a permit, shown in Figure 11-8, are the black tips of its fins as it cruises in shallow water. When permit flash by in large schools, their subtle gray-green coloration is very visible.

Fly line world record

Del Brown landed a 41-pound, 8-ounce permit on March 13, 1986, off Key West, Florida.

Snook: No schnook

A snook is a funny looking fish. Come to think of it, the word *snook* itself is pretty silly, too. A snook looks like a baby striped bass with shoulder pads. Perhaps this extra heft in the shoulders is what gives this resident of Florida and the Gulf of Mexico such pugnacity when it fights, an experience that I can compare best to the struggle of a great largemouth bass. Although

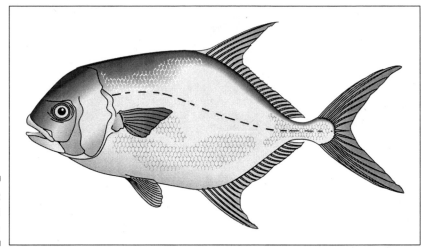

Figure 11-8:
The Atlantic permit.

snook present a fair challenge to the angler, the commercial fisherman has little trouble in harvesting this delicious, white-fleshed fish, which is why it is relatively scarce in places where it was once abundant. I can recall fishing a river on the Atlantic side of Costa Rica and coming upon two Indians in a canoe piled high with snook — maybe 200 fish. These same Indians were out there every day, pulling in a similar haul, so you can imagine how depleted the coastal creeks were becoming.

Thankfully, snook have been protected in recent years in the U.S. and have begun to make a comeback. At night, when they congregate under the lights of bayside docks, the fishing can be unbelievable. By casting a streamer, first at the outside of the group and then further into it, you can take a half-dozen nice fish before you have exhausted the possibilities in any one *pod* (small group of fish). Deceivers, Surf Candy, or flies of that class work well, and as the sky lights up, popping bugs just like the ones you may use for large-mouth bass can provide an hour of memorable action.

Though snook make great eating, they are under so much pressure that I would advise you to take them rarely, as a special treat. By returning them to the water alive, you can do your part to help bring back a classic sport fishery.

Killer gills

Dehook a snook by holding it by the lower lip — just like you would dehook a bass. Do not put your fingers in the gill covers, which are super-sharp.

The snook shown in Figure 11-9 has the bright silver sides and clearly defined lateral line that are typical of this fish.

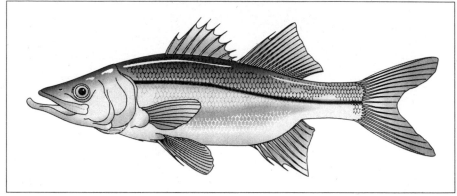

Figure 11-9: The snook, built like a bass designed by John Madden.

Fly line world record

A 30-pound, 4-ounce snook was caught by Rex Garrett on April 23, 1993, off Chokoloskee Island, Florida.

Tarpon: The silver king

The tarpon is a big fish — a very big fish — that can be taken on light tackle in shallow water. It can run forever and leap 10 feet in the air, writhing as it does so. I can't imagine what more anyone could want out of an angling encounter.

Staking a claim to tarpon fame

Tarpon, which are actually a kind of very large herring, have been taken on rod and reel for about 100 years. Claims for having caught the first tarpon on rod and reel pop up in turn-of-the-century sporting literature with the frequency (and "checkupableness") of Elvis sightings. I am partial to the claim of Anthony Dimock, an early and tireless explorer of fishing opportunities in Florida who reportedly subdued the first tarpon with sport fishing tackle in the 1880s. But then I am a fan of any guy who made and lost a couple of fortunes: Each time he was in the pink, he completely gave up Wall Street to become a full-time fisherman. His *Book of the Tarpon* has a remarkable series of photos of his fight with a huge fish — a fight that occurred nearly a century ago.

Although I caught my first two tarpon — both better than 80 pounds each — with a Zebco spincasting outfit (which goes to show that you don't need megabucks worth of tackle to enjoy catching this biggest of game fish encountered on the flats), I prefer them on flies.

A 10- to 12-weight rod is preferred because this fish requires all the force you can muster if you want to land one in less than half an hour. A long fight, in fact *any* fight, with a big tarpon can be very tiring. And the longer you have one on, the greater the chance you have of losing your fish to a shark. This has happened to me, and though exciting in its own way, it is also kind of a bummer: You catch nothing and the tarpon gets eaten. A strong rod quickens the fight in favor of the angler and also lets the angler strike hard and repeatedly in order to drive the hook home.

The great thing about a tarpon in shallow water is that it has nowhere to go but up, and this lack of room leads to a fight marked by thrilling acrobatic leaps. Many experienced anglers are happy just to hook and *jump* a tarpon and then to have it spit out the hook so that they can hook and jump another one.

With tarpon and other really big game fish, you should absolutely hire a guide until you are a real veteran. In addition to everything else (like knowing where the fish are and having the right heavy-duty gear), the experienced guide knows how to tie a super-heavy shock leader with the Bimini Twist knot, a complicated knot that, as far as I can tell, requires the knotter to be able to execute a series of 10 consecutive somersaults and a double Axel from a sitting position with the leader in his mouth.

Tarpon flies are big, usually 4 to 6 inches long and are tied on 3/0 to 5/0 hooks. A variation of the Lefty's Deceiver called a Cockroach is a good tie (throw in some neck hackle and a green or brown collar). You can also use the well-known Apte Tarpon fly.

As shown in Figure 11-10, the tarpon is easily recognizable because of its protruding lower jaw and huge eye. In fact, its Latin name, *Megalops,* means *very big eye.*

Fly line world record

William W. Pate Jr. landed his 188-pound tarpon on May 13, 1982, in Homosassa, Florida. Ten years later, on April 9, 1992, Brian O'Keefe caught a 187-pound, 6-ounce tarpon off Sherboro Island, Sierra Leone, Africa.

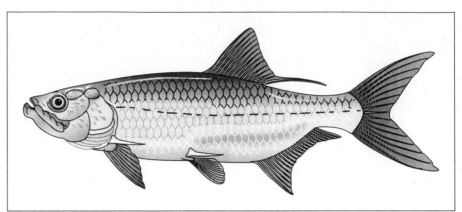

Figure 11-10:
The tarpon. Its large scales look like those of a herring, the family to which the tarpon belongs.

Chapter 12
Saltwater Baits and Flies That Work

In This Chapter

▶ What bait fish saltwater game fish like to eat

▶ Where, when, and how to find bait fish

▶ What flies imitate saltwater bait fish

*I*t is true, as the saying goes, that there are many fish in the sea, but when it comes to bait, if you know a few of the major ones, you will probably be prepared for anything that swims your way. The general rule, in angling, as in business, is "big fish eat little fish."

In saltwater, most bait fish school near the shore, sometimes coming in very close. The big fish are often right behind them, or under them, so you don't necessarily have to go far from shore to get into good fish. Most bait fish swim in schools, and the game fish pursue these schools, sometimes driving the little fish right up to the surface. As with trout fishing, or any fishing for that matter, if you can determine the bait that the game fish are eating, you will have a much better chance of giving the game fish an imitation that will interest them.

Major Saltwater Bait

There are many more bait fish than the ones listed in this chapter. And there are some that I have left out that may be the best bait in your area. West Coasters who live in squid-rich waters will notice that their favorite isn't here. True enough, but this is a good representative sampling of the most important baits that most fly rodders will come across. If I have left one out, I have two pieces of advice:

✔ Try to imitate what is in the water, not what is in this book. Books are good for the big picture, but every piece of water is a little different.

✔ No matter what, you will profit from putting your rod down and observing the action of game fish and their bait. How fast is the bait moving? At what depth? During what tide? These kinds of on-the-spot observations are the bits of knowledge that build up over a lifetime and separate true anglers from people who just happen to own a fishing rod.

Sand eel: No real slime feel

Sand eels (also known as the sand lance, and shown in Figure 12-1) are one of the favorite foods of the striped bass. They are not true eels so they aren't *Alien Resurrection*-level slimy. It is their tube-like bodies and small fins that give them an eel-like look, but they are more kin to silversides and anchovies than eels. So, yes, they aren't awful and slimy.

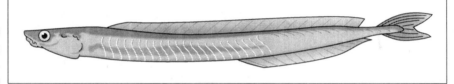

Figure 12-1:
A sand eel.

On the North Atlantic coast, look for these fish to swim in schools in early summer, usually June, particularly at dawn and dusk, in low water. They blend in with the background very well and are hard to pick out. Cast your fly line over them, however, and these nervous little guys will leap out of the water in fright. The sand eel is about 2–3 inches long, with a dark-green back and bright silver sides. You will find them in large schools on sandy beaches, in heavy surf, and in estuaries. At night, they slither into the sand to rest.

When you notice a school of these eels, sink a Snake fly or a Deceiver fly alongside or below the school itself — the fly will look like a straggler, and stragglers get picked off. If you don't see schools, look for bird activity or fish activity on the surface and cast to that. Strip your line in slowly but with a regular jerky action. In a fast current, you can vary the presentation of the fly, letting it drift along, occasionally twitching and drifting.

At night, on calm water, try a surface or subsurface fly with a slow retrieve. A Surf Candy fly works well in this situation, but a Floater Eel fly is also good for this.

Sometimes, you may actually see striper tails sticking straight out of the water. These are bass rooting around in the sand, trying to stir up sand eels. When you've caught nothing all night, this sight is an invitation to you, the fly rodder, to give it one more try. Let your fly sink and strip it slowly — you've got to get it right next to the fish's nose or he won't see it.

Silversides: Ocean-going french fries

The silversides, also called spearing, are a major type of bait fish on both coasts, ranging from Canada to the Caribbean or to Baja. They are usually 4 to 5 inches long and resemble the freshwater shiner, except that they have a bright lateral silver stripe on either side (see Figure 12-2).

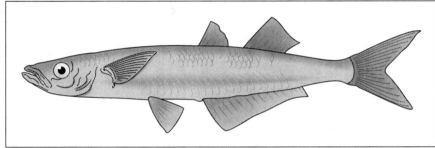

Figure 12-2:
A
silversides.

Silversides can be found all along sandy beaches, especially in the shallows around jetties, and at the mouths of estuaries. When chased by big fish, they often jump on the surface to escape. When you see this activity, don't hesitate. Fire off a cast.

Stripers and bluefish move in on silversides in the surf where they spawn. The best time to fish is at high tide just at daybreak. Bluefish actually herd and corral silversides before attacking large schools during the day. But such attacks are quick. Better, more consistent fishing can be found at night, when silversides mingle in small groups and game fish cruise in search of them.

To fish schools, use a Deceiver fly or a Snake fly in white, black, yellow, or the always fashionable chartreuse. A Surf Candy fly will also do as well. At night, use a floating slider in black. Make full 6 to 12-inch retrieves, twitching the rod tip and creating some jerkiness with your stripping hand. In fast water, let the fly move with the current. In slow water, make an even retrieve with the fly just below the film.

Anchovy: Not just for pizza

The anchovy, also called bay anchovy, rainbait, and greeny (and shown in Figure 12-3), is possibly the most abundant bait fish, serving as a main food for albacore, bonita, and bluefish on the Atlantic Coast, and for Pacific bonita and tuna on the West Coast. The best time for fly fishing with anchovies is in the fall when they congregate in huge, tight schools that are often visible. (Remember that beach scene in *Jaws II* when Chief Brody sees a shadow in the water and starts shooting at it? Probably anchovies.)

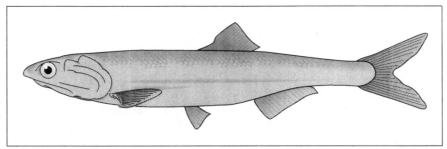

Figure 12-3:
An
anchovy.

Anchovies congregate along beaches and in open water. When there are gazillions of them and it is a calm day, they dimple the surface with a sound that is just like a steady rain. Blues and stripers pin schools of anchovies against the shore and gulp mouthfuls. It is best to get your fly under the school.

Flies $1^1/_2$ to $2^1/_2$ inches in length that match the local appearance of anchovies work best. Try a small epoxy fly, such as a Surf Candy fly or a Goddard's Glass Minnow fly.

Bunker: All in the bait fish family

These largest of the common bait fish are also known as Atlantic Menhaden (which sounds like "Manhattan," where the fish were first discovered by Europeans).

Although it can attain a length of 18 inches, the average bunker, shown in Figure 12-4, is 5 inches long. It has a blue-green back and bright, silvery, flat sides. The bunker migrates from southern U.S. waters along the Atlantic Coast in the spring and spends the summer along beaches as far north as New England, and then heads back south in the fall. When bunkers are on the move, game fish are too, often in hot pursuit.

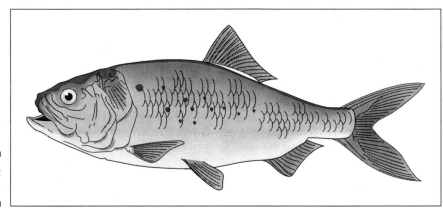

Figure 12-4:
A bunker.

A ripping good time

I was fishing in the rip, off Montauk Point, when a voice came over the radio: "White boat, white boat . . . number 8."

It was a code to designate but not advertise the fishing spots around the point.

"We're on the way," we replied.

Striped bass. Huge posses of them had penned up the bait, driving them through the surf and onto the beach. The bass chomped through the rainbait that were trapped inside the breaker line (the point in the surf where most waves break).

It was perilous water, broken up by jagged boulders. We edged along the backside of a breaking wave, leaving time for one, at most two, long casts. We switched to Clouser's minnows: Their lead heads carried them down into the marauding stripers. Had we stayed with the unweighted albie flies we had on, the flies would have slid along the backs of the striped basses' phalanxes because the stripers were so thick. Each time a striper took, we would back our boat out while we fought our fish. My partner, Gordon Hill, a placid but expert angler was an excellent fishing partner. Given the swells on the ocean, the pounding of the close-breaking waves, the swirling wind, and the furious broken field maneuvers of the bait and ravenous stripers, we had to coordinate our casts, and then, when we hooked up, we had to coordinate our fights, following our fish fore and aft, passing rods around one another.

We caught bass after bass. All except one exceeded the 28-inch limit. These were hefty, strong fish. When we tired of fighting the waves, we retreated 100 yards offshore and caught some more albacore that were busy mopping up the rainbait that hadn't been trapped inshore. Between the bass and albies, a blind cast would yield a 10-pound bluefish. Any one kind of fish would have made for a satisfying day in normal times, but this was no normal day — it was the single most intense day of saltwater fly rodding I have ever had.

Bunker usually hold in the surf and at the mouths of estuaries, but sometimes they swim out to sea, so you have to keep track of their position in case big fish move in to eat them. When blues and stripers are after bunker, they won't even sniff at a small fly. Herein is a bit of trouble: You have to cast big flies for fish taking bunker, and big flies ain't easy to cast.

Use a fly that is about 6 to 9 inches long. Sedatti's Slammer fly and Blanton's Whistler fly are good choices. You won't be able to get them out far. Use an even, smooth stripping action. If you don't want to mess with such big flies (I call them "grandma wigs"), try a largish Deceiver fly and hope for the best.

Cinder worm: On the moon tides

In the spring and summer, these worms have a spawning swarm that attracts game fish just like a mayfly hatch on a trout stream. Hatches generally occur during new or full moons on an outgoing tide. Calm, warm nights are usually primetime, but swarms can occur during the day, peaking from June through July. Worm swarms create game-fish feeding frenzies along the beach. The most common swarming worm, the cinder worm, is usually red, or some combination of red, white and black. Cinder worms, shown in Figure 12-5, are 1 to 4 inches long and swim in wild spirals.

Figure 12-5:
A cinder
worm.

Paul Dixon's Cinder Worm fly is my favorite imitation, but you could also score on a Paolo worm imitation fly that you might have left over from tarpon fishing. In a pinch, a Woolly Bugger will work well, too. Your fly must be heavy enough that it will fall through the swarm, heading nose down. Black is a good color for warm nights, so try a black Muddler fly on the surface. A Snake fly is also good for this bait.

Paolo worm: Small bait, monster fish

Knowing about this worm that never gets bigger than an inch and a half will only do you any good in the Florida Keys, which, I admit, kind of limits you. But the worm hatch is such an amazing thing to hit and affords a great opportunity to experience a soul-stirring tarpon feeding frenzy. It almost boggles the mind that such a teeny worm could summon forth such activity from such big fish . . . but it happens. In May, June, and often on into early July, the extreme low tides of the new moon allow the coral shallows to warm up. The paolo worm, which only lives in coral, gets in a mating mood when this happens, and huge swarms of them will drift out of the coral and float in the tide, looking for and finding mates. This is one of those times and one of those destinations that you have to put on your list and hit at least once in your life.

Worm Fishing 101

Sometimes the experience you gain in one kind of fishing pays off in a completely different angling situation. This point was driven home to me when I was fishing for tarpon during the hatch of the Paolo worm in the Florida Keys. We were literally five minutes from Key West Harbor when the little red worms hatched and 50 acres of water erupted with feeding tarpon. The scene looked like a trout pool filled with fish during a mayfly hatch — the only difference was that these "trout" weighed 100 pounds each.

I was fishing with Keys guide Dave Kesar and John Cole, an ex-commercial fisherman on Long Island who also wrote a number of great fishing books, among them *Striper* and *Tarpon Quest*. Residents of Maine may remember him as the editor of *The Maine Times*.

It was my turn to wield the rod when the hatch (actually a mating swarm) started. I cast and stripped, cast and stripped, getting into a rhythm. It crossed my mind that my little artificial fly might go unnoticed by the feeding fish, but I kept casting. After 10 minutes, John took a turn, and then Dave did. The rod came around to me again. I cast and talked. Dave remarked on a nice boat that was going by. I turned my head to look back, leaving my fly to hang in the current. That was the time, of course, that the tarpon chose to slam my fly.

I tried to set the hook. The tarpon took to the air and broke off.

"Hmm," John said softly (which, in a Down-Easter, passes for hysterical excitement).

I rose to the bait. "Hmm what, John?" I asked.

"The tarpon took your fly at the end of the swing, just the way a salmon would roll and take. I think if we treat this current like a salmon stream and fish it that way, we might be on to something. Anyway, it couldn't hurt," he replied.

I gave John the rod. He cast across the current, *quartering down tide* (that is, casting in diagonally across the tide and in the same direction in which it was flowing).

"Right . . . about . . . there," John said (more to himself than to us). "Whomp — tarpon on!" The fish jumped and broke off. Dave tried next, then me. We hooked a dozen fish — one of them within 10 feet of the boat. When he took to the air, he sprayed us like a Labrador retriever shaking the water off his wet coat.

Though we did not land a single tarpon, I felt privileged to have seen an observant angler at the moment he "invented" a new way to fish for tarpon. (I also liked connecting with the fish.)

Mud crab: A white sand treasure

The mud crab, shown in Figure 12-6, is found in shallow southern U.S. mud flats and has the lethal honor of being a main course for redfish, permit, and bonefish. In currents, it moves along the mucky bottom and then hides as the tide leaves the flat. This crab is about $1^1/_2$ inches wide and is brownish-green with brown-tipped claws. Look along beaches for dead crabs to figure local size and color, but the stand-by pattern is Del Brown's Crab fly. Cast the fly, let it fall and sit on the bottom, and wait. Then jerk it short and let it fall again. Wait again and repeat this motion. Permit and bonefish patterns should sink fast. This is especially important because you will often sight-cast to these fish, and (you hope) they will notice the fly as it sinks past their noses.

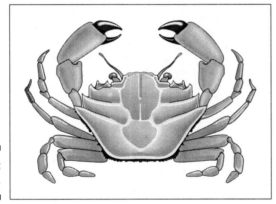

Figure 12-6:
A mud crab.

Let me not leave you with the impression that the crab is of no use in northern U.S. waters, Anywhere that you find crabs, you will also find bait fish that feed on them, notably the striper. Cast a weighted crab onto a white flat that holds stripers at high noon, and you can see one turn and follow your fly for 30 feet before breaking down and gobbling it up.

Shrimp: A great go-to bait

On both coasts of the U.S., shrimp, both shoreshrimp (shown in Figure 12-7) and the common shrimp (shown in Figure 12-8), are eaten by game fish and are of special interest to the fly rodder in shallows and flats, particularly on the edge of deeper water. They swim in open water, in an upward motion, and are sometimes active at night. In spring, small shrimp flow with the tide on shallow flats sometimes clinging to weeds. Weakfish and stripers feed on these shrimp in the shallows of bays, estuaries, and along any shrimp-hospitable bottom.

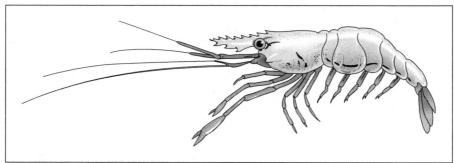

Figure 12-7:
A
shoreshrimp.

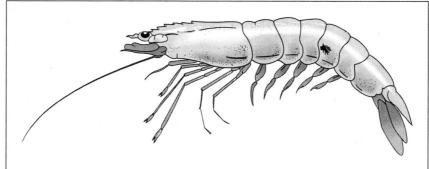

Figure 12-8:
A common
shrimp.

A fly with a tail imitates large shrimp; flies with a flared tail, for example, the Apte Tarpon fly, also work. When shrimp are visible on top, drift a fly along the surface of the water. When fishing a sinking fly, let it drift to the bottom, lift it, and then let it settle. There are many imitation shrimp patterns that are quite good. In the interest of simplicity, remember that a small Clouser's fly looks very shrimpy.

Mullet: Good in the gullet

Mainly found along the mid- and southern-Atlantic waters, the young of the striped mullet, *finger mullet,* are the species most important to fly fishing. When they are on their spawning run, they gather in enormous schools. Tarpon and snook will feed furiously. Redfish are also big mullet fans (when the state of Florida banned the netting of mullet a few years ago, redfish-fishing turned red hot). Finger mullet group along beaches and in estuaries before heading out to sea to mature. Mullet form tight schools when pursued by game fish, and sometimes they leap from the water. They are unmistakable because every fish in a school pokes its rounded snout in the air in an attempt to offer less target to marauding game fish. When you cast a mullet imitation, retrieve it with a steady 8- to 12-inch strip. Use flies 2 to 5 inches long, in white, gray, green, or brown. A mullet is shown in Figure 12-9.

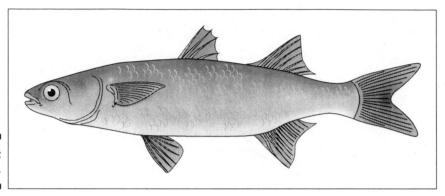

Summing up

Table 12-1 below matches up some of the most common bait fish and the most popular fly rod fish that feed on them. This is not as long a list as you can find, but it is a good all-around guide.

Table 12-1	Fish and Their Food
The Fish	**The Food**
Bluefish	Anchovies, sand eels, silversides, and herring-type bait fish
Stripers	Small herring, silversides, sand eels, bay anchovies, and bunker
False Albacore	Anchovies, silversides, and sand eels
Sea Trout	Shrimp, mullet, and crabs
Weakfish	Sand eels, silversides, anchovies, and shrimp
Atlantic Bonito	Sand eels, silversides, and anchovies
Redfish	Crabs, shrimp, bunker, and mullet
Yellowtail	Anchovies, mackerel, and squid
Spanish Mackerel	Sand eels, anchovies, silversides, and herring
Jacks	Silversides, anchovies, herring, and mullet
Salmon and Sea-run Trout	Sand eels, shrimp, herring, and smelt
Bonefish	Crabs, shrimp, and fish fry
Snook	Crabs, mullet, shrimp, and various bait fish
Permit	Crabs almost exclusively
Shark	Anything that swims

Great Saltwater Flies

Like a lot of my lists, it's just one man's opinion. Still, if you have these flies in your vest or fly box, you can pretty much feel confident that you will have a shot on most anything in the ocean that is fly roddable.

Lefty's Deceiver: A true friend

If these ten saltwater flies were a baseball team, the Deceiver (shown in Figure 12-10) could play almost every position. It works for many, many saltwater fish under a variety of conditions, and it can take big freshwater bass, too.

Thread	Red
Hook	Mustad 34007, size 2 to 3/0
Body	Silver mylar
Hackle	White bucktail, tied in at collar reaching the hook point
Cheek	Mylar strips longer than hook bend
Tail	Four white saddle hackles facing each other

Figure 12-10:
Lefty's
Deceiver.

The Surf Candy: The name says it all

I have always loved this name, Surf Candy (shown in Figure 12-11).

Hook	Mustad 34007, #2 to 2/0
Wing	Pinch a few colored strands of sparkly Ultra Hair onto shank and coat with epoxy — just enough to form a small profile and body 2–4 inches long
Eyes	Decal prismatic eye
Gills	Draw in red slash in gill area (on the epoxy; use permanent ink)
Body	Epoxy applied over the Ultra Hair

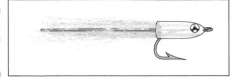

Figure 12-11:
The Surf
Candy.

Snake fly: Eels and then some

Make this fly, shown in Figure 12-12, about 4 or 5 inches long or, better yet, keep your eyes open and imitate the size you see in the natural waters. This is a tie I learned form Lou Tabory's *Guide to Saltwater Baits and Their Imitations,* which I recommend to every beginning saltwater angler. Correction, *every* saltwater angler will profit from owning this book.

Hook	Mustad **34007**, #4 to 2/0
Tail	Ostrich herl
Wing	Marabou (half as long as the tail; tie in below eye)
Head	Deer hair — spin onto the shank and trim into cone shape, flatten underneath

Figure 12-12:
The
Snake fly.

Paul Dixon's Cinder Worm fly: Summertime treat

I trust Paul Dixon's fly fishing wisdom. He catches stripers on this fly, shown in Figure 12-13. I catch stripers on this fly. You will catch stripers on this fly.

Hook	Mustad 34007, #4 to 1/0
Tail	Red marabou
Body	Dub pink Lite Bright (or similar synthetic) for the body and green-black Lite Bright atop the shank to form a small, blunt head

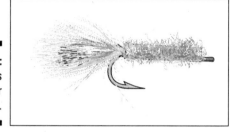

Figure 12-13:
Paul Dixon's
Cinder
Worm.

Del Brown's Crab fly: It fairly screams "eat me"

This is *the* permit fly, believe me, even though I've never caught a permit on a fly. Those who have, love it. Also good for stripers on the flats, this fly is shown in Figure 12-14. It used to be called "Dave's Merkin." Merkin is a word you really don't hear anymore. Got a dictionary?

Hook	Mustad 34007, sizes #1 to 2/0
Tail	Pearl Flashabou with 6 splayed ginger grizzly hackles
Legs	Rubber bands, cut and tied to the shank
Body	Tan and brown yarn
Eyes	Lead eyes

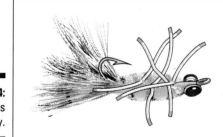

Figure 12-14:
Del Brown's
Crab fly.

The Candyman

Bob Popovics has a terrific restaurant down at the Jersey Shore, Bruce Springsteen land. Bob is a dedicated fly rodder and sometime in the 1970s, he grew very weary of having the bluefish tear up his flies after one or at most two fish. So he started coating his bucktail streamers with epoxy. As he tells the story, the flies were an embarrassing gooey mess. So if your first Surf Candies look sloppy, don't worry, the same thing happened to the inventor. Next thing you know, some of the conventional tackle guys asked Bob to tie up some of his epoxy head flies to use as teasers on their surf rigs. People liked the flies and did well with them. " I knew I was on to something," Popovics said. "After one guy came in and said he caught 24 bluefish, I started to think of it as a real fly even if it was sloppy." The big breakthrough came when Popovics started using Polar Bear hair and, later, synthetics. They gave the flies a translucent sheen that fooled even finicky stripers and super-difficult albacore. By staying at it for years and continuing to think things through, one dedicated angler and fly tier came up with a fly that enriched the sport of thousands. I urge you to keep a similar open mind and to try your new ideas. If they work, stay with them until you cannot improve them any more.

The Clouser's Minnow: The champ

Yes, that's right — Clouser's Minnow again. Just like Lefty's Deceiver, this streamer can play a whole lot of positions on the team. For saltwater, you'll use bigger-sized flies and different-colored patterns. Of course, the classic chartreuse-and-white tie works well. See Chapter 7 for the Clouser's recipe.

Part III
Fly Fishing Essentials

Initial Attempts to Capture Moby Dick

"Good one, Captain Ahab! Remember, don't rush the forward cast!"
That's it, Captain!"

In this part . . .

1 show you as best I can how to cast, find fish, catch fish, land fish, tie knots, get dressed, and all the other important stuff that's involved in fly fishing. Yeah, it's a lot to absorb, but the more you get out and fish, the easier it gets.

Chapter 13

Casting and Presentation: The Heart of the Game

In This Chapter

▶ Making a basic cast

▶ Dealing with wind

▶ Overcoming drag

▶ Feeling the sweet spot in your rod

*O*ne of the great pleasures of the sport of angling is casting a fly well. There is something in our nature that almost hypnotizes us when a cast is well executed. As in most things in angling, I would strongly recommend that you have someone who knows how to fly cast to work with you in the beginning. I can tell you from experience (mine) that if you apply yourself, you can do every cast in this chapter in two days. You won't be perfect at these casts, but you will be fly fishing. After you catch a few fish, you will want to put in those practice hours on the lawn to perfect your cast. A little success is the best encouragement I know.

The Key to Success

Remember how your Mom used to tell you, "It's not what you say, it's the way that you say it?" She may well have been speaking for all the millions of uncaught trout who have ever rejected a fly because it was delivered short of the mark or because it landed like an elephant in ballerina shoes. Presentation of the fly is the single most important skill in fly fishing. To do it well and to do it in all kinds of wind conditions require a few more casts than conventional baitcasting or spinning gear. But if you master the casts, you will be able to catch fish in almost any situation. In the words of famous part-time fly fisher, Martha Stewart, "It's a good thing."

Timing: Not Just for Comedians

When flexed, a fly rod bends into a curve. If your casting stroke moves the line at the right speed, your line will shoot off that curve in a straight path. If you hesitate too long at any point or if the arc that your rod moves through is too big, your line will no longer be able to continue the curve, and your cast will lose shape and power. Figure 13-1 shows a caster with the rod flexed properly. Note how the line smoothly continues the bend in the rod. Also note how the line curls back. This segment of line, shaped like the crook in a candy cane, is called a *loop*.

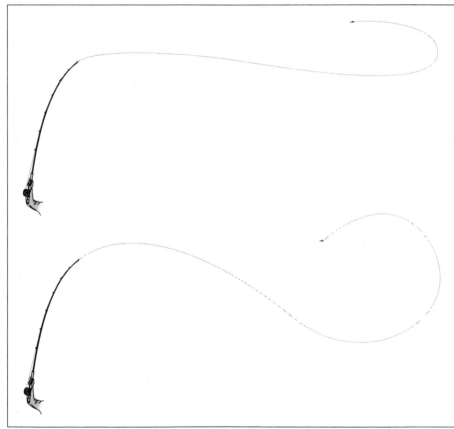

Figure 13-1:
A fly rodder with a nice tight loop and one with a sloppy backcast and a wide loop.

Keep Your Loop Tight

In the same way that a boat's prow cuts through water, the loop cuts through the air. A nice, slim, v-shaped boat will move through the water with little resistance. On the other hand, if you hook up an outboard to a bathtub, you will meet a great deal more resistance to your forward motion. The same is true of the cast. A tight loop will slice through the wind. A wide loop will just hang there like a . . . well, like a *limp noodle.*

How to Hold a Rod

There is basically one right way to hold a fly rod. I say *basically* because I use a different grip for close-in dry fly work. Many people have criticized me for it, but I was happy to see, during the few times that I fished with him, that Lee Wulff did the same thing. Still, I suppose there is something to be said for keeping it simple, so here's the classic grip.

1. **Grasp the rod as if you meant to shake hands with it.**
2. **Now "shake hands" with it.**
3. **Close your fist around the cork grip of the fly rod and keep your thumb extended, right above the reel.**

Figure 13-2 illustrates this classic grip.

The Forward (And Sometimes Sidearm) Cast

I would estimate that 75 percent of all your fly fishing casts will be a version of this basic forward cast. If you are a saltwater fisherman, make that 95 percent.

Figure 13-3 illustrates this fundamental cast.

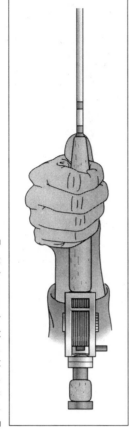

To complete a forward cast, follow these steps:

1. **Pull about 15 feet of line off the reel and pass it through the top guide.**

   Pulling line off the reel is called *stripping*.

2. **Stand sideways, or mostly sideways with your left shoulder in front if you are a rightie. (Lefties, point the right shoulder.)**

3. **Strip another 2 feet of line off the reel and hold it in your left hand.**

4. **With the rod held at a 45-degree angle, crisply lift the line in the air, snapping your wrist upward as you do. Your backstroke should stop when your wrist is at 12:00 (vertical). Momentum will carry your rod and wrist along the arc you have started.**

   The momentum of the line in the air should flex the rod backwards.

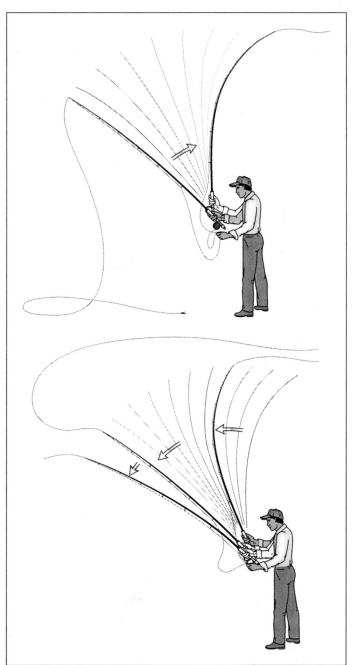

Figure 13-3:
Master the
forward
cast and
you can fly
fish right
away.

5. **As the line straightens out behind you, pause just a second (you will feel a slight pull from the very tip of the rod) and move the rod sharply forward. Again, stop your power stroke dead on 12:00; as you do so, continue to drive forward with your wrist as if you were pushing a thumbtack in.**

6. **When your rod reaches the 45-degree angle, drop the rod tip.**

If you have executed this cast well, you will feel a tug on your left hand, which is holding the extra 2 feet of line that you stripped out in Step 3, before you started the cast. Let go of the line and it will shoot out of your top guide, giving you an extra couple of feet to your cast.

Okay, what did I do wrong?

With 10 feet of line out of the guides, you probably performed a reasonable approximation of a cast. Now, do the same thing with 20 feet of line. Doing so will probably begin to show some of the problems in your beginning cast. Try to keep the line in the air as you execute a few false casts. (A *false cast* is the name given to what you do when you flick the line backward and forward before finally delivering the fly.) A false cast serves two purposes:

- ✔ It lines up your cast with your target.

- ✔ It develops *line speed,* which allows you to work more and more line through the guides so that you can hold it in the air, get up speed, and shoot a longer cast to your target. With good use of line speed, you can easily shoot line to double the distance of your cast.

But before you worry about distance, concentrate on casting mechanics. You need to get out on the lawn with your 15 feet of line and (standing sideways) watch your line in the air as you cast. This will require you to drop your arm for more of a sidearm delivery, but don't worry about that. Sometimes a fishing situation calls for precisely that maneuver.

What am I looking for?

As you watch your line, your goal is to keep the line moving in the air and parallel to the ground. If the line drops below the horizontal, you are moving through too wide an arc. You are forgetting to stop your power stroke at 12:00. I can't emphasize this enough. Stop the rod tip high, and the rod will do the work for you.

If you live in a one-story house of more or less normal dimensions, you can practice your cast by using the roof gutter as a guide, as shown in Figure 13-4. Stand roughly parallel to the roof and try to keep your forward and back casts on a line with the gutter. If you can do this, both your stroke and your timing are correct.

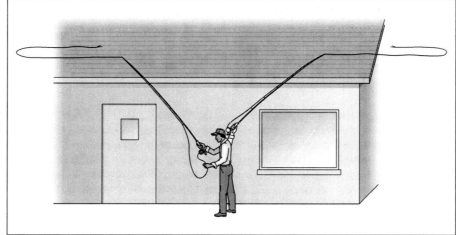

Figure 13-4:
Use your house as a guide when you practice your casts.

Don't be in a hurry

A common casting error is hurrying the cast. Casting a fly is not like shooting a bullet out of a rifle. It's not just one flick of the finger followed by delivery of the fly. In casting a fly, four things have to happen:

- ✔ You transfer muscle power to your rod.
- ✔ Your rod bends and multiplies that force over distance.
- ✔ Your line is set in motion by the action of the rod.
- ✔ The bullwhip action of the fly line develops even more speed as you finish the casting motion.

All of this action takes time. You back cast. The line straightens out and pulls on the rod. You move through the forward cast (or *power stroke*), and the line buggy-whips forward. You shoot line and drop the rod tip.

A beginner's cast often falls apart at a point between the end of the back cast and the beginning of the forward cast (power stroke). You need to pause at this part of the cast until you feel that little tug or, if you are not a great tug feeler, pause until you see the line straighten out.

If you are teaching someone to fly cast for the first time, let your student try a few casts. If he or she just doesn't seem to get the hang of it, you can demonstrate what a good cast feels like. While your student is still gripping the rod, stand behind the student, put your arms around the student's arms, and grasp the rod. Tell your eager fishing pupil to relax and see if he or she can feel how a proper casting stroke should feel. Then execute a series of false casts. Many times, getting the actual feel of a reasonable cast will fill in the gaps that a verbal explanation leaves out.

Now what? Preparing to catch an actual fish!

After the fly is out there, it might interest a fish. If order for you to catch that fish, which is the point of all this, you need to make the transition from casting the fly to fishing the fly. As shown in Figure 13-5, you wrap the thumb around the rod and extend your index finger so that holds the fly line against the rod shaft. This trick insures that anytime a fish hits, you won't have any unwanted slack in the line. Your other hand is now free to pull in line as required. This action is called *stripping in* line.

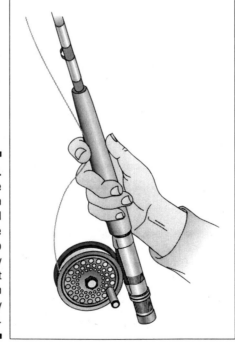

Figure 13-5.
With the right grip on the rod and line, you are ready to fish your fly or fight a fish (hopefully both).

The Backhand: A Great Tool

Looking through all the fishing books out there, the lack of emphasis that is placed on the backhand cast consistently surprises me. I can't for the life of me explain this situation. I think that, after the forward cast, the backhand cast is the most indispensable cast. Because the mechanics of it are so similar to the forward cast, it should be the very next thing you learn after you graduate from Forward Cast 101. To make a backhand cast, follow these steps:

1. **As shown in Figure 13-6, start the backhand cast by facing the target head-on (with just a slight turn to the left for rightie casters, a slight turn to the right for lefties).**

   This position has the effect of pointing your shoulder at the target when you lift your elbow in the casting motion.

2. **Begin by holding the rod out from your body with your arm crossed in front of your chest.**

3. **You execute the backstroke as you snap your wrist up, lifting your line and bending your elbow.**

   You apply power just as you do with a forward cast, described in the preceding section of this chapter. Power is added to the backstroke through an arc of about 45 degrees.

4. **Stop the backstroke when the rod is at 12:00 in the plane of the cast.**

   Your elbow is raised, and your forearm points backward.

5. **As the line straightens out or you feel a slight tug, begin the power stroke and make a quick snap through a 45-degree arc.**

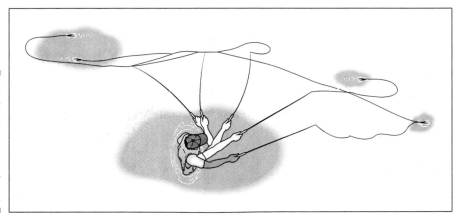

Figure 13-6:
The body mechanics of the backhand cast often make for accuracy.

This is a very powerful cast, almost as efficient as the forward cast. I use it when I find that a crosswind is driving my cast into my back or my hat. It is also great for two people fishing in a boat. If both of you are righties, the angler in the stern can throw a backhand cast while the angler in the bow uses an overhead cast. You are much less likely to get tangled, and the angler in the stern is much less likely to slam a hook into the angler in the bow.

The Roll Cast

Sometimes, you may not have any room at all for a back cast, but a nice fish is within 20 feet of you. The roll cast was designed for this situation. The roll cast is also the favorite method for picking up a fly after you fish out a cast. This cast relies on the surface tension of the water to *load up* (or bend) your rod, so I suggest that you try using this cast in a stream (there ain't much surface tension on a lawn). If you want to make sure that you have all the pieces of this cast together before venturing into the water, go ahead and try it on the land, but then try it on the water, as shown in Figure 13-7.

To execute a roll cast, follow these steps:

1. **Use any cast to get about 20 feet of line out.**

   While standing in a stream, cast downstream. On a lake, the cast's direction doesn't matter.

2. **Start with the rod at about a 45-degree angle and with your arm raised.**

3. **Begin your backstroke, which will pull the line toward you.**

   The line shouldn't completely leave the surface of the water because the resistance that is caused by the surface tension of the water causes the rod to flex and load up (bend your rod).

4. **Push the rod forward and snap your wrist at the end of your stroke.**

5. **Point the rod at your target and shoot the line toward it.**

   The movement isn't exactly like a clock pendulum, but it helps to think of one when interpreting the explanation here into an actual cast on the water.

Figure 13-7:
The roll
cast.

The Backwards Cast

Say you have a strong wind at your back (which is going to happen pretty frequently). You will have difficulty developing any momentum or your back-cast. The simple solution is to turn and face into the wind, making an ally out of an enemy. Figure 13-8 illustrates the way to use the wind with the backwards cast. (By the way, *backwards cast* is my term. I am not sure whether a commonly accepted term for this cast exists.)

Figure 13-8:
A backwards cast may be the only way the wind will let you fish.

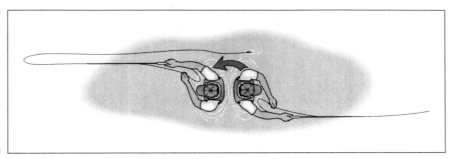

To execute a backwards cast, follow these steps:

1. **With the wind at your back, face the target.**

2. **Twist around and face *into* the wind.**

3. **Begin false casting as you would for a normal forward cast.**

   The only adjustment you need to make for the wind is to drive the forward stroke *down*.

4. **After one or two false casts, twist your head around to see what you are doing and send the backcast toward the target.**

5. **The wind will carry the backcast toward the target.**

Note: This cast is good up to about 40 feet. After that distance, I find that you don't have much of a chance. This cast is also not meant for precision placement. Instead, it can get to the fish in the general area that you want. After that, you have to work the fly to fish it properly.

Wind: Deal with It

The wind seems to blow *all* the time in two places. One of these places is Montana, and the other is the ocean. Although this is a very slight exaggeration, it remains true that if you want to fish in the mountains or by the sea, wind is your semi-constant companion. You may encounter days and weeks when it blows all the time. If you are on your once-a-year fishing trip, you need to deal with it or you won't fish. Many times, you can reposition yourself so that you can work with the wind. But there are times when the wind is blowing in your face and you need to cast into it to catch a fish. The basic rule here is "backcast high — forward cast low," as shown in Figure 13-9.

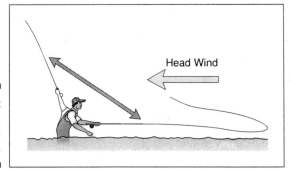

Figure 13-9:
Working
with the
wind.

To cast into headwinds, follow these steps:

1. **Position yourself for a normal forward cast, facing the target.**

2. **Toss your backcast high in the air so that the wind picks it up and straightens it.**

3. **Rather than trying to achieve distance by casting into the teeth of the wind, drive your forward cast *down*.**

   In really strong wind, think of casting straight at your feet. The line will hit the water, and about 20 feet of loop will unroll. This is a good enough cast to catch a bonefish or good enough to take trout when they are keyed in on grasshoppers.

The Steeple Cast

You are walking along the bank of a river or bass pond. You see a fish feeding 20 feet from shore. Not a difficult cast. The only problem is that reeds at least 8 feet tall are at your back. You cannot get off a normal back-cast. The steeple cast often works in this case.

1. **With the reeds (or trees or rocks) at your back, toss your backcast straight into the air and just a little bit to the rear.**

   When the line straightens out, you will feel a slight tug. Because of the force of gravity, this tug will be less than the tug you would feel if you had completed a normal backcast. Still, it will be enough to flex the rod.

2. **Come forward with a normal forward power stroke, "pushing the thumbtack" in at the end of the cast.**

When I am out in the field in the fall, hunting for grouse, I will often come upon a particularly "grousey" spot. Before I put a bird up, I look around to see where the bird has best chance of flying in the clear. That way, when the bird flushes, I have a better chance of staying on him and getting off a shot. You would do well to think of your backcast in the same way. Everybody concentrates on the fish in front, which is good. But if you can't backcast, you aren't going to get the fish. It pays to keep checking what's in back of you and to plan where your backcast is going to go. On a small stream, planning your backcast is the most important part of angling. If you don't, you may spend the whole day untangling your tackle from trees and shrubs.

Bouncing Under a Limb

In the heat of the day, any bass that has a choice is going to rest in the shade. Nice for the bass, but tough for the fly rodder. I have an unorthodox way of bouncing a fly, bass bug, or streamer under an overhanging branch. I find that my technique works better than sidearm casting because, for some reason that I have never been able to figure out, the mechanics of a sidearm cast are such that some part of your casting stroke is going to sneak above the horizontal, and your fly is going to snag on a branch.

A bounce cast calls for a forceful "pushing in the thumbtack" motion at the end of the cast.

1. **Position yourself for a normal forward cast.**

2. **Execute a normal forward casting motion but direct it so that the front of the loop hits the water just a little bit short of the limb or right under it.**

3. **As the loop hits the water, crisply "push in the thumbtack."**

   The line will unroll under the limb, and your fly will bounce into the fishing zone.

The Double Haul

Distance doth not a fly caster make. I keep telling myself this; but like most fly rodders, I like to cast to the limits of my ability and then some. This is not great angling form. The longer the distance, the harder it is to strike properly and set the hook. However, there are times — on big rivers, by a lake, or in saltwater — when the distance caster will outfish everybody else. The technique is called *double hauling* because you "haul" on the line twice during a cast. This adds power to your cast, and also aids in handling wind.

If you want to throw a fly for serious distance, you need to learn how to double haul. This technique is one of those things that you *definitely* won't master from a book. And if you are a beginner, you probably won't learn it until you have the forward cast well under control. Double hauling is one of those things on which many anglers will give you advice, until one day a light bulb goes off and you say, "Now I get it!"

Let me offer you a few hints. First, the principle involved: The fly rod, no matter what cast you try, uses the flex of the rod to develop line speed. The faster the line speed, the further the cast goes. What you are doing when you double haul is adding extra speed to your line — not by moving the rod faster, which would muscle the cast —but by pulling on the line and moving the line faster, as shown in Figure 13-10.

To execute the double haul, follow these steps:

1. **Strip about 15 feet more line off your reel than you normally would and then lay out a normal cast.**

2. **With the line resting on the lawn (or water), lean forward before you start the pickup for the double haul and grab the line just behind the nearest guide.**

   Righties grab the line with the left hand; lefties grab the line with the right hand.

3. **As you lift the line with your backcast, pull sharply on the line in your hand.**

   If you continue this motion all through the power stroke of the back-cast, your stripping arm will travel through approximately 6 feet of distance. This travel adds tremendously to line speed because it shortens the line, allowing the rod to load with just the right amount of line.

   As the backcast unrolls, the rod pulls some of the extra line from your hand and the extra line *shoots* backward, maintaining line speed.

4. **Allow your casting arm to drift back as the backcast unrolls.**

5. **Just before you begin the forward cast, reach with your line hand and grab the line near the first guide.**

6. **Begin the final power stroke and pull on the line in a long, sweeping motion.**

7. **Release the line and allow it to shoot forward with your cast.**

Figure 13-10:
The double
haul
separates
the veteran
from the
newcomer.

When you hit one of these casts right, you will know it. As with a baseball bat or a golf club, there is a *sweet spot* in your rod where it performs optimally. You will feel line being pulled from your hand. When I am saltwater fishing, which is when I use the double haul the most, I love the feel of reserve power at the end of the cast. The line slaps the rod and gives one last pull as the fly reaches its destination. Knowing that you have power to spare is always nice. This reserve power shouldn't stop you from approaching as near to a fish as you can before you cast. Double haul only when you must.

The Water Haul

I find that this is a cast that I use when I want to get distance without a lot of false casting. For the pickup, it relies on the same principle of surface tension that works for you in the roll cast. For the forward cast it requires the same kind of haul on the forward cast that you just learned in the double haul. Say you are fishing about 40 feet of line. You make your cast. You get about 10 feet of drag-free float (or 10 feet of stripping if you are fishing a streamer). Instead of continuing to strip the line over water that you have already fished, or water that you know is dead, you can use the water haul to load up the rod and shoot line. Instead of picking your line up crisply from the water, drag it along for just a bit to put some bend in the rod. The resistance of the water loads up the rod, you give a single haul on the back-cast and then shoot line right back where you want it to be.

Drag: It's a Major Drag

Now that you have an idea of the mechanics of the major casts, it's a good time to consider the problem of *drag*. After you understand drag and how to avoid it, you will understand the principles behind the casts that follow. Pay attention. You could have the best casting form in the world, but if you have drag on your fly, you will catch nothing.

When a natural fly (one that is alive or was living) floats downstream, it moves at the speed of the current. Something that moves at a much different speed does not look natural; and if it does not look natural, fish are going to pass it up.

Here's how drag happens: Say that fish are rising, as they often do, up against the shore, and you are standing in midstream, where the water is moving more swiftly. You present a dry fly to a rising fish with an upstream forward cast. For a few feet, you get a nice drag-free float. However, very

Great on the flats

As I read this, I think I may have given the backwards cast a bit of bum rap, treating it as a clumsy compromise. In fact, when fishing on the flats, it is often a more precise tool that can be your only way of hooking a cruising tarpon or striped bass. Say you are a right-handed caster approaching a good fish that is moving from left to right about 50 feet in front of you. You let go a nice cast, fish it out, and don't interest the fish which by now has moved to your right. If you turn completely around, false cast and then let the fly go, you will in all likelihood have missed your shot. However, if you use a water haul to pick up your cast, you can quickly shoot line backwards (no false casting) and still have a shot at your fish.

soon the faster midstream current starts to put a belly in your relatively thick fly line, finally pulling it across current. Back in the fishing zone, where your fly is, this current action has the effect of whiplashing your fly across the surface. The result is that your fly is moving in a direction that a natural never moves in, and it is moving at an unnatural speed. This is drag. Your chances of catching a trout are as close to absolute zero as anything ever gets in this uncertain world.

What you need is a way to cast your fly so that a trout sees it as a living insect (in other words, without drag). The following casting maneuver is designed to do just that. You will come up with some of your own casts as you follow the cardinal rule: Think about what is happening at the end of your line; think how it looks to the fish.

The Reach Cast

From one bank to another, any number of factors can affect the speed and direction of the flow of a river. Next to the bank, it is slower than it is in midstream. A rock or log may affect the flow. Underwater weed beds work in similar fashion to redirect and retard the flow of a river. Because of these factors, the fly caster has to deal with a number of varying speeds of current between rod and fly. To deal with these situations, the reach cast is designed to give your fly a float that looks convincing rather than dragging the fly at an unnatural speed.

As shown in Figure 13-11, the angler is in the middle of a swift-flowing river, and the trout is rising in the slower-moving current near the bank. The reach cast puts the line *upstream* from the fish so that when the fly is in the eating zone of the trout, the line has no slack and no drag.

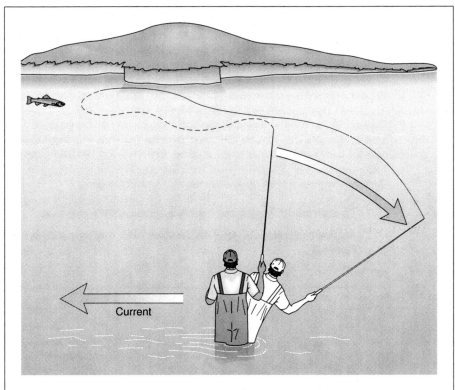

Current

Figure 13-11:
A reach
cast gets
your fly in
the feeding
zone
without
drag.

To execute a reach cast, follow these steps:

1. **Complete a forward cast up through the end of the power stroke.**

2. **Instead of dropping the rod tip straight down, move as far up current as you can while bending from the waist and reaching across your body with your arm.**

This cast can give you a good 6 to 8 feet of drag-free float before drag sets in. For very finicky and spooky trout, this cast also has the advantage of presenting the fly *before* the trout sees the leader. In ultra-calm, ultra-clear conditions, this cast may be your only way of deceiving a trout.

You can combine the reach cast with any of the other casts described in this chapter. These combined casts will be a little more contorted than the forward reach cast; but when necessity calls, you will figure a way to try your own combinations. Combining these casts takes a great deal of body English, but after a good amount of casting, you will learn how your body works in conjunction with the action of your rod and your casting arm.

The Pile Cast: Lots of Loops

If you execute a very crisp forward cast and don't drop your rod tip immediately, the result will be that the fly comes to a dead stop in mid-air and flexes the rod a little bit. The rod then springs forward and back a few times, transmitting this same motion to the line and leader. The result is a bunch of S-curves that record the back-and-forth motion of the rod, as shown in Figure 13-12. Every one of these little loops has to be pushed forward with the motion of the stream before drag sets in. This is a very delicate cast that works well with skittish trout in slow water or for getting those few necessary seconds of drag-free float that are usually all you need to entice a trout lurking behind a rock in faster-moving pocket water.

1. **To execute this cast start with a normal forward cast.**

2. **As the line uncurls, stop its motion with a slight pull backwards on the rod.**

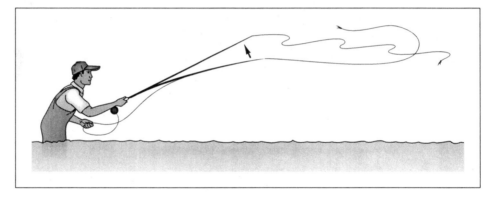

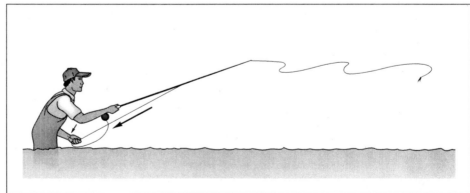

Figure 13-12:
The pile
cast.

3. **As the cast completely straightens out, the combination of the line pulling forward and your slight pull acting as a break will create a series of S-curves.**

4. **Drop the rod tip, allowing the line to fall onto the water, and fish as you would a normal upstream cast.**

Mending: A Must-Learn Technique

Perhaps the most common technique for extending a drag-free float is the *mend*. If you have seen kids playing jump rope, this is pretty much what you are doing with a fishing pole. The mend allows you to get more of your line upstream after the cast has landed on the water. It is one of the most basic of line-handling techniques and it requires a little bit of touch to execute properly, but it is well within the realm of the possible for the beginner.

1. **Lay out a normal forward cast.**

2. **After the line is on the water flip as much line as you can upstream. Take care not to flip the leader as well. Don't make the flip of the line too crisp or speedy — just give it a little oomph. Really, all you are doing is using your rod to draw a half circle in the air.**

Keeping a Dry Fly Dry (Or at Least Floating)

The whole idea of a dry fly is that it floats on the surface just like a natural fly. But fur and feathers and other fly-making materials have a tendency to get waterlogged and sink through the surface tension (no surprise here). When you consider the weight of the hook, too, you are dealing with something that naturally wants to sink after a while. So you have to do something to help the fly float. You can do three things to give your fly a fighting floating chance:

✔ **Use a floatant:** Some floatants are gloppy and some are liquid, but all floatants are designed to keep the fly on top of the water's surface film. You don't need to heap floatant on, but you should use it. I find that rubbing the stuff between my thumb and forefinger and then rubbing my fingers on the fly avoids saddling my fly with a large gob of goo on top.

✔ **Use a drying substance:** Also useful are commercial powders that work on the same drying-out, or *desiccant,* principle as cat litter. Use a commercial desiccant powder after you catch a fish, when the fly is wet and slimy, or when your fly starts to sink prematurely. Simply take the fly — no need to clip it off the leader — and put it in the desiccant bottle; then close the bottle and shake it. When you take the fly out, it is covered with white power. Blow off the loose powder. Give your fly a few false casts to remove any residual powder and start fishing again.

✔ **Use the air:** Sometimes you run out of floatants and desiccants, or your floatant may have fallen out of your vest or you just plain forgot it. In these cases, swishing the fly in the air with a few crisp false casts usually dries out all but the most waterlogged fly for a reasonable float. In heavy, choppy, water, however, you are simply not going to get much of a float without using a floatant or a desiccant.

False Casting: The Awful Truth

The act of waving your line back and forth a few times to generate line speed is known as the *false cast.* Everybody false casts and pretty nearly everybody false casts too much. In saltwater fishing, the extra 2 or 3 seconds that it takes for one more false cast will, without doubt, spell the difference between having a shot at a moving fish and having no chance at all. On a trout stream, many anglers false cast a half dozen times before dropping the fly. Don't do it. You will not catch many fish with your fly in the air. My advice: Count the number of times you are false casting and cut it in half. You may not think the fly is ready to go, but trust me, 90 percent of the time, it is.

A Great Old-Timer

It may take some time for you to get the finesse of dry-fly fishing down, but *anyone* can catch a fish with a downstream wet-fly cast. This is the way to cover a lot of water and to get into a pleasant rhythm. You cast at an angle of about 45 degrees more downstream than the bank. The fly will move through the water, usually sinking a little bit. In the last little part of the arc, it will rise to the surface just like a nymph about to hatch. This is the killing zone when you need to be ready for a strike. When you see nothing happening in the way of surface activity, this is a terrific way to find trout or bass. You cast a few times, take a few steps downstream and cast some more. As a bonus, you are not fighting current to move upstream as you often do when fishing a dry fly upstream. You will often hear this technique referred to as a *quarter cast downstream.*

GEAR

Good for wine stains, baby barf, and trout flies

Many commercial floatants were designed specifically for trout flies. Scotchguard wasn't designed for trout flies, but it really works well as a floatant, especially when you forget your regular floatant and are nowhere near a tackle shop but there's a hardware store or someone's garage nearby.

The Stripping Basket

In the 1960s, the otherwise forgettable film, *Man's Favorite Sport*, showed Doris Day and Paula Prentiss getting Rock Hudson a complete fishing outfit. With inflatable waders and a real doofus hat, Rock could not have possibly looked dorkier, except with the addition of a stripping basket, but stripping baskets weren't around in those days.

A *stripping basket* is a basket that an angler ties around his or her waist. When casting long distances from a boat, jetty, or shore, a stripping basket, which stores your stripped-in line in one safe spot, can keep your line from getting tangled, falling under a rock, or getting swept out by the surge of the waves. What could be worse than walking around with something that looks like a Rubbermaid dish drainer tied to your waist? How about not catching fish?!

Using a stripping basket makes the two-handed retrieve practical. When you need to imitate fast-moving bait fish, this retrieve is a great technique to have in your bag of tricks.

To execute the two-handed retrieve, follow these steps:

1. **After laying out your cast, place the rod in the crook of your underarm.**

2. **Now, with your two free hands, pull in line hand-over-hand for a rapid retrieve.**

   This hand-over-hand action is as fast as anything you can do with conventional tackle.

3. **When a fish takes, righties strike with your left hand and raise the rod in your right hand. (Lefties do the reverse.)**

   This double-barreled maneuver drives the hook home effectively.

Fish Near, Then Far

Everyone likes to cast as far as he or she can. This feat can really impress your friends. The fish, however, couldn't care less. All the fish cares about is this: "Does that thing with a hook attached to it look like food that I want to eat?" If that thing with the hook does look like edible food, you want to make sure that you have done nothing else to put the fish on its guard, so disturb as little water as possible. The best way to tackle a stretch of water is to fish the water that is nearest to you and to fish progressively further with each cast. If you do it the other way round, any fish that is close in is going to have been through a great deal of distracting commotion by the time that you are ready to cast to him.

Fish the clock

In keeping with the last hint, *fishing the clock* is a way to fish the water methodically and to get the most out of each position. Say you are standing in a stream, prospecting for trout with a dry fly. Before you slap your line on the water at the most upstream position, you can work you way up to it and cover many possible trout holding spots (or *lies*) in between. You begin by casting along an angle that is *downstream*. Fish out that cast and then angle your next cast a little more *upstream*. In this way, your fly is in prime fishing water for about a half dozen casting angles rather than just one. The same goes for the wet-fly fisherman who casts downstream. First, carve out a pie-shaped wedge and fish that, starting more closely in, then casting progressively farther away.

The boat clock

When sight-fishing with a friend or a guide, use the clock system to target casts, just like in the old World War II movies when the pilot says, "Bandits at two o'clock high." Your guide, who is usually positioned a little bit higher than you, will often see fish before you do and will say something like, "Redfish, three o'clock." Figure 13-13 shows what all guides everywhere mean when they call out an hour on the clock to indicate fish.

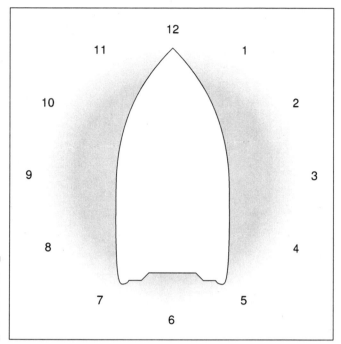

Figure 13-13:
Fishing the
clock in
a boat.

Chapter 14

The Right Time and the Right Place

Game fish, as a group, are predictable creatures although the particular fish you are fishing for may break all the rules. They will return to the same spot during the same tide or they will rise to a mayfly hatch same time every day. Do they do this in order to make life easier for the angler? Not really. They do it because that's when the food is there, and that's when you need to be there with your fly rod. Knowing *where* the fish are and *when* they are there is as important a lesson as any. Because if the fish aren't there, it stands to reason that you aren't going to catch any.

In the Zone

All animals that hunt — whether they are lions, humans, or striped bass — hunt the zone known as *the edge*. This edge can be where deep water rises to shallow, where fast current meets slow, or where grassland meets water hole. It is the place where prey lose their caution and temporarily leave the safety of their lairs for food or water (or sometimes, mates). They momentarily lose their sense of caution. Predators know this and they lie in wait until their prey is exposed. Then they strike.

As an angler, a kind of predator, you will seek out your prey in those areas where they forsake security in pursuit of their basic drives. The more food around for your prey — the fish — the easier it is for you to approach that fish.

Whatever fish you fish for, the principles in this little drama are repeated over and over without fail: The angler offers something that looks like food to the fish. Fish bites. Angler hooks fish.

Going with the flow

The basic fact of life in a river or stream is moving water. Food is carried along by the current. Bait fish dart out into the current while seeking bugs, worms, and the like. Game fish move out into the current to eat the same things the bait fish eat (and they eat the bait fish, too). You should look for those places that provide space for predators to securely hang out but are also close to the food being carried on the watery conveyor belt of the stream.

Riffle, pool, riffle

A normal free-stone river (a *free-stone river,* by the way, means what it says: a river with a great number of stones lying around) is made up of two areas:

- **Riffles:** Rocky areas with fast-moving water
- **Pools:** Deeper areas where the current slows

In trying to visualize a free-stone river, think of a typical, small mountain river with boulders and rocks (you can also call this a free-stone *stream* — streams are really just small rivers).

Another kind of stream is the *spring creek,* which, as its name implies, rises from a subterranean source. It is usually more gentle and slow-moving than a free-stone river and it usually has weed beds and undercut banks.

As illustrated in Figure 14-1, a typical riffle pool system has a number of likely places for game fish, particularly bass and trout.

1. **The riffle.** In the riffle, rocks break up the current flow. Water gets more oxygen from this turbulence and provides a rich habitat ground for insects and other aquatic life. Game fish hang out in the lee of the current; that is, behind or directly in front of rocks or at the margins of the streambed where the current slows and undercut banks may offer shelter. In these conditions, with food zipping by, fish tend to strike quickly at anything that looks like food. You'll need bushy, very floatworthy flies. Exact imitation is not as important as it is in slower water.

2. **The head of the pool.** As the current rushes into the head of the pool, it often digs a nice hole. Fish will hold in the depths and rise to take the food which flows through the funnel that you typically find at the entry to a pool in a classic riffle-pool system. Typically the current will enter in a V shape. At the outside edges of the V, you can also prospect for fish. (They often show themselves as they feed on floating food.)

3. **Deadfalls, logs, rocks, debris.** Anything that obstructs the current offers a place for a predator to lie in wait. Don't forget the "pillow" of water on the upstream side of a boulder.

4. **The middle of the pool.** This is usually the place where the current is slowest. In many rivers, it is also the place where the fishing is the slowest. You will occasionally find big fish in this part of the pool, but for the most part, little current means little edge (which means not-so-great fishing). If the current is clipping along, however, try your luck in this area. You never know.

5. **Eddies.** The *hydrodynamics* of some pools — that is, the physics of the water flow as it interacts with the structure of the pool — creates calm areas that collect many of the dead insects and shellfish that float downstream. The pickings are easy, so in the case of trout, you will see very gentle feeding activity. A delicate casting hand and a quiet approach can reward you with a nice fish. For some reason, rainbows are partial to the scum line that often forms in an eddy.

6. **Tributaries.** Where water from a smaller stream enters the larger stream, it is usually cooler and more oxygen-rich. You may well find game fish just downstream of the outlet of a feeder stream (the place where a tributary flows into a larger body of water). As far as the local fish are concerned, they are at the head of a pool, where a current brings them a great deal of food.

7. **Weed beds.** You usually find these structures in slower streams and spring creeks. Weeds offer shelter, and they are often rich in fish food, such as freshwater shrimp and insects of all types. Predator fish hang out in or near weeds because it puts them conveniently close to their food supply.

8. **Spring holes.** Subsurface springs beneath rivers and creeks bring cool water in the hot weather and warmer water in the cold weather. Often, the water temperature of a spring is close to the optimum for fish activity. Wherever you find an underwater spring, you may find nice fish. How do you know where a subsurface spring is? Someone tells you, or you figure it out after fishing a particular stretch of stream in all conditions. Say it's the middle of a heat wave in the summer, and you catch a few fish at a particular spot in the depths of a pool. The odds are you have hit upon the location of a spring hole. Mark it by taking note of natural landmarks — trees and boulders — and remember it next year when heat strikes again.

9. **Shade.** Bankside trees offer shade, a thing that fish seek on bright sunny days. Shade also offers fish some protection from the view of predatory eagles and ospreys.

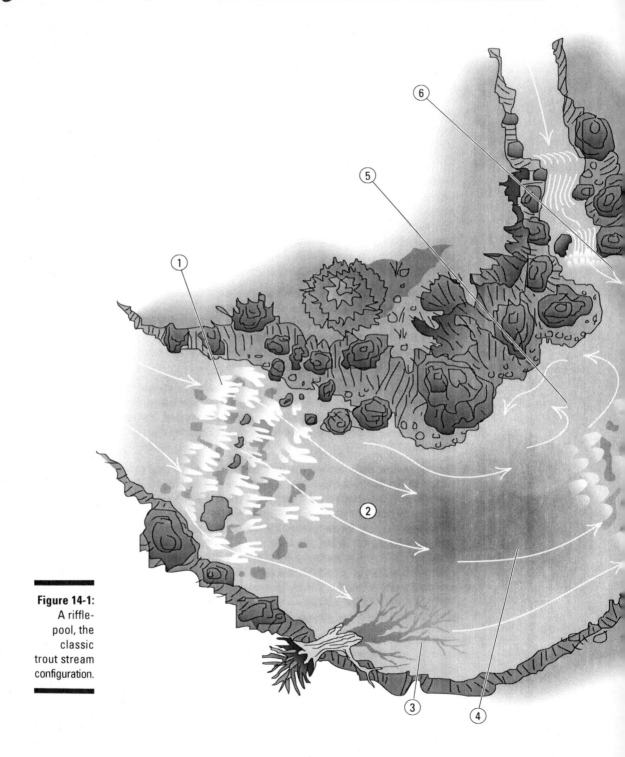

Figure 14-1:
A riffle-
pool, the
classic
trout stream
configuration.

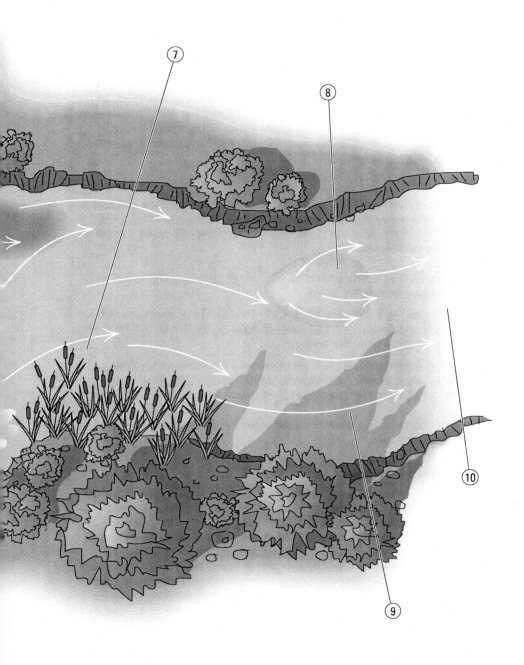

Bankside trees and shrubs offer rich habitat for all kinds of insects. As mentioned in Chapter 5, aquatic insects hatch out of the water and often spend a day or two in the trees and shrubs before returning to mate over the water. So if you see mayflies in the shrubs during the day, look for a spinner fall nearby at night. Also, trees and bushes that are in bloom attract non-aquatic insects that sometimes find their way into the water.

10. **The tail.** As the water leaves the pool to enter another riffle, it often shallows out and may get very glassy and slick. When a great deal of insect activity takes place, game fish often venture into this shallow water and slash about, which makes for tricky fishing, and the fish can be spooky (but also exciting in a special way). I can't really describe this situation other than to say that the water looks pregnant with the possibility of good fishing.

Down by the river

The first time you step into a huge river like the Yellowstone, you will find so much fishy-looking water that you really won't know where to start. I have found that the best thing to do in these cases is to think of a really big river as a bunch of smaller rivers.

- ✔ If there is an island in the middle of a big river, treat each channel as if it were a separate, smaller river.

- ✔ Treat the island as if it were a big rock in the middle of a stream. Fish will hang just upstream and just downstream of the island, where there is some protection from the current.

- ✔ If you are fishing from the bank and a current line (the edge of the current) is about 20 feet out from the bank, fish the 20 feet of river between the current and the bank as a separate stream.

By breaking the big problem down into separate parts, you tackle the task at hand in manageable bites.

Dead water: Keep moving

When fishing a lazy river with big bends and slow deep pools (the Delaware River in New York State is one such river and almost any Ozark stream would be another), remember that trout and bass concentrate in areas where there is at least some current. Those long, slow, mid-pool stretches look like inviting spots to fish, but nine times out of ten — make that 99 million times out of 99 million and one — you will not catch anything in this kind of water. If you are floating downstream in a boat or canoe, pass such a pool by and save your casting for water that fits the fish-holding profile (unless, of course, you actually see a fish).

Catastrophic drift — no danger to the angler

Sometimes the insect or shellfish population can outgrow the capacity of a particular weed bed. When this happens, whole battalions of little organisms abandon their native weed pocket and take to the current in search of new food. This activity is known as *catastrophic drift.* If this happens while you are on the stream, you will be treated to a major feeding frenzy. The upside is that the fish are feeding like crazy. The downside is, with so much food in the water, the odds aren't great they will take whatever you are throwing at them. Still, a feeding frenzy brought about by catastrophic drift provides a unique fishing opportunity.

Lakes and reservoirs

Lakes and reservoirs are both standing bodies of water with a few important differences for the angler:

- ✔ A reservoir is a more recent creation than a lake. (After all, most lakes have been around since the last Ice Age, but reservoirs are man-made and are relatively recent creations.) Reservoirs haven't had time to evolve all the subtle habitat features of a good old-fashioned lake.

- ✔ Reservoirs can have their level raised or lowered and are, therefore, subject to tremendous fluctuations in depth. Not only does this fluctuation have the obvious effect of determining how much water is available for the fish to hang out in, it also means that significant parts of the reservoir bottom can dry out in periods of low water, affecting the long-term survival of shallow-water bait fish, insects, shellfish, and aquatic vegetation.

Reading a fishing hole

I promise that I won't give you a diagram full of little fish marks and 30 different kinds of structures to look for. If you have ever read a how-to fishing book before, you know what I am talking about. "Fish for walleye on drop-offs. Try bass over gravely bottoms. Look for northerns by weedy shores." Such suggestions are all true; but collectively, they are a big chunk to swallow in one gulp.

It's much better, I think, to remember the idea of *the edge* (mentioned earlier in this chapter in the section titled "In the Zone"). Look for current, changes in depth, shelter, or anything that breaks up the uniform character of the water. When you discover an edge, realize that game fish and bait fish have to deal with it in various ways. Some fish feed on one side of it. Some lurk on the other side.

I guess this whole concept does require a picture after all, but I'll keep it simple.

Figure 14-2 represents a lake that exists nowhere but in a fishing book. It has a little bit of everything that you might find in any lake from the Arctic Circle to Patagonia.

1. **Inlets and outlets:** Wherever water flows into or out of a lake, bait follows, and game fish concentrate to feed.

2. **Drop-offs:** Wherever the structure goes from shallow to deeper, you may find game fish lurking in water that is in a comfortable temperature zone. This set of circumstances usually puts game fish *under* bait fish (which they can ambush from below).

3. **Weed beds:** Weeds can be a haven for bait fish, a breeding ground for crustaceans and insects, and because of this, a magnet for game fish. Weed beds also offer a place for game fish to hide from prey and predators.

4. **Rocky points:** Rocky points can block the wind, divert a current, offer shade, and the like. In other words, rocky points provide classic edges.

5. **Shade:** Trees on the banks and lily pads in the shallows both offer shade (which affects water temperature). Shade also affects the view of dangerous predators, like herons and raccoons, and therefore limits their ability to prey on game fish.

6. **Underwater stuff:** Sunken islands, drowned trees, and fallen trees all offer structure which translates into lots of hiding places for predators and habitat for bait.

TIP

Dog day afternoons

In the summer, when rivers and streams drop, the trout go deep and sometimes the fishing is a little slow. Take this downtime as an opportunity, leave the rod in the car, and go wading with a pad and pencil. You don't have to be an artist or map maker — all you have to do is be able to scribble your way to making a diagram of some of the major structures of the river or stream that are exposed by the low water. Knowing exactly where big rocks drop off or the steepness of the side of a pool can make a serious difference when normal water depth returns and the fishing is back on. But do try to make your sketch clear enough to read later. A bunch of squiggles without any labels or arrows will probably just confuse you.

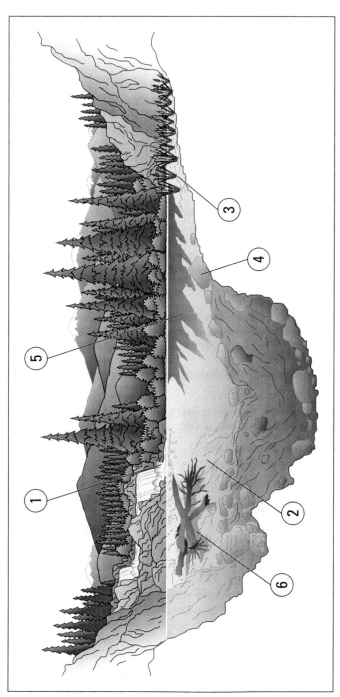

Figure 14-2:
Turn this page sideways to see an all-purpose, typical lake.

Bird signs

Feeding birds are always a sign that bait is available — whether it is in the form of insects or bait fish. This situation is a no-brainer. Fish where the birds are.

Other bird signs are more subtle. For example, a blue heron (or any other wading bird that is known to feed on bait fish) is a promising sign for anglers. If you see one in the same pool day after day, chances are that Mr. Heron knows that this pool is a regular food source. (You can count on Mr. Game fish to have reached the same conclusion.)

"How deep should I fish?"

This is a question that only the fish can answer. Obviously, you need to fish where the fish are. Water temperature has a great deal to do with their location. If you can figure out the depth where the water is at the optimum temperature level, that's a good place to start fishing. Some electronic devices take the water temperature at various depths, but (as with all electronic devices) they cost money.

If you don't have a sophisticated gauge for reading temperatures at different depths, you can do the following. Say you want to find out what the temperature is at 10 feet of depth. Here's a simple way to do that:

1. **Tie an inexpensive (but accurate) outdoor thermometer to the end of a line.**

2. **Let out 10 feet of line (you can guesstimate this) and attach a bobber to the line at the 10-foot point.**

3. **Then put the thermometer in the water, let the thermometer sink and bob there for a minute or so, pull it up quickly, and take a reading.**

   To check the temperature at other depths, just let out 5 more feet of line (for example), move the bobber 5 feet up the line, and you get a 15-foot reading, and so on.

Saltwater

Most saltwater fly rodding is done close to shore — under a mile out —in less than 100 feet of water. When you narrow your fishing grounds down to this strip of shallow coastal waters, the overwhelmingly big ocean begins to take on the characteristics of a combination of river and lake. I don't want to give you the impression that there is no fly rodding farther out to sea in (deeper) *blue water*. Marlin, sails, sharks, dolphin fish are all pursued in deeper water. If you are a beginning fly rodder or belong to the 99.9 percent of the angling world that can't afford a big ocean-going boat, you will do your blue water fishing with a guide in the guide's boat, using the guide's equipment. The only thing I can add by way of advice for this situation is: "Do what your guide tells you to do. He's the guide and you're not."

Where the baits are

When the notorious stick-up man, Willie Sutton, was asked why he robbed banks, he gave a sensible answer: "Because that's where the money is." If you want to catch fish, go where the bait is. Think of the ocean as a bank filled not with money but with bait. Just as when fishing in a stream or lake, the first thing to look for is feeding fish. The second thing to look for is bait. And the third thing to look for (actually it's two things) is current and structure.

The tale of the tides

Anyone with any saltwater angling experience knows that tides are critically important. They move a lot of bait, and game always follows bait (it wouldn't make a lot of sense the other way around). There are two high tides and two low tides each day. For fishing, this means roughly dividing the day into 6 hours of *incoming* water and 6 hours of *outgoing* water (followed by 6 more hours of incoming water and 6 more hours of outgoing water). When the tide is moving, you will find a current coming in and out of creeks, back bays, and the like. Treat this current just as you would treat a river or stream and fish the moving tide accordingly. If a current sweeps by a rocky outcropping, look for fish just as if they were holding behind a subsurface rock in a trout stream.

However, it's not all exactly like reading a trout stream. Ocean tides are a lot different than river current. Tides move back and forth, ripping this way and that, often with a lot of turbulence. Time of day and month (actually, the moon) affect the depth of the tide. There is also a lot more water moving around in the ocean than in a trout stream, which means a lot more space for fish to roam. Where stream trout will hang in a pool and wait for the current to bring food to them, oceangoing bluefish will chase all the way down a beach after bait that are running with the tide.

Here are some additional tips for fishing the tide:

✔ Try to fish when the tide is moving. At *slack tide* — in other words, still water at the end of a tide — there is very little action that would cause bait to concentrate. Consequently there is nothing to concentrate game fish.

✔ At low tide, examine exposed flats to see the contours of the bottom. You will find holes, troughs, and subsurface structure to cast to later during high tide.

✔ When fishing shallow flats, the incoming tide will often bring nice fish out of deeper water as they follow bait onto the flats.

✔ Be mindful of the phase of the moon. The full moon will bring abnormally high and low tides. This situation will affect ocean access and safety. Know the territory, especially at night!

Lake-like too

The tides make the ocean behave like a stream. But the ocean is also a *very big* lake. As you would in a lake, look for structure, drop-offs, and channels. Weed beds hold food and hide predators. Underwater wrecks provide all kinds of hidey-holes. Because nature works with so much greater force in the ocean, underwater structure changes more dramatically from year to year on the ocean. However, the need to look for the edge still holds. You just have to figure out where the edge is.

Bays

Take a look at Figure 14-3. This is a typical coastal bay situation. Water moves into the bay at high tide and out at low. So do the bait fish. Water also moves into the bay from the smaller, marshy tributaries. You probably know without my telling you that you want to fish just inside the mouth of the bay on an incoming tide and just outside on a falling tide. This is the place where you will find the greatest concentration of bait fish. It's just like a multi-lane merge on the freeway. Further up into the bay, where the tribs flow into it, you will find the same situation. Predators can also pick up bait fish here, but there must be enough depth to give the game fish a sense of security. Bigger fish also wait at the mouths of the tributaries as the tide goes out. Notice that the middle of the bay is not a prime location, but if the bay has a white sandy bottom and you have a shallow draft boat, you will often find nice fish cruising over the flats in bright daylight.

Points

Think of a point of land in much the same way you would a boulder in a stream — three-quarters of a boulder. The tide rushes at it from one side, wraps around, and makes an eddy (see Figure 14-4). Often, the last two hours of incoming tide and the first two hours of outgoing provide the best fishing.

Usually, but not always, the best fishing is straight out from the tip. In many cases the slope of the ground continues past the point under the water. This contour will frequently produce a rip (a tidal cross-current). This is a great edge to fish.

Jetties

Put on your cleats — you're going to the jetty. A jetty is a narrow, man-made poke of rocks extending into the ocean. Jetty fishing can be rough — the surf can pound you. Game fish like to hang off the tip in the seam created by

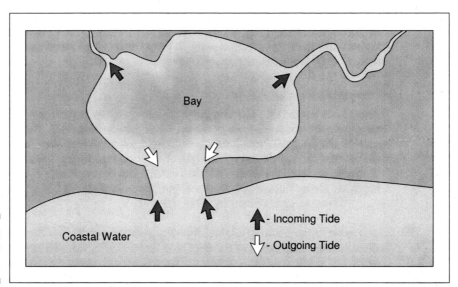

Figure 14-3:
A typical
coastal bay.

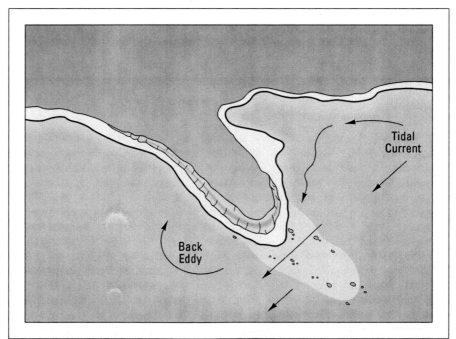

Figure 14-4:
The
dynamics
of a point.

water moving into or receding from either side of the jetty. Other times they hug the sides of the jetty, following bait as the tide peaks. As high tide carries bait up to the beach, game fish will cruise the length of the jetty up to the sandy bowl where the jetty meets the beach.

Always watch the birdie

If you see a battalion of diving gulls all bunched up together, you can bet there are bait fish underneath them. What happens is this: The game fish encircle the bait fish and force them to the surface; and then, while the bait fish are penned up this way, the gulls have easy pickings. My advice: Follow the birds. My other advice: Follow the bird (as in *one* bird). Sometimes, a lone bird diving repeatedly in the same place indicates that a feeding striper or a cruising sailfish is nearby. Check it out.

Don't trust terns. *Terns* are little birds shaped like swallows. They have flattish heads, orange dagger-shaped beaks, and forked tails. You will see them dipping and diving along the shore. While diving gulls are a pretty sure bet as a sign of game fish, terns are a 50-50 shot. If you get under a flock of terns, cast a bunch, but if you catch nothing, move on. All that commotion means that the terns have found food but the game fish haven't. On the other hand, in the fall at the peak of the albacore run, the gannet, another small bird, is usually the first to feed on the schools of bay anchovies when the albies have them penned up. Bottom line: It helps to know a little about the habits of shore birds.

Beating Old Man Winter

On the third of January, 1997, my daughter Lucy and I went fishing in New York Harbor with pioneer New York Harbor guide, Joe Shastay. Normally this would be a suicidal time to be on the water or, at the very least, not much fun. But on that January 3, the air temperature stood at 60°F at eight o'clock. We walked from our house down to the Brooklyn Bridge and through the bar of the swanky-but-angler-friendly River Cafe where our fishing clothes stood out from the designer outfits worn by the well-heeled clientele. Joe picked us up at the landing by the side of the restaurant and we made our way up the East River. The water was 44 degrees and there was no sign of fish. At 9:00 p.m., the current reversed as the tide came in, bringing with it warmer ocean water. In the lights around the cargo docks we began to see swirls. Stripers were chasing little spearing. I put on a popping bug and took half a dozen schoolies. They would not have amounted to much in any record book but I can't begin to tell what great satisfaction it gave this angler to be surface fishing with a fly rod in the dead of winter. The night was completed when my daughter, who had gone to a spinning rig, took a 20-inch fish that had been tagged by the Hudson River Foundation. The icing went on the cake when, a month later, we found that Lucy's tag had been drawn from a hat and she was to receive a prize of $100.

Again, take the temperature

Fish when the water is at the right temperature and you will catch fish. Fish when the water is the wrong temperature and you will catch nothing. It's that simple. As in freshwater fishing, a thermometer (or a more-sophisticated electronic monitor) is one of the most practical angling aids you can buy. As noted in Chapters 9 and 11 and on the Quick Reference Card, all fish have an optimum temperature range. Seek it out.

The Time Is Now

The quick answer to the question, "When do I fish?" is simple: Whenever you get the chance. Most of the time, you can find a way to catch *something*. You may not be able to fish for the big guys, or you may have to forget about some of the glamour fish and go for panfish, shad, or whatever. Still, it's fishing. The other thing to remember is this: Game fish don't go to sleep during the day; they just go to different places. Sometimes, they go to deeper water. Sometimes, they visit reefs or nooks in a rocky shore. But they are *somewhere,* and they can be caught if you know where to go and how to fish. The important thing is to fish whenever you can.

While traditionally it may be true that the early bird catches the worm — and logically, the early worm catches the fish — it is more accurate that the bird on the edge, very early or much later, is the one that catches at all. For this reason, dawn and dusk are very productive times. When the world changes over from those animals on night duty to those that come out in the daytime, you have a certain kind of edge. This particular edge is not a physical edge, but an edge in time. The important thing about all edges is that they are *transition* zones, and some creatures have a natural advantage in making that transition. The skillful predator exploits that advantage. Just as the trout grows bold and loses caution when many mayflies are on the water, many predators grow a little bolder in dim light. Maybe, in dim light, the bait fish feel that they are less visible; they get a little cocky, and the game fish know that the pickings will be good. Anglers observe this behavior, and that's when *they* are on the water.

Good times

Sometimes, the fish totally ignore the rules and come out to feed when all the books say they have no business being out and about. But of course, if fish didn't make fatal mistakes like that, no one would ever catch them. For most fish, most of the time, here's when you want to be fishing:

✔ At dawn and dusk.

✔ On cloudy, overcast days (which have similar light conditions to dawn and dusk).

✔ An hour either side of high and low tides. You will quickly find out if your area is good at high or low or both tides.

✔ For trout, fish the pleasant time of the day. Water temperature in spring and fall is usually optimal for insect activity in the warmest part of the day. In the summer, the prime insect time is when things cool down a bit.

✔ Apple blossom time. For shad, trout, smallmouth bass, and probably a good many other fish, the locals will tell you, "Don't fish until the dogwood blooms," or "Wait until the redbud leaves are as big as squirrel ears." What these tips all mean is that generations of anglers have noticed that when spring really starts to put some early flowers and leaves out, it is a sign that the air and water are warming. This is when fish are going to stir from their winter doldrums. And when you wake up after a big winter nap, what do you want? Yes, a snack.

✔ For flats fishing, the only rule is that you should fish when there is enough water on the flats to allow the game fish to come up and feed. Your best times are the hours of peak visibility, so contrary to everything you have heard, you have the best shot on a clear day with the sun overhead.

When the barometer's moving, rent a movie or clean your closet

In my opinion, you can hang it up right after a big barometric swing (though there are some anglers who have exactly the opposite opinion). Time and time again, it has been my experience that a change in the weather means that fish are going to need some time to adjust to the change. A Finnish fisheries biologist (who I ran into years ago while fishing with the Rapala brothers on one of the lakes near their hometown) said that it was his belief that bait fish don't have sophisticated organs to compensate for pressure. He believed that a falling barometer meant that bait (or at least Finnish bait) had to go deeper to equalize pressure. When the bait fish went deeper into the water, the game fish followed, and anglers who were using dry flies and poppers were out of luck. According to his theory, a rising barometer should have the opposite effect and should make for good topwater action, but I have never noticed that effect. If you play the odds, my advice is give the fish a little time to adjust to a change in the weather.

"Real guys fish at night"

If you hang around Montauk Point, you will hear that the hard-core guys (supposedly the guys who catch the big babies) fish in the middle of the night, dressed in wet suits and using miners' lamps for illumination. I can tell you right now that I have seen 50-pound striped bass pulled out of the surf at nine o'clock in the morning under a bright sun. I have seen such striped bass on top of the water, boiling under bait all through clear fall days. So, no, you don't have to fish when it is dark to have a chance to catch big fish.

However . . .

Unless you have a flats boat that allows you to prowl the white bottom flats, you will probably catch more fish in low-light conditions than you will catch in the heat of the day. You will catch more fish on cloudy days than you will catch on sunlit ones. You will have a much better chance in shallow water when darkness provides bait fish with the feeling, but not always the reality, of security from predatory game fish.

No Matter When or Where You Fish, Remember This

Here are a couple of pointers that I want you to remember. All of them have to do with getting your fly to the fish without scaring the fish away. Scared fish don't eat, so no matter what you cast to them, no matter how pretty the cast, they will stay away.

Keep a cool head

You see a fish that is finning quietly just below the surface. (No scene is more enticing to an angler, and at no other moment is a fish so skittish.) When approaching a fish like this (in fact, when moving through *any* water where you think you might find fish), steady yourself, concentrate, *breathe,* and follow the rest of the rules here.

Go slow

The faster you move, the more likely you are to make a disturbance. In really calm water, moving slowly is a matter of taking a step, waiting a second for the waves to subside, and then taking another step. The same goes for rowing your boat or canoe — do it slowly and steadily.

"Be vewy quiet": The Elmer Fudd method

Be careful about banging your oars, scraping rocks with your boots, or walking with heavy footfalls. Sound really does travel well underwater, and it transfers very well between land (underwater rocks, riverbanks, and beaches) and the water. Take it easy, take it slow, and if you must do anything, do it quietly. Remember that sound travels much better underwater.

Don't show yourself

In most cases, if you can see the fish, the fish can see you. This rule is not always true, however. For example, if you are downstream of a rising trout, it will probably not notice you. Still, the basic rule is this: Stay out of the line of sight of wary fish. Here are some tips you can follow to do that:

- ✔ **Blend into the background:** Although you don't need full camouflage, wearing clothing that is the same color as the background against which the fish will see you is a good idea. (Remember that fish are not used to seeing fluorescent exercise outfits.)
- ✔ **Keep a low profile:** Just like the guy who wants to keep his head on his shoulders while hiding in a foxhole, the angler should stay low and out of sight.

Be vewy, vewy quiet

I just want to emphasize how important it is to stay cool, calm, collected, and *quiet.* The more enticing the fish, the harder keeping quiet may be. But the only way that you are going to be sure not to scare off a trophy fish is by being quiet.

Wading

Most every fly rodder wades at some point in his or her fishing career. Trouters do it just about all the time. Just like walking, it is something you have to learn how to do.

And even though wading is just walking, it requires much more skill and care than walking down the street does. First, you are often dealing with the force of moving water. Second, you can't see the ground in front of you that well. And third, underwater rocks and plants can be slippery. For all of these reasons, there is one cardinal rule of water: *Take it slow!*

Come to think of it, there is a second cardinal rule: Test the footing in front of you before you take the weight off your back foot.

Drop-offs, unseen rocks, and current surges are often invisible, so you need to wade slowly and cautiously, one foot at a time.

Thy rod and thy staff

I do most of my wading without a staff, but there are times when one really helps, either as a probing device or as a third leg.

Although a stick lying around on the ground may make a serviceable wading staff, what do you do with it after you are in the middle of the stream? For greater convenience, many people like commercial wading staffs that can be tied to a belt. If you can't find such a staff, a cheap and easy alternative is a ski pole with the little rubber circle cut off the bottom. I say *cheap,* because in the summertime, ski poles are not a hot ticket, and you can often pick up a bunch at bargain-basement prices. Because many trout fishing destinations are also at or near ski resorts, you are very likely to find some ski poles right in the town where you are fishing.

Thy friend, too

You would think that if one person can easily slip and fall in a stream, then linking two people is a sure recipe for a dunking. But the opposite is true. By linking arms together, two anglers can actually gain strength and stability. If one of you is a stronger wader, that person should take the upstream position because that is the more difficult one. (This is also a good way to get a new angler a little more used to handling moving water.)

Think like a fish

When a fish is hooked and it wants to use the force of the current to fight you, it turns broadside to the current. This may work fine for a fish trying to escape. For an angler trying to wade, it is precisely the wrong thing to do. You want to present the thinnest silhouette possible. In other words, stand sideways to present a more streamlined surface to the rushing water. I realize that some of us older anglers may have a shape that looks more like a soup spoon than a steak knife, but sideways is still the most efficient way to deal with the physics of moving water.

Lead with your rear

You see a nice fish rising behind a midstream rock. Inch by inch you begin to wade across the treacherous stream. It's slow going, but you are slowly getting in position for that perfect cast. And then the bottom drops sharply and you realize there is no way you are going to make it. Whatever you do, don't turn around and wade out! This action simply presents the broadest part of your body to the flow, and it is a great way to get knocked off your feet. Just take your time and back out, inch by inch.

If you fall

One of these days, you are going to take a tumble into the water. If you are careful, you will tumble much less often than you think. In 25 years of angling, I have fallen into the stream exactly twice. I've come close to falling more often than that, but in terms of real bona fide butt-soakings, that's it. That makes me lucky. If you fall in, you should be able to right yourself pretty quickly. It helps if you keep your waders tightly cinched with a belt. If the current does take you, don't fight it: The river always wins. If possible, keep your feet in front of you so that if some part of you strikes a rock, it probably won't be your head. Although taking an involuntary ride is a little scary, try and remember that most dunkings will leave you in calm water in less than half a minute. And if you just can't manage to stay safe and hold on to your rod, let the rod go. After all you can buy a new rod faster than the rod can buy a new you.

Chapter 15
Catching and (Often) Releasing

*Y*ou have spent a great deal of money on gear. You have stolen precious time to get a few hours (or a few days) to try and catch some fish. You have learned how to cast, tie knots and flies, but none of this makes you an angler. Anglers catch fish. In order to do that, you need to know when to strike a fish, how to fight it, how to complete the fight and land it, and then how to kill it humanely or set it free.

When Should I Strike?

Different fish have different takes. By *takes,* I mean the ways in which the fish takes the bait into its mouth. A trout may slurp a dry fly or slam a streamer. A tarpon inhales a fly along with a bucketful of water. A bluegill takes a popper quickly off the surface. There is no *one* general rule for when to strike. To be an effective angler, you need to know your fish and its behavior.

A savage strike doesn't require a savage response from the angler. Usually, all this sort of response does is ensure that you pull your fly away from the fish before you have a chance to set the hook. You need to *come tight* to the fish: All the slack must be gone from your line, and you must feel the weight of the fish before you drive the hook home.

Some fish, like the tarpon, require a couple of good, slamming pulls on the rod to embed the hook in its tough mouth. The trout, on the other hand, needs just a slight jerk to set the hook. With bass and pike that slam and gnaw on a fly, you need to let them run with it for a second or two. To get a fish securely on your hook, follow these steps:

1. **Lift the rod tip to make sure you have taken up all the slack.**

2. **Hold the line in your free hand and the rod in the other; pull back to set the hook.**

   The gentlest motion will secure a trout whereas a tarpon needs a couple of slams with all your might.

   If you have a stiff rod with a fast tip, your fish should be on (hooked) at this point.

3. **Come to think of it, if you've got a tarpon on your line, whack it again for good measure — maybe twice.**

Soft rods require even more forcefulness in the hook-setting motion. Some rods, although they are nice, safe casters, are too soft ever to set the hook. If you follow all of my recommendations and just can't seem to set a hook, you may need a rod with a faster tip.

Fish On! (Now What Do I Do?!)

Having a fish on the end of your line is like any other emergency situation: If you have never been through it before, you may lose your head. Remember this piece of advice: It's an emergency for the fish, not for you. If you maintain your cool, you can win this fight. Millions of anglers have done it before you, so it isn't magic. Still, you do need to know what you are doing. Fighting and beating fish is one art where, I promise you, you can learn from your mistakes because you will replay them a thousand times in your head. The better the fish, the more times you will tell yourself, "Gee, if only I'd. . . ."

And then, after you finally learn how to fight your average fish, you will hook into a big one someday, and it's a whole new ball game (with a whole *new* set of mistakes to make and learn from).

Rod up

When many fly rodders first strike a fish and get it on, you may notice them holding the rod high. This technique accomplishes two things:

✔ First, it reduces the amount of slack line right away.

✔ Second, holding the rod high keeps the fish's head up, out of the weeds and away from the rocks. This technique is good to use when fishing with conventional tackle as well as fly tackle.

For you physicists, raising the rod increases the angle that the rod makes with the water. This, in turn, increases the mechanical advantage of the rod which acts like a lever against the fish.

The Fight

Having a fish on and not knowing what to do can be a source of much anxiety. It shouldn't be. Having a fish on is the fun part of fishing. That tug. That pushing and head-shaking and throbbing. That wildness. These are the prime thrills of fishing. It's you against the fish, and the fish is in its element. That *you* will win is not a foregone conclusion (although the more fish you fight, the better your chances). Win or lose, the fight is always a thrill and the main thing in fly rodding. You will learn to savor it.

Your rod is your best weapon

A good fishing rod can be a great tool *if* you remember to let it help you fight the fish. Let the rod do some of the work. It was designed to do just that. Follow the advice of Izaak Walton and keep the fish under the bend of the rod. This advice means that you should be holding the rod at an angle that allows it to bend. It doesn't have to bend double, but it has to bend. This flexing of the rod, more than anything else, will tire (and eventually conquer) a fish. No matter how far the fish runs, no matter how much it jumps or shakes, the rod will flex, putting pressure on the hook, which is buried in the mouth of the fish.

Help from the reel

When fighting a fish, the drag mechanism on your reel is another potential ally. If you have set the drag properly, the drag acts as a brake mechanism that can further tire the fish. In most cases, the time to set the drag is before you cast. Adjusting the drag while you are fishing becomes just one more thing that you can mess up, and I don't recommend doing it.

The other thing about drag is that you don't need a whole lot. You need more for saltwater game fish, and saltwater fly reels offer the ability to add some serious pounds of resistance to the line. You'll need some, but not all the drag a reel has to offer; too much drag can put too much stress on the leader and tippet. You should use just enough drag that the fish does not easily pull line off the reel, but not so that the fish can hardly budge the drag.

The line helps too

When a large fish runs off a great deal of line, the resistance of the water against the line creates even more drag. This factor can work in your favor if you have a sense of how much added pressure your tackle can take. The added drag can also break your line if you don't take it into account. Only practice will teach you this lesson.

The reel thing

Many newcomers to fly fishing get a fish on and panic because they're stripping line — they inevitably drop this line to start reeling and have just dumped a bunch of slack on the fish, a real gift. You can deal with this situation one of three ways:

✔ With a smaller fish, you can strip him in, using your rod hand to hold the line between strips.

✔ Or you may brace the line with your rod hand, quickly reel in the slack, then fight from the reel, using the bend of the rod to fight the fish as you take up slack.

Most times, if you have a lot of line out, you can strip, reel, strip to get rid of slack and get down to fighting the fish from the reel. But understand that you will not always fight the fish from the reel as you do in spincasting or baitcasting.

✔ The third situation, with bigger, running fish, is to guide — but don't grab — the slack line with your hand as the big fish runs away with it. Ultimately he will take up all the slack and then the fish will be running line off the reel. In this case, you have no choice but to fight from the reel.

Heads up!

Heads up means that the head of the fish points up. If you are able to keep the head of the fish up, *you* are directing the fight. With its head up, the fish is disoriented and bewildered and can't see where to go (that is, it can't see a rock to slip under or a weed bed to dive for). If the fish can get its head down, you are in the position of reacting while the fish picks where it will take the fight.

Keeping the head up doesn't mean rearing back at all costs. Sometimes a little pressure to the side or from side to side will do the trick. You are in contact with the fish, and you just have to feel your way through this one, responding to its twists and turns by pulling back, easing up, or changing direction — whatever it takes.

Use the current

A fish is going to run away from the pressure of hook, line, and rod. If you have hooked your fish in moving water, try to position yourself downstream from the fish. That way, the fish is not only fighting you and your tackle, but it is also fighting the current. This move may not always be possible, but when it is, do it, even if you have to back out of the stream and walk downstream.

Running for cover

If the fish burrows into the weeds, you may well have lost it, but not always. True, if you rear back and bend the rod every which way trying to get the fish out of the weeds, you will probably break off sooner or later. However, if you point your rod tip straight at the fish, reel up tight, and start walking backwards, you *may* coax the fish out of the weeds. The best defense is to know where weed beds are, and when your fish moves toward one, hold the rod high and steer the fish away from going into cover. Yes, easier said than done.

"What a jump! Hey! What happened?"

If your tussle with a fish *concludes* on a jump, it can mean only one thing — the fish has jumped free, and your fight is over. It may have broken the line or shaken the hook, but either way, it's off. When a fish goes airborne, I bow (drop my rod tip). When I bow to a fish, I mean literally *bow* — I bend from the waist, drop my rod tip, and extend my arms like a waiter offering a tray full of appetizers. As soon as the fish falls back to the water, I come tight again. When a fish is airborne, it may reach a point in its trajectory when all of its weight and momentum snap against the line. Without the buoyancy of the water to act as a shock absorber, knots can break under the added force of gravity. A hard-mouthed fish, like a tarpon, may not be very deeply hooked to begin with. The force of a jump may be all that is needed to dislodge a hook. Bowing to a jumping fish neutralizes drag and momentarily pays out line to the fish so that as it jumps, it is not pulling hard against a taut line.

Rod up, reel down (pumping a fish)

Most newcomers get a fish on and reel for dear life. This technique will do you no good. It can even do you harm by causing bad line twist.

As indicated in Figure 15-1, *pull up* to try to bring the fish toward you. Then drop the rod tip and, as you do, reel up line. Sometimes the fish will still take line as you pull up. That's okay; you can do nothing about it but hang on. **Remember:** As you reel in, drop the rod tip so that you have someplace to go when you pull up again. When fighting a fish, the idea is to tire the fish and to recover line that the fish has taken off the reel so that you can eventually get the fish close enough to grasp or gaff. The reeling up is the longest and most tiring part of the fight, and it's one that doesn't come naturally.

Remember, too, that every pull up is not going to bring the fish in. Sometimes a fish will take a lot of line before you are able to recover any. Or you may have gained a great deal of line, and then the fish sees the boat and tears away on another run. Keep the pressure on — it's the only way to land the fish.

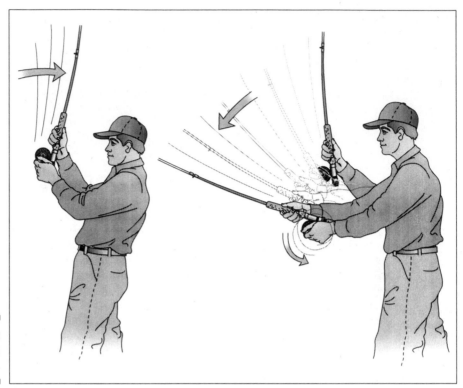

Figure 15-1:
Pumping
a fish.

Playing the fish

You should always try to get the fish in as soon as possible, especially if you are going to release it. The longer the fish fights, the more lactic acid it builds up in its muscles (lactic acid is the same stuff that makes you cramp and get stiff), and the harder it is to revive. Releasing (letting go of) a fish that you have fought to the point of exhaustion before you have spent the time to revive it often makes no sense because the fish may well die of exhaustion anyway.

In the ocean, ending the fight quickly is even more important (even if you are keeping the fish) because a long, splashy fight is a great way to attract a predator (like a shark) who will end the fight for you as he takes a meal. This happened to me in the Florida Keys with a tarpon that weighed well over 100 pounds. I fought hard, but I could have fought harder and followed my guide's advice and have gotten the tarpon into the boat within 10 minutes. Instead, I prolonged the fight, and my heart was broken as, 200 yards out, I saw a tremendous commotion and then felt my line grow slack as a huge shark devoured my tarpon.

Light tackle takes longer

While it is more sporty to subdue fish on lighter tackle, you need to use enough tackle to do the job. Using an outfit that doesn't let you bear down on the fish may still land you a fish after a long fight; but if the fish is totally exhausted when you land it, you probably have a style of fishing more suited to heavier gear that allows you to muscle the fish rather than finessing it.

Landing or Boating the Fish

After you have subdued a fish, your next task is to land it or boat it. This section gives you the lay of the land (or the water) for most fish that you can land by yourself. I am going to assume that if you are going for big game, you either already know what to do or will be fishing with a guide or some-one with experience. Landing a big fish is not something to do on your own with only a book as your guide, unless you are a real dummy. (That's a word my publishers asked me to avoid in this book, but I can't think of another word to describe someone who tussles with a big and dangerous game fish without actual physical help and personal experience.) You will, however, be able to handle 99 percent of the fish you get on the line by yourself.

Should I use a net?

For trout and bass, "the experts" say that you definitely should have a net if you want to release fish back into the water in the hopes that they will live and reproduce. The theory behind this reasoning is that, if you use a net, the fish will be less exhausted when netted rather than landed by hand.

Having said that, I can tell you that I rarely use a net when trout fishing (or when bass fishing, for that matter). I find, at this stage of my angling career, that I can get most fish within my grasp when they still have some life in them. With trout, I reach under the belly and lift up until I am cradling the fish gently. Then I lift it out of the water. For bass, I grab the fish by the lower lip. If I have a really big fish, I use a net. You may want to use a net for all fish, and that's perfectly fine. A net does give you someplace to secure the fish momentarily while you tuck your rod under your arm or ready your camera. Just be quick about it and keep a netted fish in the water.

If you use a net, you should flip it over so that it is hanging in front of you as the fight concludes. Make sure the net is wet so that you do not damage the protective mucous-like slime that coats the fish. As shown in Figure 15-2, hold the rod tip high and slip the net under the fish. Remember to keep the fish in the water until you have the net around it. Lifting the fish out of the water and then trying to net it is a classic Three Stooges move.

Figure 15-2:
The classic
landing net
position.

Maybe a gaff?

Certain things in life are designed so well that you take one look at them and you know what they are for. A gaff is one of them. It's really nothing more than a humongous hook on a long shaft.

When you gaff a fish, most of the time you are going to keep it, but you don't necessarily have to. For example, a lip gaff is not quite the heavy artillery of a standard gaff, and it is often used by tarpon fishermen who want to release their catch. But for most other cases, you gaff and kill.

Surf fishermen have short hand-held gaffs that are great for bluefish, but most gaffs are long-handled and are designed to be used while leaning over the side of a boat. With smaller fish (in saltwater, anything up to 30 pounds), you can probably do your own gaffing. Try to gaff the fish somewhere in the head, gill, or shoulder region. With bigger fish, don't try it until an expert has shown you how.

Killing and Not Killing

Fishing, like hunting, is a blood sport. But it is also very different in significant ways. The pursuit in hunting ends with a dead animal. In fishing, it ends with a live fish in hand. After you shoot a deer or bird, it's a goner. You can't release it back into the wild. A caught fish is different: You can always return it. So the angler always has a choice: "Do I kill the fish, or do I let it go?" The quality of this killing is much different than killing in hunting. It is difficult to kill a deer or bird completely, instantaneously, with one shot. Most fish, however, can be dispatched quickly and cleanly.

The decision to keep fish is up to you. Don't let anybody tell you that you are immoral if you decide to kill fish. If you intend to eat them, killing them is okay with me. However, and this is a big however, if we *all* killed *all* the fish we caught, fishing (in the words of Beavis and Butt-head) would suck.

This is especially true of the glamour fish like trout. They are the top predator in their environment; and the way Nature has set things up, fewer numbers of top predators are out there relative to the prey animals lower down the food chain, which means that if you take a bunch of trout out of a stream, the fishing quality in that stream will *definitely* decline. The same holds for big game, like marlin and tuna. The world just doesn't have that much big game. If you thin out the "alpha predators" (the top dogs), that much less remains for the next time you hunt.

Words to fish by

"Of all the sports of capture, fishing is the most merciful. There is no need to kill unless you choose. The fish that gets away lives to be hooked another day. On the conscience of the fisherman, there are no wounded ducks, no paunch-shot deer. You catch your fish. If you don't want him, back he goes, none the worse for wear."

—Gifford Pinchot, Founder of the U.S. Forest Service and Lifelong Angler.

I like to eat trout. I like to catch them even more, so I pretty much return all my trout to the stream. The same goes for bass. I don't care for pike, so they go back, too. Fluke I keep. Stripers go back. Bluefish I keep some of the time. Tarpon, bonefish, and snook all go back.

That's how I do it. I have a standard and stick to it. As a responsible fly fisher you, too, will have to make up your own mind about what you want to do. Perhaps you have a special dinner planned and you set out purposefully to catch and keep some trout. That's fine, as long as you don't do this every week of the season. As the years go by, you may (as I have done) kill fewer and fewer fish even as you catch more and more.

Before you catch and release

If you intend to release a fish, you should follow these few general rules:

- ✔ Make up your mind whether to catch or release when you set the hook.
- ✔ Try to set the hook quickly so that the fish cannot swallow it too deeply.
- ✔ Minimize the time of the fight because an exhausted fish is not a strong candidate for survival.
- ✔ Consider using barbless hooks. (Some stretches of trout water require barbless hooks.)

Treating a fish properly

These tips increase a fish's chances of surviving:

- ✔ Leave the fish in the water as much as possible.
- ✔ Handle the fish as little as possible.
- ✔ Use forceps or pliers to remove the hook.

✔ Use a wet rag (if you have one handy) to hold the fish. (This technique causes less damage to its scales and protective coating.)

✔ Wet your hands before handling the fish.

✔ If the hook is very deep inside the fish's mouth, cut off the leader. In many cases, the hook will eventually rust out or work itself free. Most fish, particularly trout, do not have much time to swallow a fly before you set it.

Letting him go

Sometimes, releasing the fish is relatively easy. You simply remove the hook and the fish wiggles vigorously, which lets you know that it is ready to take off for freedom. Sometimes, the fish won't wait for you to release it. Instead, it will wriggle free and hightail it.

Often, however, the fish is totally exhausted. If you simply released it right away, you would have a belly-up, soon-to-be-dead fish on your hands. Before you *release* you need to *revive*.

A good rule to follow in figuring out if a fish needs reviving is this: If the fish lets you hold it and doesn't struggle, revive it. After all, any self-respecting wild animal will take off like greased lightning to escape the clutches of a strange creature. To a fish, a human is a strange creature.

Follow these steps (illustrated in Figure 15-3) to help insure that a caught-and-released fish survives:

1. **Hold the fish gently and keep it under the surface of the water.**

   Cradle it from below if you can. If you cannot, hold it gently by its sides. You may grasp some mid-size fish (salmon and stripers, for example) by the tail.

2. **If you are in heavy current, move to gentler current.**

3. **Point the fish upstream.**

   On lakes or in the ocean, however, current isn't a factor when reviving a fish.

4. **Move the fish backward and forward so that its gills are forced to open and close.**

   When properly done, this technique delivers oxygen to a heavily oxygen-depleted fish. Bringing the fish back enough so that it can swim under its own steam may take a few minutes. It lets you know that it is ready to be released when it starts to wiggle.

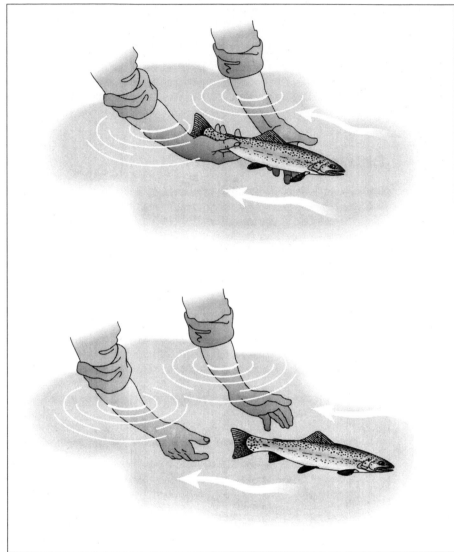

Figure 15-3:
By moving the fish forward and backward, you supply the force to open and close its gills while the fish is still too weak to do this on its own.

5. Release the fish.

It should swim slowly away. If it rolls over on its back and lays there, this is not a good sign. Bring the fish back under your control and continue to revive it. The fish that gives you a real hard shrug and bolts has been revived just fine.

Catch, shoot, and release

The point of catch-and-release is that the fish survives. Shooting a photo gives you a tangible memento of your fish while still allowing you to release it. Here are some things to keep in mind if you want to give your fish a fighting chance at surviving:

- ✔ Since shooting a photo of a fish involves keeping it out of the water, you are adding stress to an already stressful situation. So speed helps — both in landing and in shooting.

- ✔ As long as you hold the fish in the water, facing upstream (if there is a current), the fish will survive a long, long time. When you want to snap a picture, lift the fish out of the water, supporting its body as you do so. (Remember that the fish's internal organs are normally supported by the buoyancy of water.)

- ✔ If you have a friend helping you, let the friend hold the fish in the water until you are ready to snap a picture. Focus on your friend's hands (so you don't have to focus when the fish is in the air) and then have your friend lift the fish for your shot.

Remember, anybody can take a picture of a dead fish. Getting the shot and letting the fish go requires a little more finesse.

Chapter 16

The Fly Fishing Wardrobe

*I*f you are dressed for the weather, you can pretty much fish in any conditions. If you are not dressed well, I guarantee you will be miserable. The cold feels colder; the heat feels like the inside of a Weber Kettle; the wet gets into your bones and stays there for days. Even though we live in gear-obsessed times, you don't need all that much to dress comfortably. I'm not promising that you'll look great, but who's looking? This is fishing, not a dinner party. The fish don't care. There is a bit of a tradition among British fly fishers to dress tweedily and wear neckties and nice hats. My friends, there's no need for you or me to get so dressed up — we wouldn't look right, feel right, or cast right, and how would our families recognize us?

Take It Off!

Weather changes from day to day, and even more importantly for the angler, it changes *during* the day. Mornings are cool, afternoons are hot, cold fronts blow through, showers start and stop. The one thing you can usually depend on is some change in the weather during a fishing session, which means that no matter how you are dressed when you start fishing, you will have to put on or take off clothes at some point. Make sure you have what you need on hand. Long ago, striptease artists discovered that the more *layers* they took off, the more the audience liked the show. It's the same with angling. What I mean is that by dressing in layers, you can take off (or put on) articles of clothing as the day goes along and still stay comfortable. Most of the time, I start out the day wearing a T-shirt with a turtleneck over it, followed by a fleecy pullover. And if it is windy, I add a rain jacket as a windbreaker. When it's cooler, I wear a wool shirt over the turtleneck, and when it's warmer, I just wear a long-sleeve cotton shirt over the T-shirt. I go with jeans when it's cool and shorts when it's hot.

The Well-Dressed Fly Rodder

The following basic wardrobe will serve you in most places, most of the time. The only time I modify it is when it is ultra-hot, like in the tropics when there is no chance of anything remotely cool happening, or in the opposite — when it's cold and going to stay that way, say, for instance, Lake Michigan in November. But let's leave the extremes for a second and talk about being prepared for weather from about 40°F to 90°F, which is the range at which most of us fish.

✔ **Underwear:** Regular old cotton T-shirt and shorts. (Don't fall into the superstition of having a lucky pair of drawers. Eventually the washing machine will eat them and you'll suffer a mental block.)

✔ **A long-sleeve cotton turtleneck:** This gives overall covering of your torso and protects your neck and chest from wind. (You can pretty much always count on wind while boating.)

✔ **Long johns bottoms:** I like the silk ones in particular because they are light, cheap, and warm. Even if you don't need them while fishing, they take up little space and you will be glad you have them when your jeans are wet and you haven't brought spare clothes for the drive home. (But if you stop off at a 7-11 or a bar, remember to put your jeans back on — wet or not.)

✔ **Hiking or athletic shorts (with pockets):** Have them in your gym bag in case it's a warm day. P.S.: This means bring a gym bag with a change of clothes.

✔ **Jeans or khakis:** There's a reason that people just naturally wear them when given a choice. They're comfortable, they break the wind, they keep the sun off, and so on. Some experts have a thing against cotton because it feels cold when it is wet. My solution is to have an extra pair.

✔ **Long-sleeve cotton shirt (warmish weather):** When it's hot, I always wear a long-sleeve cotton shirt to keep the sun off. At this stage of the game, I think most of you know that prolonged exposure to the sun is rough on unprotected skin. And fly fishing is a sport that gives you about as much sun as any human activity.

✔ **Long-sleeve wool shirt (cold weather):** Wool can stay warm from body heat. For early spring and autumn fishing, I prefer it to cotton.

✔ **Socks:** Your feet are going to perspire if you do any wading. Wool socks, preferably merino wool, will stay warm. In really cold weather, put on some silk undersocks as a first layer, and then wool.

✔ **Fleece pullover (Polartec, Polarfleece):** There are a lot of brand names for that soft fleecy synthetic material that most outdoor stores sell these days. I think that this stuff is one of the few great synthetic things.

✔ **Rain jacket:** You can buy very high-tech, very expensive rain jackets that "breathe." That sounds good, but the only thing that I have ever found that keeps you dry in an all-day soaker is a *completely impermeable* rain jacket. I always have one along when I am on a boat, not just for rain, but also to break the wind when I'm making a move from one fishing spot to another. Get one that fits *over* your fishing vest. Make sure that it has a hood. If you're going to be wading, a waist-high rain jacket works best, or else you'll look like a bride trailing a green rubber train.

If you don't feel like shelling out for a rain jacket, or if you forget yours, you can make a poncho out of a lawn-size garbage bag. Cut holes for the head and arms and, in a pinch, you're in business. Nope, doesn't look great at all, but style loses to dryness and warmth.

Dress like Robin Hood (except for the green tights)

If you can see the fish, the fish can see you — so, yes, color does make a difference. If you blend into the background, you will scare fewer fish. English fly fishers wear green for the same reason that Robin Hood did: They want to blend into the background. In the American West, tans and browns work well. Out on the shallow ocean flats, you are going to look like a big silhouette, no matter what you do, so stay low and far away, unless you own a Romulan cloaking device like in *Star Trek*.

Hat = Luck

They say that 40 percent of your body heat is lost through your head. In my opinion, anglers who don't wear a hat are also losing 40 percent of their brain power. You need a hat when you fish. It keeps your brains from baking when the sun is out. It keeps the rain off. It shields your eyes so that you can see what the fish are doing when the sun is low in the sky — which is, coincidentally, the best time of the day to fish. The most popular hat is a plain old baseball cap, and that is what I wear most of the time. Some anglers, and I am one of them, prefer a long-billed hat for early morning and late afternoon fishing. In cold weather, a stocking cap does just fine.

If Sherlock Holmes played baseball

What the baseball cap design lacks is any sun protection for the neck and ears. Enter the most dweebish-looking hat ever invented, the *flats* hat. It was devised for fishing the sun-drenched bonefish flats of the Caribbean, where

Right next to the wine glasses

I have always treated baseball hats like baseball mitts. They just get older and more worn and full of salt stains from perspiration. My neighbor's teenage son taught me how to use the dishwasher to clean my favorite hat. You just put in on the upper tray, where you usually put cups and glasses, and run the washer normally. The hat will still be wet when the cycle is through, but don't put it in the dryer; just let it air dry. Your hat may not look brand new, but you (or your spouse) will see a large improvement in its general funkiness.

anglers spend a whole day in the sun. It has a reinforced flap in the back that fits over the ears and shades the neck as well, just like those Foreign Legion hats. It also has a long bill that is especially helpful in shielding your eyes from late afternoon and early morning sun, when it's particularly important to see well because that is when so much good fishing takes place. Recently, they have started to make these hats with a chin strap — another silly-looking but practical feature, which I am sure you will seek out after you lose your ninth or tenth hat by having it blown off your head while speeding along in a boat.

Made for shade

The long-billed hat is not the only possibility for anglers. In very hot direct sun, where you are fishing in the heat of the day, I like an open-weave straw hat with a reasonably wide brim. It throws shade on your head and shoulders and is well ventilated to let cooling breezes through. Some clown might say you look like Minnie Pearl, but I think Huck Finn is closer to the mark.

Waders: Like a Kid in a Snowsuit

If you are going to do any stream wading or surf casting, you need *waders*. The first thing you need to know about them is that they all leak sooner or later. It doesn't matter how much you pay or how well you take care of them, they are going to leak. Sometimes you will be able to find the leak and patch it, and sometimes you are just going to have to shell out for another pair. There are two basic models and one variation.

- **The boot foot (chest high):** This type of wader is a one-piece outfit. The boot is attached to the legs, which is the most convenient design for getting in and out of it in a hurry. It is also the *only* design for surf casting because there is no way for sand or pebbles to find their way into the boot.

- **The stocking foot (chest high):** Stocking-foot waders do not come with a boot attached, so they require wading shoes. Many anglers prefer this setup because they say a sturdy wading boot gives them extra support while wading. On the minus side, these waders take a long time to put on and take off. Once they are on, you are basically committed to staying in waders until you are done fishing for the day. To prevent abrasion of the stocking foot, you should always wear a pair of wading socks *over* the foot of the wader.

- **Hip boots:** These waders are great for fishing streams in the summer. You can't get in nearly as deep as you can with chest-high waders, but if the river never gets that deep, why roast inside of chest-high waders?

Face it, waders are an inconvenience. You wouldn't wear them if you didn't have to. There is a range of wader materials that vary in durability and comfort.

- **Neoprene:** This is the material used in wet suits. If you are fishing in cold waters, neoprenes are the waders of choice. Walking around in them on a hot day, you will feel like a baked potato in a microwave oven. And they are nasty when they spring a leak: You have more chance of pitching a perfect game in the major leagues than you do of finding a pin-sized hole in neoprenes. So why get them? As I said, they are the *only* thing to fish in when the water is cold, say below 60°F.

- **Rubber and rubberized:** When I started fishing, I bought rubberized canvas. You can still buy this material, and it works as well as it always did — which is pretty good. It doesn't get high marks in the mobility department, but it still moves more freely than the rubber waders that have lived in the trunk of my car since 1984. That pair cost $39.95, and although they are not super-comfortable, they are indestructible.

- **Flyweights:** Made of lightweight rubberized synthetic, flyweight waders are great for traveling because they can roll up very tightly in your duffel bag. They offer no insulation, but a pair of sweat pants, or better yet, polar fleece pants or long johns— and thick wool socks worn under the waders can help.

- **Breathables:** Made of Gore-Tex and its clones, these types of waders are the new kids on the block. They are pretty pricey but ultra-comfortable. The jury is still out on durability.

Not for codgers only

When I was a kid, we always had a laugh at the "old guys" who wore belts and suspenders. I still think it's kind of overkill for streetwear, but with most waders, wearing both is a must. You wear suspenders to hold up your waders, and the belt keeps water from rushing in if you get a dunking. This is a serious safety precaution. You can drown if your waders fill up and you go under. But don't let me panic you too much. It is actually the air trapped in your waders that can flip you. If your waders fill completely up, the water has no effect. After all, you are floating in water. Getting out of the stream, however, is more difficult in water-filled waders.

Save your Nikes for B-ball

In the heat of the summer, I prefer to wet wade if at all possible. That used to mean sneakers for footwear, but I took a couple of spills on slippery rocks. If you have stocking foot waders, then you probably have wading shoes. Wear them over a pair or two of heavy socks. While fishing in the South Pacific a few years ago, I picked up a pair of the felt-bottom shoes used by pearl divers when they walk on sharp coral reefs. These "reef-walkers" are now found in most dive shops and a few tackle stores. These little rubber booties, more costly than the $9 pair I bought in the town of Banana, on Christmas Island, usually zip up the side and are snug enough to keep out sand and gravel.

Feltless and fancy free

You can buy waders and boots without felt soles, but you shouldn't. When rocks are covered with algae, wet leaves, dead seaweed, or unidentifiable slime, they are very slippery. Felt is clingier and helps counteract the slipperiness. Felt also wears out after a few years and you have to replace it. It's worth it. Felt is cheap. A broken fishing rod or bent reel is not.

Wear cleats: This means you!

A couple of years ago, I was fishing on a jetty that juts into the Atlantic. The guys on the end were into a run of false albacore. When I saw about half a dozen rods bent over I felt compelled to hop the big jetty rocks to make my way out to the fishing. I was wearing felt, but it didn't matter. I hit a slippery spot and took a hellacious fall on my casting arm. Somehow I managed to grab onto a rock before an incoming wave swept me right off the jetty. I was lucky (although it took a couple days and a lot of aspirin before I felt unsore enough to feel even remotely lucky). If I had been smart, I would have worn a pair of strap-on cleats. There are a few different kinds that you can buy. One is like a pair of rubbers with metal cleats on the bottom. They are murder to get on, but they never slip off. I prefer Korkers, which are more like a sandal with studs on the bottom. Either way, the metal makes for a very sure grip when it rubs up against stone. If I don't have them, I just won't go out on a jetty anymore. They are also very helpful when wading a strong river like the Yellowstone.

Gloves: A Cold Weather Blessing

When pursuing cold water species, you might encounter some cold weather: cold air, cold rain, sleet, and snow. No matter — if the fishing is good, you're staying out there. It would be nice, though, if you could still tie a few knots or feel your line as you strip in. Nothing, short of leaving your zipper open, feels as chilly as fast as fingers. Wear gloves. I use neoprene gloves and they work well for me. Just about anywhere that people fly fish the surf or cold rivers and streams, you will find these kinds of gloves in the tackle shops. Yeah, yeah, I know how some people say wool may get wet but it stays warm. That's true if there is some kind of wind break between the wool and the air. Exposed wool can be pretty frigid. Invest in a pair of neoprenes and pack them in your vest.

GEAR

And God made duct tape . . .

I have only one mounted fish on my wall. He's a 6³/₄-pound brook trout with a bite taken out of his tail, no doubt suffered in his careless youth when he got too close to a pike or even another trout. I caught him on a stream in Labrador in early August. When I hooked him, I worked my way over to the side of the stream to continue the fight where I had a chance of winning. This required me to fanny walk across a number of midstream boulders. As luck would have it, one of those boulders had a sharp edge that tore a 5-inch gash in my flyweight waders. When I had calmed down from the excitement of my gorgeous brookie, reality set in. When you're in the middle of Labrador and the nearest store is over a hundred miles away, you can't just hop in the truck and get a wader repair kit at the nearest tackle shop (and there are no roads there anyway). I did have a roll of gaffer's tape, also known as duct tape, that lived in my duffel bag since I had worked as a gofer on local film crews. The first thing they teach you on a film production is how to rip gaffer's tape with your teeth. It has a thousand and one uses on films, and it earned a thousand and one thank-yous from me when I ripped off a piece and ran it over and around the gash in my waders. I got another two full seasons out of them, and in the end, it was the seams and not my patch that gave out. Moral of the story: Always carry a roll of duct tape on a fishing trip.

The Vest: More Important Than Your Underwear

The vest is such a common sight that it's hard to imagine fishing without it. Yet until Lee Wulff had the bright idea of sewing some blue-jeans pockets onto a denim vest about 60 years ago, there were no fishing vests. You can buy vests with a gazillion pockets, and you can stuff every one of those pockets. And you can also make sure that you have every possible gizmo hanging off the little snaps and rings that many vests have. I know that some of you will because fly fishing has its share of gear freaks. However, I recommend that you take as *little* as possible in your vest. You'll experience less confusion and have less weighing you down.

When you buy your next vest, consider the following:

- **Two large, outer front pockets suitable for holding a couple boxes of flies:** The pockets should open and fasten *from the top*. If your vest has pockets that open on the side, someday you will forget to zip up, and you will lose a box of expensive flies, which will leave you feeling really stupid (at least that's how I feel when it happens to me, which it does every couple of years no matter what).

- **Four inner pockets:** These are smaller, and it's okay if they only have Velcro and no zippers. I like to put a box of strike indicators, or split shot, in one pocket, tippet or leader material in another, and bug repellent in another.

- **Four small, outer pockets:** One should have a zipper for an extra car key. The rest are for a small box to carry a limited fly selection of the stuff I think I will need that day, floatant, a small extra pocket knife with scissors, and this and that.

- **A metal ring:** I tie my clippers onto the ring. They do make retractable pin-on gadgets that are designed as clipper holders, but I have broken every one I ever bought and lost my clippers each time. I save old fly line for these kinds of jobs. I tie my clippers on with them. This little trick also makes a free alternative to Croakers for holding your sunglasses when you want to keep them handy.

- **Outside back pouch:** Put your rain jacket in here, or maybe your lunch, water bottle, extra reel, tape measure, and small scale, and so on.

- **Drying pouch:** Most vests come with a small piece of fleece pinned on the left-hand breast pocket. You're supposed to stick your flies on this so they can dry, but invariably, one or more flies get embedded and you end up tearing up the fleece and tearing apart the fly trying to get it unstuck. So I don't like them and don't use them. Then again, I might be lazy. You can put a fly here temporarily to let it dry, but remove it soon before the barb gets driven in. Your call on this feature.

What's in the best vest?

- **Safety pin:** Just pin one, or better yet, two, to your vest. They're useful for cleaning out glue from the eye of a fly, as emergency nail knot tools, and as on-site clothing menders.

- **Sunscreen:** Use it for *all* daytime fishing, even if the sun doesn't seem particularly bright or patchy clouds are out. Ultraviolet rays can still get through and burn you.

- **Insect repellent:** You will feel like a real genius the next time you walk two miles to the fishing and the bugs are out in force *if you bring something to keep them from biting you.* You can also try netting to protect your face and head, but you'll need repellent for your hands and arms.

- **Clippers:** For cutting leader and trimming knots, clippers are preferable to the teeth because clippers don't need to go to the dentist, and they make a cleaner, swifter cut.

- **Thermometer:** Fish bite at certain temperatures and not at others. A thermometer tells you if you are wasting your time. Many tackle shops sell inexpensive thermometers designed to withstand being tossed into the trunk of your car along with your vest, waders, and rod case.

- **Dip net:** Any store that sells aquarium supplies also stocks these little nets that are about the size of a tea strainer. When you see a lot of nymphs floating by, or spent (dead) mayfly spinners, you just dip into the surface film and scoop up a bunch. This tool is very helpful in identifying what the trout are eating.

- **A plastic garbage bag:** You may not keep fish as a rule, but every so often, you will want to, and who needs a vest full of fish slime? You don't need a lawn-size Hefty Bag; a wastebasket liner is more like it. Then again, a lawn-size bag can be your back-up poncho.

- **Forceps:** They help remove hooks more easily, which is helpful for the catch-and-release angler who wants to get the fish back in the water in a hurry. And they help when you're dealing with fish with sharp teeth.

- **Rain jacket:** It doesn't take up much room and it makes a big difference, especially when it rains! Fold it and wedge it into the big back pocket.

- **Spare car key:** Everybody loses the car key sometimes. It's a bummer if this happens when it's dark and cold by the side of a trout stream 20 miles from home.

- **Flashlight:** They make small flashlights that you can clip on and aim so that you have two free hands for knot tying, removing hooks, and so forth. Then, walking back to the car, spare key in hand, you can see where you are going. Don't leave home without one!

- **First aid kit:** With the current boom in outdoor sports, it's easy to find a compact first aid kit. Buy one and keep it in your vest. You may never need it, but if and when you do, you will be most appreciative. If you are allergic to bee stings or other insects' stings, make sure you have something to treat severe allergic reactions.

Sunglasses: Function, Not Fashion

You need sunglasses. On a sunny day you will suffer much less eye fatigue if you wear them. But even more importantly, *polarized* glasses cut down on glare and enable you to see down into the water. You will see fish that are hardly visible to the naked eye. And if you can see fish, you have a much better chance of catching them. Polarized glasses provide the most assistance in seeing into the water when the sun is high in the sky. When it is low, the surface looks like one continuous, glaring sheet. Polarized lenses also cut that glare and let you pick out a dry fly. As the light gets lower, you face a trade-off because even though you are cutting glare, you are also letting in less light. At some point, you just can't find your fly anymore. When this happens, I try to fish without my sunglasses, but to tell you the truth, it rarely works. As for color, I fish with gray lenses that are said not to change the true colors of things. Many saltwater anglers prefer brown and amber, especially on the flats.

Chapter 17
Knots: A Few Will Do

In This Chapter

▶ The three most important knots

▶ A couple of other pretty important knots

▶ How all good knots make sense

*P*eople have opinions about knots in the way they have opinions about politics. Often, people express them just for the sake of argument or for that "mine-is-better-than-yours" kind of snottiness. But while your political opinions may not affect your day-to-day life that much, your ability to tie knots well is the difference between catching big fish and catching no fish. Learning how to tie proper knots takes time, but once mastered, you don't forget them.

Why Knot?

At last count, the experts in knotology say there are about 3,000 different knots. I do 90 percent of my fishing with three knots. These three knots are not the prettiest knots, but they are the easiest, and they are as strong as any knot you can name.

In this chapter, I try to describe some knots (including my three favorites) and illustrate them. (Actually, I didn't really illustrate them myself. I can't even draw a smiley face. The figures in this chapter, like all the other figures in this book, are the creations of Ron Hildebrand, who gets a big thank-you from me.) But the best illustrations and the clearest descriptions are, at best, just a guide. Whenever I read angling books and attempt to learn the knots shown in them, I find myself trying to turn my head upside down or doing almost-impossible contortions. The long and the short of knot-tying is that you just gotta do it (and do it again and again and again).

I will say this: Every knot has a logic to it, and every time you learn a new knot, there comes a point in the learning process when you will understand *why* the knot works and precisely *what* it does.

A brief vocabulary of knots

Most knot-tying instructions use a few standard terms. These terms are pretty self-descriptive, but just to make sure that we are all on the same page, here they are:

✔ **Tag end:** The end of your line. This is the part that does the knot-tying. When you are finished tying, the tag end is the sticking-out part that you clip.

✔ **Standing end:** The rest of your line. You tie the tag end around it.

✔ **Turn:** Sometimes called a *wrap*. A turn is created when you pass the tag end through one complete turn around the standing end.

The Fisherman's knot

The real name of this knot is the *Improved Clinch knot.* But back when I started fishing, many people called it the Fisherman's knot because every angler knew how to tie this knot, and it was often the first knot they learned. Use the Improved Clinch knot to attach the tippet to the hook.

If a knot ever fails on you, 99 times out of 100, the place where it fails is right next to the hook, so the knot you use at this critical place should be the most reliable one that you can tie. Since I began fishing, I have read many claims for many other knots; some of the claims were quite learned and passionate. But guess what? The Fisherman's knot still gets the nod from me. Here's why:

A few summers back, my oldest daughter, Lucy, went to The Catskill Fly Fishing Center. This Center's wonderful two-day introduction is held on the Willowemoc River, which is about as close as you can get to holy water in fly fishing. You may think that the folks at the Center taught Lucy some knot that could only be learned by people who had a reading knowledge of Latin. Wrong. They taught her the Improved Clinch knot, and they called it the Fisherman's knot.

Here's how you tie one (follow along with Figure 17-1):

1. **Run the tag end of the line through the eye of the hook and pull 8–10 inches of line through the hook eye.**

2. **Wrap the tag end around the standing end for five wraps or turns.**

3. **Now pass the tag end through the loop next to the hook eye.**

   You will have formed another loop that includes your wraps.

4. **Pass the tag end through that loop.**

5. Wet the loops with some saliva to lubricate the knot.

6. Hold the tag end and standing end in one hand and the bend of the hook in the other; then pull with *steady pressure*.

   If you are not sure about safely holding the hook, grip it firmly but not super-firmly with a needle nose pliers.

7. Tighten slowly.

8. Clip the tag end so that only $^1/_8$ inch is left.

The Surgeon's knot

Twenty-five years ago, I was on the Beaverkill River in the Catskills. No one was catching fish except for this one guy. He had silver hair, and he laid out line like he was shooting a laser. He caught fish after fish. After a while, he left the stream. When he passed me on the bridge, I complimented him on his fishing prowess, and I offered him a pull of bourbon that I had in a flask to ward off the early spring chill. As we talked, I learned that he was the well-known fly fishing author, Doug Swisher.

While looking at his fly, I noticed the ugly knot joining the last length of tippet to his leader. I asked about the knot, and by way of reply, Doug demonstrated the Surgeon's knot. This knot got its name because it's the same one that surgeons use to close up their handiwork. I use it to join two pieces of monofilament that are close to each other in diameter, namely, the last sections of a knotted leader and tippet. For me, the Surgeon's knot takes the place of the more-complicated Blood knot, a well-known knot which is not described in this book. While the Surgeon's knot is not as prettily tied, it is stronger than the Blood knot and more practical.

More than one fly fishing buddy has turned his nose up at my scraggly-looking Surgeon's knot. Hey, it may not *look* great, but it *works* great. And if a surgeon feels that this knot is dependable enough to close up a wound, I am willing to trust it to haul in a fish.

Two hands are better than one

When tying knots, remember that there is no law against changing hands while you are tying. Sometimes you can hold the standing end in one hand, and sometimes you can hold it in the other. If you try to tie a knot by starting with the standing end in one hand and keeping it there until the end, you will end up in a pretzel position. Again, try to understand how the knot functions; then use whichever hand works best at the moment.

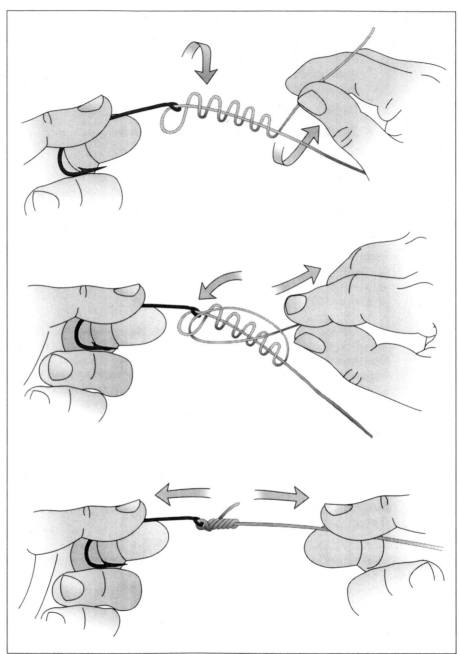

To tie the Surgeon's knot, just follow these steps, which are illustrated in Figure 17-2:

1. **Lay about 10 inches of tag end on top of your standing line.**

2. **In one hand, hold about 4 inches of standing line and the tag end and make a loop.**

3. **Pinch the loop together between thumb and forefinger.**

4. **Take the other end of the tag end and the end of the standing line and, passing it through the open loop, wrap them twice around the two strands of your loop.**

5. **Using both hands, pull evenly on all four strands.**

6. **Wet the knot with saliva when you are just about ready to finish pulling the knot tight.**

7. **Clip the tag ends.**

After a little practice, you will see that the Surgeon's knot is easy to tie. After you know how to tie this knot very well, practice tying it in a dark room or step into a closet and tie it. Knowing how to tie a simple knot in the dark can be a handy skill. (I leave it up to you to explain things when someone opens the closet door and finds you standing there with two lengths of fishing line in your hands.)

The Perfection Loop

The Perfection Loop is another of those less-than-gorgeous-looking knots. I use it to connect my leader to the butt of the fly line. I also use this loop to make droppers for 8-ounce sinkers when I am fishing live eels for stripers 80 feet down in the currents of Hell Gate on the East River in New York (even a fly rodder will be forced into bait-dragging desperation from time to time). In a nutshell, the Perfection Loop is a versatile knot. It is very fast to tie, and (like the Surgeon's knot) you can do it all by feel in almost total darkness.

Check out Figure 17-3 and follow these steps to tie a Perfection Loop:

1. **Create a $1^1/_2$-inch loop and pinch it between thumb and forefinger.**

2. **Repeat the action, creating another smaller loop around the first loop, and pinch again.**

3. **Run the tag end between the two loops and continue to hold everything pinched together.**

4. **Pull the second, small loop through the first loop and start to tighten the knot, providing the final tightening with a pair of pliers.**

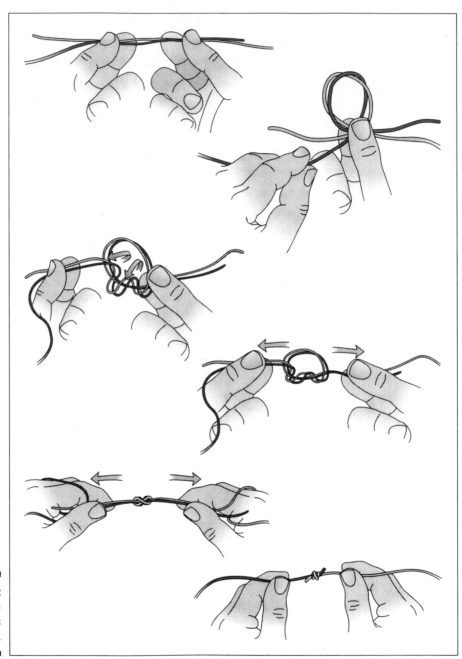

Figure 17-2:
The
Surgeon's
knot.

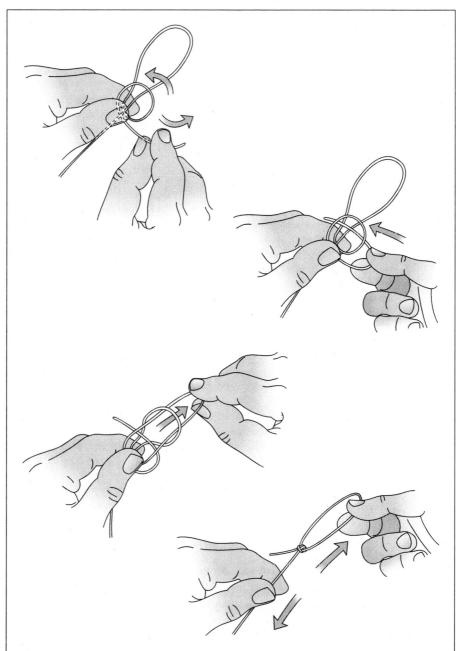

Figure 17-3:
A perfect
Perfection
Loop.

Good-to-Know Knots

The three basic knots that I have discussed in this chapter can get you through most fishing situations — not *all* situations, but *most* situations. You won't be able to lift a tarpon into your boat with these knots, and they are not designed to be tied with metallic materials. But in terms of basic light to mid-range fly fishing, you are covered. Now, here are a few more knots that can take you even further on the road to fishing success.

Line to reel

There you are — casting away into a pod of feeding fish. Thwack! Your rod bends double, and you feel the pull of the biggest fish you have ever felt in your life. It keeps pulling and pulling. You are getting more and more excited. You are down to the last couple of wraps of line on the reel. You decide to chance it and apply a little extra pressure, hoping to turn the fish and recover just a few feet of line. You lean into the rod, it bends more, the fish starts to turn, and BLAM — disaster strikes. The rod springs back as you watch the end of your line pass through the guides, and away goes Mr. World Record Fish with 75 feet of fly line, 150 yards of backing, and a nice fly in his mouth (about a $55 loss), all due to a insufficient knot. It's times like these that can make a person feel the way that Wile E. Coyote feels when he runs off a cliff and his legs keep going until he looks down and sees where he is, at which point he plummets like a stone.

Actually, you should finish fighting your fish (or the fish should finish with you) a long time before you get to the knot that connects your line to your reel. But even if you never get into this extreme predicament, you need to tie the line to your reel.

Figure 17-4 illustrates the Arbor knot. Here's how you tie one:

1. **With the backing line, pass the tag end around the center post of the reel spool and tie a simple Overhand knot, passing the tag end around the standing end.**

2. **Take the tag end and tie another Overhand knot with it.**

3. **Pull on the standing line until both Overhand knots come tight against each other and against the spool.**

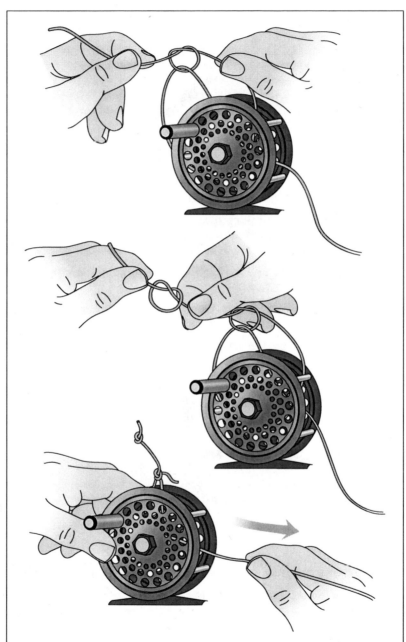

Figure 17-4:
The Arbor knot is one of the best and easiest ways to attach line to a reel.

Another loop

I often use the Uni-Knot (also known as the *Duncan Loop*) for such things as bass bugs or big steamers, both of which need unrestricted movement. I guess that the reason that I like the Uni-Knot is because it is so much like an Improved Clinch knot, and like most anglers (and fish as well), I am a creature of habit. This knot also works in place of the Arbor knot for attaching line to your reel.

The Uni-Knot is illustrated in Figure 17-5. Take these steps to tie one:

1. **Thread the tag end through the hook eye and run it parallel and right next to the standing line for 3 or 4 inches.**

2. **Bend the tag end back toward the hook, making a bowed loop; then wrap the tag end six times down and around the parallel lengths of tag line and standing line. Slip the tag end up through the loop.**

3. **Pull on the tag end to tighten the loop until the wraps are fairly snug against each other.**

4. **Pull on the standing end until the loop is the size you want it to be (just enough to give the lure room to swing freely).**

5. **Pull on the tag end with a pliers to make the knot good and tight.**

When a fish strikes, the knot slides up against the hook eye, closing the loop. Because the loop closes, you must retie this knot after you have unhooked your fish. A minor pain, but at least you caught a fish.

Joining fat line to skinny line

When joining wire to leader or backing to fly line, I use the Albright knot. This knot works well even if the two pieces being joined are very far apart in diameter.

Here's how you tie an Albright:

1. **Make a 3-inch loop in the heavier piece, as shown in Figure 17-6.**

2. **Pass the tag end of the lighter line through the loop for 7 to 8 inches.**

3. **Pinch the loop and the light line together and take the tag end and wrap it six times.**

   As you do this, try to include the new wraps in your pinch.

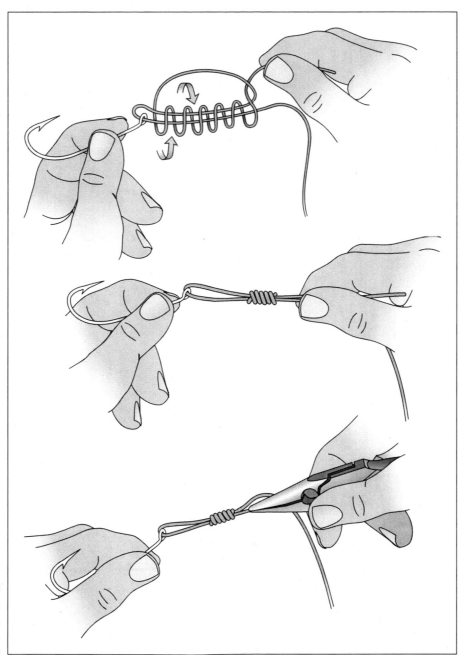

Figure 17-5:
The Uni-
Knot.

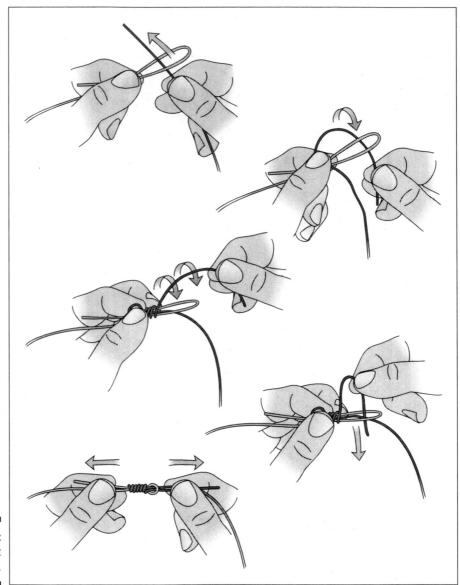

Figure 17-6:
The Albright
knot.

4. **Pass the end of the line you have been using for wraps back through the loop on the same side that it entered.**

5. **Pull gently on both ends of the lighter line so that the wraps slide up against the end of the loop.**

6. **When everything is lined up and fairly snug, you can give a good firm pull (not a yank) to finish the knot.**

The Albright knot is one of those knots that sounds and looks a little complicated, but as you tie it, you see that there is a logic to it. It really isn't hard to make.

Don't trust your knots

No matter how well you tie a knot, it will weaken the line to some degree. The more fish you catch with one knot, the weaker that knot, or the line just next to it, becomes.

After every fish you catch, you should check your line for abrasions and nicks. And after catching a few fish, clip your knot and retie the fly. After you lose a painstakingly tied dragon fly imitation or lose a big fish, you may come to agree with me that retying is better than losing fly and fish.

Part IV
The Part of Tens

The 5th Wave   By Rich Tennant

"You're really out of control, you know that? Anyone who uses a vise and bodkin to tie an apron string is seriously out of control."

In this part . . .

1 give you my ten favorite instructional fishing books, my ten favorite fishing stories, the ten best fly fishing magazines, and the ten best fly fishing Web sites. If you haven't already guessed, this part contains top-ten lists.

Chapter 18
Ten Good Books for Guidance

*B*ecoming a complete fly rodder involves uncovering many secrets. Thankfully, enough writers are also out there that you can pretty much count on somebody having spilled the beans, no matter what your question. Quite a few very good instructional books are available (not to mention the one in your hands), and at some point it is worth turning to each one of them because you can always discover something that will make your fishing better. Study what's in these ten favorites, and you'll know much more than I do.

Numero Uno

McClane's New Standard Fishing Encyclopedia and International Angling Guide (enlarged and revised Second Edition) by A.J. McClane; 1974 Henry Holt

If you had only one book, this is the one. It's the first place to go for anything to do with any kind of fishing. The research is great, the writing is a joy, and the information is accurate. McClane has assembled the most comprehensive fishing reference book ever.

Perfectly Simple

Streamside Guide to Naturals and Their Imitations by Art Flick; 1969 Crown

Everybody knows that trout fishing with a fly can be very complicated, but it took Art Flick's wonderfully small and straightforward book to show that it can also be simplified. His explanation of why, when, and how certain flies work is crystal clear, and his advice to forget 90 percent of the fly imitations out there is about the single best piece of advice I have seen in print.

Knot to Worry

Practical Fishing Knots by Mark Sosin and Lefty Kreh; 1991 Lyons & Burford

I don't know of two men who have fished more or more productively than these authors. Every angler needs to know a few knots. This book has every knot you could possibly need. The drawings are clear, and so are the instructions.

Simple, Direct, and Right on the Money

The Orvis Guide to Flyfishing by Tom Rosenbauer; 1984 Lyons & Burford

So many fly fishing books make you well aware of how much the author thinks he knows and how much you don't know. Not Rosenbauer's. His book is complete, informative, and has a very accessible voice and attitude. He wants you to understand, and this book is set up so you will.

Gentlemen, Start Your Bodkins

Talleur's Basic Fly Tying by Dick Talleur; 1996 Lyons & Burford

This handsome, well-organized book shows how to tie a great variety of flies. Step-by-step instructions, enhanced by good photographs, take you through the process. Talleur writes the fly tying column for *American Angler* and is a master of the craft. Even better, he has taught so many people how to tie that his instructions are full of neat tips that I guarantee will help you.

He duh Man

Fly Fishing in Salt Water (revised edition) by Lefty Kreh; 1996 Lyons & Burford

Having Lefty Kreh talk to you (through his words on the page) about saltwater fly fishing is kind of like talking to one the Wright Brothers about airplanes. Lefty was one of the first salty fly rodders when no one else really knew that much about the sport. This book has both story-telling and instruction, and therein lies the enjoyment of reading it. These are fish tales told by the man generally held to be the greatest modern angler. The man fishes for everything and he does it well.

Surfin'

Flyrodding the Coast by Ed Mitchell; 1995 Stackpole

Although this is a book mostly about northeastern fly rodding in saltwater, it can be read usefully by anyone who has taken up the sport. Mitchell's understanding of how water works in different coastal situations helps the newcomer get a handle on how to spend time profitably. This book is about finding the edge, hitting the tide on time, and fishing productively.

Fly Fishing in a Whole New Light

The Fly and the Fish by John Atherton; 1997 Freshet Press

Atherton was an artist and well acquainted with the properties of light and water. He also was an angler well acquainted with trout and salmon. His discussion of why flies work, how they break up the light, and his application of this knowledge was a true inspiration to me early in my angling career. His beguiling tales about the classic waters of North America are a terrific bonus.

If Art Flick Fished Montauk

Saltwater Baits and Their Imitations by Lou Tabory; 1995 Lyons & Burford

This smart little book simplifies saltwater bait and tells you how to recognize the most important baits, how to tie the most productive imitations, and how to fish them. Tabory is one of the pioneers of the salty fly rodding boom, and this volume simplifies his broad experience.

A Modern Master

The New American Trout Fishing by John Merwin; 1994 Macmillan

If Merwin knew any more about these fish I would recommend that he be checked for gills. As editor of *Fly Fisherman* and *Rod & Reel,* and as the author of a dozen books, John Merwin has helped to shape the angling style of a generation of fly rodders. What he knows about trout is staggering. This book goes beyond the basics of a beginner's book and takes the reader deeper into an understanding of trout and the art of angling.

Chapter 19

Ten Great Reads

For some reason, fly fishing has produced more good writing than any other sport. I know my love of fishing with a fly rod makes me a biased observer, but still, I think that the sheer amount of fly rod writing dwarfs other sporting writing; you are bound to find a few gems when that much volume is turned out. You may have others that you would include in your top ten list, but I am sure that you will include at least a few of these.

For the Trout Obsessed

Trout Madness, by Robert Traver; 1960 St. Martins Press

Traver, whose real name was John Voelker, was a small town district attorney and judge in Michigan's Upper Peninsula. The publication of his thriller *Anatomy of a Murder* brought him enough money to retire and trout fish at his little cabin in the woods. The full title of this book is *Trout Madness, being a dissertation on the symptoms and pathology of this incurable disease by one of its victims.* I understand the disease, and I also think Traver understood you, me, and anyone who loves to fish.

The Second Time Around

Tarpon Quest, by John N. Cole; 1991 Lyons & Burford

After a lifetime of fishing for stripers (about which he has written beautifully) John Cole discovered tarpon. Not many of us are given the chance to fall head over heels in love when we reach middle age, but that is how I would describe Cole's affair with the fish they call The Silver King.

Now You Know How Capt. Ahab Felt

My Moby Dick, by William Humphrey; 1978 Nick Lyons Books

Having obsessions about big fish is a very American tradition. When William Humphrey discovers a humongous brown trout in a little New England stream, he sets out to catch it with the determination of the trout-obsessed.

The Angler's Angler

Spring Creek, by Nick Lyons; 1995 Grove/Atlantic

Most of us first became acquainted with Nick Lyons through his essays in *Fly Fisherman.* In this short book, Lyons employs the same easy, almost liquid, style in the chronicle of a month spent on a beautiful, little-fished spring creek in Montana that is chock-full of great trout. He leaves you with the feeling that you have shared a unique angling experience.

The Master

Any book by A.J. McClane. These days you are more likely to find McClane in collections with other writers (rather than whole books just by him). If you find such a book, buy it. Ten pages by McClane is worth ten thousand by most other angling writers. For simple style and deep knowledge of the sport, the United States has never produced anyone like Al McClane.

Made in the USA

American Fly Fishing: A History, by Paul Schullery; 1987 The Lyons Press

Schullery is a fine writer and a respected naturalist. As Park Author at Yellowstone National Park in Wyoming, and the former curator of The American Museum of Fly Fishing, he brings deep knowledge and a sportsman's passion to the most complete survey of this sport in America.

Fly Fishing and the Meaning of Life

Sex, Death, and Flyfishing, by John Gierach; 1990 Fireside

Ah, yes, two of my favorite things. Gierach's work is both story-telling and a meditation on fly rodding. His gruff, aging hippie, "don't tread on me" attitude captures the spirit of many modern anglers who find truth, beauty, and the measure of themselves in the pastime that Lee Wulff called "this wonderful sport."

Fly Fishing to the Rescue

Flyfishing through the Mid-Life Crisis, by Howell Raines; 1994 Anchor Books

Not all of us suffer a mid-life crisis, but all of us have tough times in life. In mine, fishing has always had the ability to pull me through the bluest day. Apparently the same is true for this *New York Times* editor who writes from the heart, the head, and the funny bone.

Talk Softly and Carry a Big Rod

Fishing Talk, by Gifford Pinchot; 1993 Stackpole Books

History records Pinchot as the founder of the U.S. National Forest Service. For that, anglers owe him a debt. In this book, he reveals that he was also a master and sensitive angler. He would fish anywhere, anytime, and love it.

He Wrote. He Fished. It Was Good.

In Our Time, by Ernest Hemingway; 1996 Scribner Paperback

When Nick Adams gets off the train at St. Ignace (the beginning of "Big Two-Hearted River"), modern fishing writers are presented a model against which all other angling literature in this century can be judged. Hemingway's fishing writing is astonishingly real and intimate.

Chapter 20
Ten Top Fly Fishing Magazines

In This Chapter

▸ Great resources for fly rodders

Fly fishing has spawned a whole spate of magazines that suggest where to go, how to fish, what fly to use, and what gear to buy. Some of the information in them consists of very useful pointers and some of the stories and pictures are fun to look at and dream about. Like the *Playboy* centerfold when I was a youngster, or the *Gourmet* centerfold now that I have put on some years, some of the things in these magazines are attainable only in my dreams, but dreaming about a perfect anything always tends to lift my spirits.

I don't expect you to run out and get subscriptions to all these magazines, but every one of them is worth picking up from time to time to keep yourself informed about what is going on and where the sport of fly fishing is headed. The evolution of fly fishing has been so fast in the past 30 years, it's as if we went from the biplane to the Stealth fighter in a couple weeks (in fact, some fly rods are made from the same high-tech materials that go into super-duper military machines).

Fly Fisherman — Numero Uno

Founded in 1969, *Fly Fisherman* was the first all-fly-fishing magazine in the country. From the time that I started reading it, I found two main attractions — make that three.

✔ First, the articles taught me so much. And I think that is as true today as it was then.

✔ Second, the ads. I've seen ads for little cabins in Maine, fly rod guides in the Keys, and places to buy rooster necks out in California. *Fly Fisherman* is the first magazine where I can truly say that I, and thousands like me, read the ads as carefully as the articles.

✔ And the third benefit was the writing of Nick Lyons. More than anyone, certainly better than anyone, he lets the reader in on how it felt to love fly fishing and to do it well. *Fly Fisherman* is a showcase of some of the best writing about fly fishing being published right now.

Gray's Sporting Journal — A Young Classic

When I first heard the name, *Gray's Sporting Journal,* I thought this magazine had been around for a long time and I had missed it — the name sounds stereotypically old or British. But this elegant-looking, colorful magazine has been around even less time than *Fly Fisherman*. This journal is about the outdoors in the way *Sports Afield* is — it covers it all. The emphasis changes from issue to issue: In the spring, fishing is the main interest; in summer, fishing and hunting are considered; as fall and winter issues appear, the articles cover mostly bird and game hunting. Most of the stories in here are just that — stories. You won't find any direct, how-to instructions with diagrams and step-by-step directions. You have to read the articles to find out how things happen. The writing here is very literary — this is the only outdoor sports magazine I know of that regularly offers poetry. Hey, why not?

Fly Rod & Reel — What's in a Name (Change)?

Fly Rod & Reel first appeared in 1979 as *Rod & Reel,* a general, all-tackle fishing magazine under the guiding hand of John Merwin, whose books on trout fishing and whose term as editor of *Fly Fisherman* marked him as one of the most knowledgeable fly rodders of the last quarter century. After a few years of trying to be all things to all anglers, the editors found themselves focusing on fly fishing. The name changed to *Fly Rod & Reel* in 1989. The magazine is published bimonthly and is similar to *Fly Fisherman* — lots of articles on destinations for trips, studies of rivers, and much focus on trout. A number of well-known fly fishing writers, such as John Gierach, publish articles here. The differences between *FR&R* and *Fly Fisherman* aren't tremendous (they even have the same advertisements in the same places), but *FR&R* does have a regular saltwater department, and it seems to have a more playful tone all around. Want to know the truth? I read them both.

Trout — The Good Guys

No organization has done more to preserve and enhance quality fly fishing than Trout Unlimited, known throughout the fly fishing world as T.U. You should support them for no other reason than that doing so will give you good fishing karma. But if you do become a member for the current, reasonable fee of $35, you will get a free subscription to this magazine. The "Budget Angler" feature alone will probably earn you back the cost of membership as it tells you where to fish, how to get there, and where to stay, all on a budget. The writing of troutologist Bob Behnke of the University of Colorado is always enlightening on the favorite fly rod quarry.

American Angler — Trout Again

This 20-year-old bimonthly-monthly premiered as *Flytier* but later became *American Angler*. It is subtitled *The Magazine of Fly Fishing and Fly Tying,* and though it may have its share of advertisements for fly fishing the Bahamas or going after Mexican largemouth bass, the articles focus heavily on domestic, "cold water" fly fishing, that is, trout and salmon (pike rarely get any billing). The editor, Gary Soucie, is one of the most knowledgeable angling writers and editors in the business whose years at *Audubon* also established him as a leading conservationist. The regular columns are a wealth of practical information; I always read Rick Hafele on entomology (that's "bugs" to the rest of us) and the incomparable Dick Talleur's "Fly Tyer" department.

Saltwater Flyfishing — Just Like Teenage Lust

Eventually, a saltwater fly fishing magazine had to appear — too much of it was going on for the magazine world not to notice. This magazine, edited by Joe Healy, who is a pretty fair fly rodder, was the first one to come along since the original *Fly Fisherman* that had me reading everything down to the tiny little ads. Salty fly rodding has hooked me, and a lot of other people, the way fly fishing for trout first did, and for this I am grateful. How many times do you get to fall head over heels in love in your life and have it work out fine?

Fly Tyer — Yes, Virginia, There Is a Magazine All about Fly Tying

The pictures are big, understandable, and clear. Great writing by regulars includes C. Boyd Pfeiffer and Dick Talleur. Just like a good cookbook, this magazine makes the technique look simple and easy, and that is half the battle for any beginner.

Warmwater Flyfishing — Finally!

By now you know that I think that bass fishing with a fly rod is on a par with the traditionally more aristocratic trout and salmon fishing. This magazine is what you might call the "alternative" freshwater fly fishing magazine, getting away from the "tail water, spring creek, riffle-pool-riffle" world of much fly fishing writing. Bass, pike, and panfish all receive their long-overdue due, to coin a phrase. Because serious treatment of this sport is so new, almost everything in this magazine breaks new ground. It may even help to remove some pressure from over-fished trout streams, a real win-win proposition.

Sports Afield — The Granddaddy

The first issue of *Sports Afield* appeared in 1887, making it one of the oldest magazines in the world. Of the Big Three fishing and hunting magazines (which includes *Field & Stream* and *Outdoor Life*), *Sports Afield* has the most modern fly fishing feel, largely because of its design. It also has a great angling history: John Alden Knight published his famous solunar tables in *Sports Afield,* and the great Jason Lucas also wrote here frequently (as did A.J. McClane for a number of years).

Field & Stream — The Other Granddaddy

Since 1895, *Field & Stream* has billed itself as "The Soul of the American Outdoors," and if you had to pick one magazine about the outdoors, this is the one that more people know than any other. It has published the greats, like Hemingway and the lion's share of McClane. Under the stewardship of Duncan Barnes, it has taken strong conservationist (but not anti-hunting) stands. One of my old fishing buddies, Tony Atwill, is now a regular (and terrific) writer and sportsman to boot. As with *Sports Afield,* fly fishing is only one of the outdoor activities covered in *Field & Stream,* but it has covered the sport for more than 100 years and done it well. Plus, you can find it at any newsstand in the U.S.

Chapter 21

Fly Fishing as an Interactive Sport

In This Chapter

▶ What the weather is like where the fishing is

▶ What shape the streams are in *before* you fish

▶ How to find the right outfitter for you

▶ When the next tide will be

The Internet is like one of those bulletin boards at the supermarket full of ads for handymen, house painting, free kittens, garage sales, old boats, and church trips: You have to wade through a whole bunch of unorganized stuff before you find anything that is remotely useful. A good deal of junk is out on the Web, and you can waste time surfing it as effectively as any time-wasting thing I can think of. Still, I do find a few spots genuinely useful.

The United States Geologic Service

http://webserver.cr.usgs.gov/public/monty/

The first thing you want to encounter on a fishing trip is fish. The next most important thing is weather. Get flooded out (or "droughted" out) once and you will agree that it helps to know ahead of time what is going to happen weather-wise at your fishing destination. The United States Geologic Service maintains a site with a number of good weather links, including:

✔ U.S. forecasts by zone and region from National Weather Service

✔ An interactive weather browser

✔ Maps of the U.S. overlaid with infrared, radar, and satellite photos

Coastal Marine Forecasts

www.weather.bnl.gov/

Knowing what the ocean is going to do on a given day can mean the difference between great fishing and a long swim. I'm talking safety here. Is a storm coming up the coast? Is there a strong east wind? Are the waves coming high, fast, and furious? You better know what's coming. Take a look at this site — it provides coastal marine forecasts from Boston to Washington, as well as the southeastern U.S. These forecasts include easy-to-read charts with surface analysis, sea conditions, and temperature.

Real-Time Hydrologic Data

http://h2o.usgs.gov/public/realtime.html

Driving for hours only to arrive at a high and muddy river hardly makes sense. Hydrologic conditions can change quickly, especially in mountainous areas, and conditions on one river can affect those on nearby or connected rivers. This USGS site gives real-time stream conditions for most of the United States' fishable rivers. Although I hate most graphs, the ones at this site are actually quite good.

Tide Predictions

www.ceob.nos.noaa.gov/tideframe.html

Game fish follow the bait fish. Bait fish move with the tides. The successful angler is often ahead of them both. Maintained by NOAA (the same folks who make the coastal marine broadcasts), this site provides a nationwide table that tracks tides and predicts the next high and low. Fish the right tide and you will find fish. Fish the wrong one and you would swear there isn't a live fin in sight, and guess what — you're right.

The Virtual Fly Shop

www.flyshop.com

Maintained by *Fly Fisherman* magazine, this site is as thorough and rich as its in-print parent. This very good, all-around site offers a great deal of information, mainly on freshwater fly fishing. You'll find a very useful nationwide fly shop search function, magazine-style features, product information, reviews of new tackle, and tips about what fly patterns are catching fish in various waters across the country. The site also includes a chat room and bulletin board.

Orvis Online

www.orvis.com

Billed as the "total fly fishing resource," it just about is. Everything here is either Orvis-made or Orvis-approved — so it is as much a commercial site as it is an informative one. But because Orvis is a serious fly fishing company, that doesn't detract a bit from good and helpful information. You can find stores and dealers state by state and worldwide. You can look into fishing schools and fly fishing vacations. And a feature called *Orvis News* reports on new tackle and innovations that are worth knowing about.

Reel-Time: The Internet Journal of Saltwater Fly Fishing

www.reel-time.com

The Internet doesn't have that many sites that cover saltwater fly fishing, and this one is probably the best. It offers a ton of information and seems to be updated often enough that the information is accurate. I like *Fish Wire* — a weekly report of catches and conditions at prime locations on the Atlantic and Florida coasts. This site also regularly offers fly recipes that are enhanced by good graphics. You can also find forums on fly tying, places to fish, and rods and reels. The site contains lots of photos, too.

Trout Unlimited

www.tu.org/index.html

Trout Unlimited has a limited and praiseworthy goal: conservation and protection of cold-water fish and their environment. This site doesn't contain a whole lot of fishing information, but fishing won't exist if the environment goes to pot. The site offers up-to-date features on environmental legislation and initiatives across the country, stream and river clean-up efforts, problems affecting fish populations, and information on ways you can get help to protect trout, salmon, and their waters. Get involved!

Fly Fishing Questions and Answers

rec.outdoors.fishing.fly

This newsgroup site records multiple hits every day (that is, it gets a lot of visitors) and is a very good place to get questions answered. It's also a pretty civil site, so seemingly simple questions or differing opinions are usually dealt with good naturedly. I find that this site is one of the best ways to get really up-to-the-minute information about what fish are hitting what imitations and where the fish are. Skip the occasional non-fishing stuff, like "XXX — Tour Moscow Brothels!" (At least I think that's a non-fishing topic.)

Fly Tying Newsgroup

rec.outdoors.fishing.fly.tying

Yes — thousands of people are chatting in cyberspace about tying flies. You can often find good information and advice about what fly patterns are working well and where. (The first day I checked out this site I found a recipe for a catfish fly I had never seen.) A couple of the listings I saw recently were "Advanced Saltwater Tying Seminar" and "Animated Knot-Tying Programs." Again, some unwanted junk shows up on newsgroups like this, but with so much other good stuff, you can easily ignore the garbage.

Sharon's Fly Fishing Links

http://underthesun.com/UTS/Truly/fish.htm

I try to stay away from Web sites with first names, but I'll point out this one because it does offer a ton of links — most of which actually lead to useful information! It also offers many links for the growing number of women fly fishers, a trend I applaud.

AltaVista: A Very Useful Site to Help Find Other Useful Sites

www.altavista.digital.com

The Internet has a bunch of sites designed specifically to help you search out what you're looking for. As of this writing, the very best one (and easiest to use) is maintained by the Digital corporation. Your Web browser will probably suggest a few others as well, and you should feel free to try them. I, however, am pretty sold on AltaVista.

"Go ahead, Louise — pick one."

Index

• **G** •

• H •

• S •

• X •

• Y •

• Z •

CPSIA information can be obtained at www.ICGtesting.com
Printed in the USA
BVOW02n2313200514

354077BV00003B/11/P